They Used To Call Us Game Wardens

VOLUME TWO

William H. Callies

Technical manuscript formatting, cover preparations, proof reading and editing by Shawn Nevalainen

Proofreading/Editing by Ivy Hanson and Amber Callies

Special thanks to Michelle and Ken Strukel

Manufactured in the United States of America by Callies/Hanson Publishing, and printed by Bang Printing of Brainerd, MN

First Edition, January 2007

ISBN: 978-1-4243-0076-1

Venison For Sale cartoon used with permission from the
St. Paul Pioneer Press

To order books, send $17.00 for each book ordered to cover costs, tax and mailing. Send a check or money order to Callies/Hanson Publishing, 3308 1st Avenue, Hibbing, MN 55746 or call 218-258-7831. Reseller discounts are available.

"...Enjoy and understand why it is so important to be good stewards of our land, our resources and our animals."

William Callies

To. Bill Collins
With best wishes.
Wendell R. Anderson
Governor

This is the second volume of stories our Dad wrote. He, Bill Callies, became a Minnesota State Game Warden in 1960. This was huge career change at 43 years old. He had been in the floor-covering business when he decided to take the test and pursue his dream of becoming a warden. How this all happened is in the appendix of volume 1. Eleven hundred men took the test in 1960. Bill was one of just a few wardens hired. Bill gave up an income that was more than three times that of a warden and our mother, Patricia, gave up a job as head of the office staff for Donaldson's at Southdale in order to go with Bill to follow his dream. The new job was a major financial change for his family.

He was stationed at Waskish for fifteen years, but he also spent time stationed at Crosby-Ironton, Orr and Baudette. He retired while at Baudette in 1980. Bill wrote these stories after his retirement.

After a period of training with other game wardens, Bill was assigned to Waskish and told to report to his station on January 16, 1961. There was a huge log house at Waskish owned by the state that the game warden could rent very reasonably. Chief Fran Johnson told Bill that he would try to get money to fix up the house if Bill would do the work and maintain the house and grounds and outbuildings.

Before Bill moved to Waskish, a resident of the area, Bill Kues, was advertising in the St. Paul Pioneer Press that he had venison for sale. He was also threatening to kill a moose and sell the meat, and even threatened to kill a game warden. Waskish needed a game warden.

This volume, like the first volume, contains stories Bill Callies wrote about people and events as he saw them during the twenty years he was a game warden. He had record numbers of arrests many years, won commendations for saving lives, was given an award as an outstanding warden; and generally had the time of his life doing a job that he thought was the best job in the world. He was a tough, fair warden who was hired to enforce the laws of the State of Minnesota, and he worked very hard to do so.

In this volume in the appendix, we also included three stories Dad wrote about hunting and fishing that are not really game warden stories but we thought the readers would enjoy them. We also included some pictures that might help readers visualize important events and people in Bill's life. He was a wonderful father—an extraordinary man who led an extraordinary life.

We hope you enjoy the stories as much as we have enjoyed them. There are people whose names are in the book who will not like what he wrote—he always called a spade a spade. He was willing to write these stories for us, but we were given instructions that we could not publish them until after he died. If Dad gave instructions, we listened.

Ivy Hanson and Fred Callies

Photo of Ivy and Fred taken by Bill

PERSONAL EXPERIENCES AS A MINNESOTA CONSERVATION OFFICER

BY

WILLIAM "BILL" CALLIES

Game Warden Patch from 1960

TABLE OF CONTENTS:

Appendix

Obituary

Chapter 1/ WASKISH WARDEN STATION

DURING THE MONTH OF SEPTEMBER 1960, I was sent to Baudette to work with Game Warden Harland Pickett at the opening of the grouse season. I had heard that the station south of Baudette had been transferred from the section of game to the warden service. I also heard that the department was hard-pressed to get a man to bid on the station. In fact I heard that the station had been open for two years and was getting token policing from the neighboring wardens.

My curiosity was aroused so one day Pickett and I stopped at the Waskish station house. I liked what I saw even though the state house was in dire need of repair. The furnace, water heater and sump pump had been spirited out of the house to other buildings belonging to the section of game. I contacted Al Markovich at Warroad who was the last man to occupy the station. He let me know that there were some good things about the station but it seems there were some individuals he could not tolerate. In fact he let me know I would be out of my mind if I bid on the station.

Being inclined to use my own judgment, I submitted my bid for the Waskish station in November of 1960. In December of 1960, I was advised that I was the only bidder and I would be transferred to this station on January 11, 1961.

My family was living in a rather comfortable home in Edina, Minnesota and I was quite concerned about how they would take the transition from the metropolitan area to a small town. Time would tell.

Because our two children were in school—Fred in the ninth grade and Ivy a freshman at the University of Minnesota, we elected to hold off selling our home and making the big move until June of 1961. Also it would give me time to make repairs in the log house and get it in a livable condition.

Fortunately the district forest rangers, Roger Anderson and Hugo Kornell, allowed me to move into a side room in their office and I was allowed to use their stove and refrigerator in a back room of their office building. There was no running water, so with the help of two pails, I got my water from an outside spigot at the ranger's house. I usually got two 10-quart pails at a time. Roger used to kid me that I could have running water if I would move faster. Toilette facilities were located about four rods southeast of the office building. There were some times in the middle of the night when I would get the call and I would be resting on that cold, hard seat and it was 40 below zero outside that I started to wonder what ever possessed me to bid on this station. I never spent a lot of time in this building and no one else ever seemed to use it–it was my private dubisary. Fortunately, I am a poor cook and due to all of the work I had to do to fix up the state house besides learn my territory, my body consumed 90% of the energy and there was very little waste to contribute to the dubisary.

Finally, come spring, things started to look up. The house was all freshly painted, the new furnace was in, the water was hooked up, and a new water heater was installed. My thoughts started to turn to planting a garden south of the house and getting my equipment in shape for the coming fishing season opener.

The time was at hand to move my family to our new home. We sold our house in Edina for a lot less than what we thought we should. By the way, shortly after we sold it, it was sold for three times the amount we were asking for it.

The warden service had a large enclosed truck for moving their personnel from station to station. Several wardens in the metropolitan area were assigned to come to our house to help us load the truck. My wife and children had our belongings pretty well packed—boxed and contents noted.

So away we go over the road headed for Waskish. We arrived about 8 p.m. and several of the local citizens came to help us unload. We got all of our belongings into the house but in the process, we also let in a jillion mosquitoes. I thought before morning, I would have to nail my family's shoes to the floor and tie them in. I had a hard time trying to convince three people that this would be a good place to live that night.

Come morning, the sun came up and it started to look somewhat better to my family. Of course during the five months I had been there, I got to know some of the people. There were a lot of people that were friendly and there were as many that were suspicious of me. Lets face it—a game warden in those days was not the most desirable person to have around and I understood that.

A game warden's main duty is to enforce the game and fish laws. The second most important thing is to take care if any and all complaints concerning wild animals versus the local citizenry. You are supposed to contain the complaints in your assigned district. To have a complaint get to your supervisor or, worse yet, to the St. Paul office will bring worse than the wrath of God down upon you.

With all of the forgoing, I will tell you of one incident that occurred that summer. I received a letter from Milton L. Babin. He complains of deer damage to his garden. His letter was dated July 6, 1961.

Dear Sir,

> *I ask that you come up to my place and advise me what you can do about deer getting in my garden and eating up my garden stuff. Last night they ate up 7 cabbages. They like best of all cabbage, carrots, beets, spinach and parsnip. They leave sweet corn and potatoes alone. Our garden is ½ of our living. This year on account*

of the weather and time we have a poor garden,
planted a month later than usual. I have a woven
fence 5 feet 6 inches high but that means nothing
to them. We are ½ mile north of Hoglin's.

Yours truly,
Milton L. Babin

Mr. and Mrs. Milton L. Babin taken at an anniversary party at
Leonhardt's

I had never heard of this party before so I asked the postmistress, Bertha Halvorson (who, by the way was about the only person willing to give me any information at that time), if she knew this person and what kind of an individual he was. Also, I needed to know where and who were the Hoglins. She told me Hoglins lived in the last house in Konig on the way to Pine Island on the south side of the road.

As to Milton Babin, she assured me that he and his wife were real nice people but that Milton Babin was a letter writer and he wasn't afraid to write his congressman if he didn't feel he was being taken care of. I also called my neighboring warden, Leo Manthei of Blackduck, because he had told me he had been taking care of complaints in the Waskish area after Markovich left. I read him the letter and then he told me just how to handle this problem. He said, "You go up to Babins, introduce yourself and then listen to Mr. Babin tell you the whole story over again." Also he said, "I am sure he will take you out in the garden and show you some deer tracks and the places where the deer fed. When he gets done, you tell Mr. Babin that you will come up tonight with a big flashlight and a high-powered rifle and that you will have to kill those deer and then you should ask Mr. Babin if you can bury the deer guts in his garden." Leo went on and said, "You had better be ready to run if Babin has a gun handy. He will run you off his place. Those people love those deer and they enjoy seeing them."

So, armed with all of this information from Bertha Halvorson and Leo Manthei, I went up to the Babin farmstead. I met Mr. And Mrs. Babin and everything went just like Leo said. When we got to the garden, I noted that there were tracks of two deer—a small doe and one fawn. So now it is time to go into my act. With a lot of macho, I told Mr. Babin what I would do and asked him where in his garden I should bury the guts from the deer.

To my surprise, Mr. Babin said, "Fine and you can bury the guts over in that corner of the garden by the fence. I will dig the hole this afternoon and have it all ready so we won't have to be doing that after dark." On our way out of the garden he asked, "Can I have the meat?"

This isn't the way it was supposed to work out. I got in my car and drove back to the station. I went out to our garden and I checked and noted that we had every kind of vegetable that he had lost. Fortunately, while we were talking in Mr. Babin's garden, I had written the number of the various plants he claimed to have lost. So, I gathered up some pails and boxes and started digging up the proper number of each vegetable plants. I drove back to the Babin home and transplanted and watered all of the vegetables they had lost.

I then got a bunch of rags and tacked them to about half a dozen five and six foot stakes and shoved them into the ground in and around the garden. I left instructions with Mr. Babin to relocate the rag flags everyday and told him that I hoped that the flags would deter the little doe and her fawn from coming back.

Mr. Babin seemed somewhat satisfied however, I have a feeling he would have enjoyed some nice tender venison chops better.

I did not hear from Mr. Babin anymore that summer so obviously, the rag flags were a deterrent for the deer and that minor problem was history.

Chapter 2/ GABBY LEONHARDT

Eric Leonhardt, better known as Gabby Leonhardt, owned and operated Gabby's store in Waskish, Minnesota located at the intersection of Minnesota Highway 72 and the Tamarac River. He had ten fishing boats that he rented out to fishermen. He sold bait, groceries and tourist trinkets, and he also rented cabins.

I was assigned to the Waskish Warden Station in January of 1961. I did 90% of my grocery shopping with Gabby. He had a meat counter in his store but he never had any meat in it. I had to drive to Blackduck (thirty-five miles to the south) to get a pound of hamburger. That was soon to change.

It was in Gabby's store in February of 1961 that I first met Otto Herman, a very cocky farmer, a part owner of Rocky Point Resort, and a carpenter. A former game manager had advised me that he was a game and fish chiseler. On meeting him, he made the remark, "Now that we have a new game warden, I can go back to killing deer."

I told him, "I am pleased to meet you and if you choose to go to violating the game and fish laws, then we both will have something to do."

Sometime that spring I heard Gabby had gone to Baudette to have a part of his stomach removed. He had a history of drinking alcoholic beverages. The whole community just accepted his drunkenness.

Gabby was in the hospital for about ten days. Then he came home to finish his healing period. The doctor was very emphatic that Gabby was to stop drinking or it would kill him.

About two or three weeks later, I came into his store and found him with a bottle of beer in his hands and that was not his first one. I said to him, "I thought the doctor told you to lay off that stuff."

Gabby's response was, "Those doctors don't know everything, sometimes they are wrong. Anyhow, I'm only testing to see if they did a good job on my stomach." It wasn't long and Gabby had reverted back to his old drinking habits according to local information.

Eventually we came to the opening of the fishing season. I stopped in his store the day before the walleye season was to open. The store was packed with customers. Gabby was in the center of this mass of people. He had a cap on that had the word 'guide' on the front. Any time anyone asked Gabby, "Where can one expect to catch his limit of walleyes?"

Gabby would respond with a wide sweep of his right arm towards Red Lake saying, "Out there."

Also I noted he had a carpenter's apron around his waist that he used to keep his money in and make change on the spot. Fortunately, his wife and two daughters were down in the store to sell the merchandise and take in the money. Otherwise, in six weeks, Gabby would be broke and out of business—I'll leave the reader to figure that out.

On his shirt was pinned a highly polished brass deputy sheriff's badge for Beltrami County. How he ever conned

Sheriff John Cahill out of that piece of jewelry is more than I know. I would assume there was a super generous donation to Cahill's election campaign fund. I questioned Gabby as to his justification to wear that badge. He admitted he really had no legal authority. It was just to kind of keep his customers from getting too abusive in his place of business after partaking too much of the grape.

Later on that summer, one day when I stopped in to pick up some groceries, he commented on a list of people that had been picked up by me and run through justice court in Kelliher in the weekly <u>Kelliher Independent</u> newspaper office. I used the Justice of the Peace Court in Kelliher overseen by Justice of the Peace Clara Quale. He asked me, "Does she get paid?"

I told him, "Yes. She keeps the court costs, usually five dollars. The fine is split between the county and the state general fund."

Then he told me, "I have been elected as the justice of the peace by the people of Waskish and Konig Township. I would like for you to use my services and keep that money in the area it was generated in."

I told him, "I will be glad to use your services. It will save me thirty miles of driving plus the time to make the trip."

Later on that afternoon, I picked up an Arthur Duhamel, from Brooklyn, Michigan. The charge was "Angling without a fishing license". I booked him into Gabby's Justice of the Peace Court that same day. I called Justice of the Peace Eric Leonhardt and told him, "I picked up an individual that was angling without a license. Justice Quale usually fines individuals on this type of violation ten dollars plus five dollars court costs, which will be your fee. This party knew of you and your place of business and will be in this evening to take care of the matter."

In one of the following days, I stopped in to Gabby's store to see how he had made out as a justice of the peace. He said he just followed the procedural instructions he had received from the county court. The man pled guilty and paid his fine of ten dollars and five dollars cost.

Then Gabby went on to say, "Bill, we've got to make some improvements in this Justice of the Peace Court system. Did you know that Mr. Duhamel had rented one of my cabins and one of my boats? You created an awkward situation for me. In the future, you check with anyone you pick up on a game and fish violation. You check and see if they are one of my tenants, or a tenant of Davidson's that operates the Sunset Resort, or one of the locals, or a relation of a local person. Then you send those individuals to Justice of the Peace Clara Quale in Kelliher. If they don't fit any of those, I will handle the case."

I said, "Gabby it doesn't work that way. Either you take any and all misdemeanor cases I pick up or I will not send anyone to you to be heard."

That was the first, last, and only case our fearless Justice of the Peace Eric (Gabby) Leonhardt ever handled.

Chapter 3/ OHIO FISHERMAN

It was the fifth day of June 1961 at Waskish, Minnesota. It was a nice day with little or no wind. I told Patricia I was going out on the lake and check fishermen. At this time, I was using an old Model K 16 foot Alumacraft that belonged to the section of game. They only used it when Herman Anderson came down from Norris Camp to go fishing or if Vern Gunvalson came up from Bemidji to go fishing.

By the way, later Gunvalson found out I was using the boat to check fishermen so he told Herman to lock the boat up so I couldn't get it.

I used my own eighteen horsepower Johnson motor to run the boat on this particular morning. I moved out onto Upper Red Lake and started checking licenses and the number of fish.

The walleyes were really biting so there was a good chance for over the limit somewhere.

I had moved down the lake into a group of fishermen. I pulled up to one boat when I became aware of three men in a boat scrambling to pull up their anchor and lift in their stringers of fish. They had lots of fish. The man in the back was busy getting the motor started and away they went headed for the Tamarac River.

These three men had, in my opinion, done something wrong and wanted to leave the area immediately. This aroused my curiosity. I told the people I was checking I would be back later. I started my outboard motor and took out in pursuit of this boat with the three men. They were about a quarter-of-a-mile ahead of me and appeared to be going as fast as their boat would take them. I gained some on them because we each had similar boats and motors. However, with three good-sized men, they had a lot more weight in their boat than I had. As we turned into the Tamarac River, I could see they were throwing something out of the boat as they moved. I slowed down a bit where I first saw them throw something. It turned out it was a walleyed pike floating belly up.

I took my dip net and scooped it up. Then I opened up the motor again, wide open. Ahead I could see another walleye floating belly up. I kept on full speed ahead operating the motor with the tiller bar with my left hand. I had the dip net in my right hand and as I was passing this next fish, I scooped it up. However, at this speed the net was almost torn out of my grip and I felt as though I had dislocated my shoulder. That was enough of that. I was afraid of losing them. From then on, I just kept count of the fish as I passed them.

We went up river passed all the resorts. I was quite close to them, maybe one hundred fifty yards when they turned into shore on the left side. The three men almost knocked each other down in their haste to get out of the boat and run up to a little shack. In they went and closed the door. I pulled along side their boat, climbed into it, and found they still had about thirty walleyes on three stringers. They would be allowed to have a total of eighteen, which would be their possession limit on any given day.

I walked up to the shack and rapped on the door. It was real quiet inside so I hollered at them, "I am a Minnesota Game Warden. Open this door now, or else!" Again I was met with absolute silence. So I backed up a few steps and slammed into that door with my left shoulder. I had noted the wood had long since seen its best days. The door popped open and I could hear pieces of metal hitting the wall and the old stove. I assumed it was door hooks or a door bolt.

Anyway I was inside and these three guys were ugly—especially the oldest one. I told them, "Just calm down. You have enough trouble now without asking for more."

Then the oldest guy said, "You busted our door all to pieces."

I told him, "I had no other option. You wouldn't open up when I knocked and told you to open up."

Then I spied some big coolers. I started to open one up when this older guy says, "You have to have a warrant."

I then asked, "Can I see your licenses?" They dug them out of their billfolds. They all had non-resident angling licenses. They were from Ohio.

The older man said, "This is my property."

So I showed him in the fishing synopsis he had been given when they bought their licenses that the possession limit was six walleyes per licensed fisherman. I also showed him Subdivision 97.50 Section 3 whereby I was empowered to search any property for illegal game. I told the men, "You have already still got over your limit out in the boat plus all those fish you threw out coming up the river." With that, I opened the coolers and they were full of filleted walleyes and ice. As I remember, they had close to one hundred walleyes.

Bill setting up a booth for the North Beltrami Sportsmen's Club

I made out the summons and seizure slips for all the fish and loaded them in my boat. I took one man in my boat and instructed the other two to get in their boat and follow me to my office and residence on the Tamarac River. There we all transferred into my patrol car and I hauled them to Kelliher before the Justice of the Peace Clara Quale. She fined each man $15 and $5 costs or fifteen days in jail. That was considered a pretty tough fine in those days.

Chapter 4/ *FOSSTON PREACHER*

I'm out on upper Red Lake on a fantastic, warm summer afternoon checking fishermen. Life is good; I've got the best job in the State of Minnesota. The state furnishes me with a sixteen-foot Lund boat, a fifty horsepower Mercury motor, and a pair of seven-foot oars, all the gasoline and oil I need. They even furnish the clothes I've got on and all I have to do is see to it that the people obey the laws of the Department of Natural Resources. They even pay me.

I left home after lunch with my wife, who by the way was my secretary. She took all the complaints over the phone and in person when I was out on patrol. She did more work for the State of Minnesota than I did and she never got a nickel for it. She was my best friend and the only person I could really trust.

I went out the Tamarac River to Upper Red Lake. I decided to move up along the north shore. There was no wind; the lake was as smooth as a newly laid blacktop highway. I checked a half dozen boats out of Hudecs Resort.

There was one couple that was real excited to see me. There had been a boat fishing near them that had way too many fish and had pulled up anchor and gone back in the vicinity of the Tamarac River. They wondered if I had intercepted them. I said, "No, every boat I checked only had a part of the number of fish they were entitled to take." I then asked how they knew they had so many fish.

Then both the man and woman were so excited to tell me their story. It seems the other man and woman, the fish violators, were anchored when the two informants came out from Hudecs Resort. When these people saw the alleged violators pulling out so many fish, they anchored near them to partake of the good fishing. They told me, "We caught about a half a dozen but nothing to what the couple that we watched caught." In fact, they were sure when the other couple left they had to have at least fifty walleyes, maybe even more.

Bill on patrol

I asked what kind of boat they had and the man said it was white and it had the number 9 on it. I said, "That boat is from Johnson's Resort, half way between Hudecs and the Tamarac River." I asked what the occupants looked like and was told they were a young couple in their late twenties. I thanked them for this information and turned back to the Johnson Resort boat canal.

I came in on the canal to the lagoon where the boats were docked surrounded by the cabins. I located boat number 9. It was tied up to a small dock. I looked all around the dock and boat to see if there were any fish on stringers. There were none. So I went up to the cabin and knocked on the door. A young man opened it and I asked if he just came in from fishing and what kind of luck he had. The young man said fishing was fabulous and they had their limit of real nice fish. I knew he could see who I was but I confirmed it by telling him I was the local Minnesota State Game Warden. I told him I wanted to check his fish and their angling licenses.

"Sure, come on in. The fish are in the sink, I haven't

cleaned them yet," he said. The fish were on a stringer and I counted twelve walleyes, which was what two licensed fishermen could have in possession.

I then asked, "Are these all the fish you have?" I said I wanted to check around. I looked everywhere—inside, outside, and in the fish cleaning shack. There were no other fish.

Then I told this couple someone had said they saw you catch at least fifty walleyes. To this the man said, "Oh, we caught more than that but most of them were so small we released them back into the lake if they were not hurt too badly. We just sorted until we got our twelve pike that were fair size."

"There is nothing wrong here, sorry to have bothered you," I told them.

"No bother," he said, "glad to see you guys working."

Then I said, "I would like to see your license." He offered me a combination husband and wife license. The wife's hair was a different color than the license denoted, however, I had learned years before that a woman's hair color had a way of changing. I thanked the man for the license and he put it back in his billfold.

Then the young lady said "Don't you want to see my license?" as she offered an individual angling license. I checked it and thanked her for it. The man looked upset but there was no violation there for me. So I took leave of their place.

I did stop and explain the whole situation to the informants. I thanked them for their courage to alert me of what on the surface looked like a violation but this time it was a mistake.

So, I continued on down the lake to the west. I could see ahead of me a small runabout with two men trolling. When I was about a quarter mile from them, I saw something silvery being thrown up in the air from the boat. I thought it was a small walleye. So many fishermen have to have this macho attitude and throw the smaller unwanted fish as far as they can. Not like the young couple at Johnson Resort who had obviously released the small walleyes carefully and quietly back into the lake.

When I got closer, I saw it was a shiny aluminum beer can. I took my dip net and scooped the can out of the water. The two men were sitting on real nice padded fishing boat seats facing to the back. They each had one line in the water. I pulled along side of the boat, took hold of the gunnel on their boat, shut my motor down and told them I wanted to check their angling licenses and their fish. They complained that they hadn't even had a bite yet. I told them I was a Minnesota Game Warden and I wanted to check their angling licenses. I noted they were from Fosston, so I asked if they knew the warden at Fosston. They knew him and the older man said he was one of his parishioners. I then asked, "Who threw the beer can in the lake?"

The older man said, "It wasn't us." There were two six packs in the boat. Both six packs had five cans of beer in them.

The young man had a can of beer in his hand. So I said to the older person, "You must be the one that threw the can in the lake." Again he denied it. I then showed the numbers on the bottom of the can to the man and also lifted up my dip net with the can in it so I could read the numbers on the bottom. The numbers matched the other five in the six-pack.

Still he denied he threw the can. I said, "That's all right. I'll write a summons against both of you and then we will let the judge sort it out. Also, I will have time to get the fingerprints lifted off the beer can. No hands will touch that can until I can get to the B.C.A. for the fingerprints."

That was too much for the young fellow and he said, "My father-in-law threw the can in the lake." I was reasonably sure of that so I wrote up the preacher.

Later on when I met the Fosston warden he said, "When my preacher told you I was one of his parishioners, couldn't you have backed off a little?"

Chapter 5/ LEO'S HELPER

I don't know why, but before the deer season in 1961, Leo requested of Supervisor Tarte an assistant to work with him during the deer season. That same year, Bud Breezee offered to go up north to work with a northern warden during the deer season. So Supervisor Tarte made arrangements for Breezee to go to Blackduck to work with Leo.

It was on the night of November 13 that Leo came up to meet me north of Saum to show off his assistant. When Leo pulled up to my patrol car, he said, "Look at this guy." I looked at the passenger in the front seat and he was sound asleep. Leo said, "His head rolls around so much I'm afraid he will break his neck. When he is awake, he keeps saying, 'You guys are crazy with the hours you work and the chances you take.' I am stuck with him for the whole deer season." Leo wanted me to take him for a few days.

I told Leo, "No way. You asked for help, you've got help." I don't believe I ever talked to Breezee, we couldn't wake him up.

Leo and I decided to work that area that night. There was a small borrow pit north of us on the west side of the Range Line Road. I would go south and pull in on a logging trail where the Battle River Road meets the Range Line Road.

Along around 10:00 p.m., Leo called on the radio and said, "I have a car going by, driving slowly and it has turned west on a dead-end road that ends at the Mohsted Farm." Leo followed the car without lights down to the corner. He said, on the radio, "I can see the car is shining and is in the process of turning around. Start up that way without lights. I have Breezee awake and I am going to have him lay along side the road at the corner and then I will attempt to block the car at the corner." Breezee was schooled by Leo that when Leo blocked the car, Breezee was to jump up, jerk the car door open and holler, "Game Warden," and if he saw a gun in the car, grab it.

I am several miles south coming as fast as I dared driving without lights. Leo announced, "The shining car is here. I'm going to block him now." At that same instant, I saw a pair of headlights coming from the west and turning south towards me. Then, I saw Leo's red flashing light and I knew the stop had been made. Leo hollered in the radio, "They got around me and Breezee has been knocked down!"

Leo had to turn around and pick up Breezee to follow the car. I turned on my lights so I could drive fast. When I got near them, they turned west on a farm road into an abandoned farm when I hit my red lights. I followed them right in and got them blocked between an old building and my car. There were four men and I got them out of the car and up in front of my headlights. I checked the car and there was no gun or spotlight. About that time Leo came on the radio and said, "I thought something had been thrown out of the car as it passed over the bridge over the North Fork of the Battle River. I'll check it out."

Then Breezee came on the radio and asked, "Did you catch the car?"

I told him, "I have and I am holding the men."

Then Breezee came back and said, "Good, get their names and addresses. I'm going to sue them for knocking me down when I opened the door."

Then Leo came on the radio and said, "I found the rifle and five cell flashlight. The gun was loaded."

With that, I got identification from the men and told them, "You are all under arrest for deer shining. If you give me any problems, I will seize your car."

They told me, "We haven't seen any deer and we have hunted all day." It was the opening day of the deer season. "We have yet to see a deer much less to shoot at one."

The guy that owned the car was on the verge of bawling. He said, "My wife will kill me if I have to pay a fine and I lose my car."

I just told all of them, "Just hold still and behave yourselves. I'll talk it over with my partners when they get here."

Leo and Breezee drove in. Breezee was all for throwing them in jail. I could see he wasn't hurt. I figured it had to be as much his fault as the violators. I then told Leo, "They are a bunch of dummies. They are so scared I'll bet they pissed their pants. A couple of them were actually shaking." I told Leo, "I think we ought to charge them with a misdemeanor, 'Attempt to take deer in closed hours'. The justice of the peace will whack them $100 each. We will seize the gun and light and void their deer hunting licenses after court the next morning."

Leo said, "I'll go along with that."

So I went to these men and told them we could take them on a gross misdemeanor. They could be fined in District Court up to $1,000 and/or a year in jail. They would lose the car, gun, and light.

I also told them that they seem like a bunch of opportunists, and if we could get some assurance that they would never pull a dumb stunt like this again, Leo and I could just charge them with a misdemeanor—"attempt to take deer in closed hours". I said, "I'm sure the justice of the peace in Kelliher will hear you in the morning. She will no doubt fine you the maximum fine she can fine you, $100 plus $5 costs each. If you get smart with her she can also have you committed to the county jail for up to ninety days. Also, after court we will void your deer licenses. You are all done deer hunting this year. We will also seize and confiscate the gun and the flashlight."

I told them Bud Breezee threatened to sue them. I said I don't think Bud is hurt. These sorts of things go with the job. However, if Bud decides to sue them, it will have to be in civil court.

The men came in to Clara Quale's Justice of the Peace Court in Kelliher the next morning. They pled guilty and were fined $100 and costs. Their licenses were voided. Their deer tags locked. They lost the gun and light. I am sure they learned a good lesson the hard way.

Bud did not sue them.

Chapter 6/ ROY CYRUS IN LAKE OF THE WOODS COUNTY

In the fall period in 1961, prior to the goose season, my neighbor to the north, Harland Pickett, contacted our supervisor, Dick Tarte, and made a request that he not be available that opening weekend of the goose season. I don't know what his excuse was but our supervisor granted him the time off.

J. C. Richards of Big Falls and I were instructed to go to Baudette and take over in Pickett's absence. We were to be there Friday through Monday. We were not to stay in any motel or hotel. We were to bring our sleeping bags and some grub and hole up out in the bush.

Harland contacted me and suggested I bring the state Model K Alumacraft and the old green twenty-five horse outboard motor. He also told me Cyrus would know he was gone and if we would work Four Mile Bay on Lake of the Woods, we just might catch that old fox violating the game or fish laws. Harland went on to say, "If you just catch Roy Cyrus, I'll be happy."

I don't remember where I met Ces, but I do remember the two of us cruising Pickett's area trying to figure out just where the best place to work would be. Herman Anderson, the refuge patrolman from Norris Camp over south of Roosevelt, did call us to one big farm. He had a radio in his car with our same frequency. He told us he had two goose hunters out in pits all set up with lots of decoys. We asked Herman, "Have you seen them doing any shooting?"

His answer was, "No."

I told him via our radio, "If you think they might be doing something wrong, go out on the field and check them out."

Herman came back with "I don't have my credentials to check the men out."

Herman talked us into where he was. He pointed the two men out in their pits surrounded by about three dozen decoys. Then Herman said, "The goose season doesn't open until tomorrow and these men aren't supposed to put their decoys out until an hour before the season opens."

Then we told Herman, "That only applies to public waters. On private land they can have decoys out year around."

Later on that evening we came upon an old abandoned tarpaper shack. We moved our gear inside, cut a mess of spruce boughs for mattresses and sacked out for the night.

The next morning we rustled up a mess of grub. It was then that we decided to go over near the Morriss Gap on Four Mile Bay and put our boat in. We ran the boat down into some bullrushes on the southwest end of Four Mile Bay. We could see off north of us a lot of boats going out into the gap and some in the bay anchoring their boats and fishing.

We sat there for at least two hours telling lies and smoking cigarettes when we observed a small flock of honkers coming down the middle of the bay toward us and about thirty yards in the air over the water. About this same time, we witnessed a small boat with a fast outboard motor and one occupant who seemed to be trying to intercept this flock of geese. The operator was close to underneath them when he rose up with a pump shotgun and fired five shots toward the geese all the while maneuvering his boat through and past some fisherman.

We immediately assumed we were in business and proceeded to pole our boat out into open water with the two aluminum oars. The water was shallow and there were a lot of small boulders.

Ces was up in the bow checking for depth and rocks. He finally announced the water was deep enough to lower and start the motor. I did this. We went about thirty feet and bang—I hit a boulder. I tipped the engine up and I could see one of the three blades had broken off. Also, on further check, I found that the pin had also sheared. That is when I discovered that my little toolbox with spare shear pins had inadvertently been left in the car.

We looked out to the party that had shot at the geese. He had shut his motor off. It was a red motor which we guessed was a thirty horsepower Johnson, manual start. He was just finishing loading his shotgun and laid it down. He stood up to pull the starter rope on the motor. He pulled and pulled but the motor would not start.

I quickly installed the oars into the oarlocks and commenced rowing. Ces spit a stream of tobacco juice into the water and said, "Forget it, this is not our day." I kept on pulling and in my exuberance pulled the pin out of one of the oarlocks.

I told Ces to hold that oar down into the oarlock so I could keep rowing. And, wonder of wonders, we got to the goose shooter's boat and grabbed his gunnel.

I told him who we were and I wanted to see his hunting license. He produced that for us and I noted there was no federal migratory stamp on his license. Also, I told this man you are not allowed to shoot at migratory waterfowl from a motorboat underway in open water. He had a Model 12 Winchester shotgun uncased with no case in the boat. Checking the gun showed it to be unplugged and reloaded with five shells in the gun. Then, I noted the name, "Roy Cyrus".

I didn't say a word about the name, I just handed the license to Ces. He almost swallowed his snoose, caught himself, shot a stream of tobacco juice into the lake and announced, "Roy you're just wrong in too many ways."

I asked Roy, "Do you know what is wrong with your motor?"

He just said, "I've been having a lot of trouble with it."

I then asked him, "Do you have a spare shear pin and a pair of pliers that you can supply?" He did. So I changed my shear pin and we towed Roy and his boat back into his property.

We made out one charge and a seizure slip for his shotgun and told him Harland would set the court date and all the additional charges that would be placed against him when he got back.

About a week later, Harland notified Ces Richards and myself of what day we were to be in court to testify to what we had witnessed before Judge Sherwood in Municipal Court. Our nickname for this judge was "Wheels".

Ces and I testified to all of the violations. Then the judge turned to Roy Cyrus and asked him how he would plead. Cyrus pled guilty to all the charges.

Then the judge turned to Harland and said, "I understand you seized Mr. Cyrus's only shotgun."

Harland told him, "That's correct and we could have seized his boat and motor but because no geese were brought down only the gun was seized and it will be confiscated after court today."

To which the judge said, "A man's shotgun is one of his tools and if you persist in keeping it, it is going to have a big influence in the amount of monetary fine I plan to assess."

Harland came back with, "The maximum fine on each of the charges, which were misdemeanors, could be $100. If you assess $100 for each one, then I will consider returning the shotgun."

The judge became real insistent that Harland assure him the gun would be returned before he pronounced sentence.

Harland conferred with Ces and I and we told him it was his area, his judge, and his arrest. Whatever he chose to do was OK with us.

Harland turned to the judge and announced, "The gun will be returned."

The judge confronted Harland and asked, "Now, do I have your solemn word the man's gun will be returned to him?"

Harland then responded, "Yes, your honor."

At this time, the judge swiveled his chair toward Roy Cyrus who was still sitting in the witness chair and he said, "Roy, this is a serious thing you have done. The fine will be $15. If you're a little short right now you can make arrangements with the clerk of court."

Ces, who was standing near the wall to the right of the judge's bench, turned to the wall and with the base of his fist of his left hand, he hit the wall while muttering, "Ain't that something?"

The judge then said, "Another outburst like that, and you will be charged with contempt of court!"

Chapter 7/ THE STOVE PIPE DEER HUNTERS

The first time I was aware of these people was Sunday night of the opening weekend in 1961 at Waskish, Minnesota. This was my first deer season at this station.

I knew of a hundred places I should be to watch for illegal activity. I had selected a place in Konig Township where I might catch a deer shiner.

Around 11:00 p.m., I got a call on my radio from Dick Florhang, the Minnesota State Highway Patrolman, that he just came across a dark colored Chevrolet station wagon that was crossway on Highway 72 about two miles north of Ludlow Island. He slowed way down when he passed them. He was able to get the license number. The station wagon was headed south.

Dick was stationed in Baudette. I thanked him for the information.

I drove out to Highway 72 and then up to an approach that led into Irv Davidson's to watch for this station wagon. It wasn't too long before it passed my hideout and I followed it into Waskish and directly to a Waskish resort. They parked along side a cabin that overlooked the Tamarac River. It looked like five or six men got out of the vehicle and went in the cabin.

I waited and watched for about a half hour then it seemed as though they were in for the night. I slipped up close and found eight or nine big bucks hanging from a tree next to the cabin. Now I was reasonably sure these boys were hunting illegally. All the deer were properly tagged.

I had, since the day I started at Waskish, become aware that many resorters would not give me any assistance. Some were only interested in swapping the resources for money. All of the deer hanging were shot in the head. That is typical of a spotlighter's shot.

Around 1:00 a.m., I knocked it off and went home to bed. I had to be up in Baudette for court for four shiners I had caught Saturday night.

It was about 7:00 a.m. Monday morning when I left Waskish en route to Baudette to process the four night hunters through court. I was driving north on Highway 72 and as I topped the rise at Ludlow Island, I could see down the road ahead a vehicle parked on the west side of the road. As I got closer, I could see several men out on the bog walking around. Apparently, they were looking for something. Then I realized that the car was the station wagon Florhang had seen in this area the previous night.

I could not check things since I had to be in Baudette for court.

I met Warden Pickett who was stationed in Baudette. He took me to meet the county attorney of Lake of the Woods County. Then the three of us went to the county courthouse where we picked up the hunters from the jailhouse. Then we took them before District Judge McRae. They all pled guilty and were fined. I then seized their car and rifles in the name of the State of Minnesota. I would have to auction the car off at a later date in front of the Lake of the Woods Courthouse.

After court, the county attorney, Pickett, and myself went to a local cafe for lunch. When we came out of the cafe, I saw the station wagon that Florhang had alerted me to. It was being parked up in the next block.

I pointed the car out to the county attorney and Warden Pickett and told them of my suspicions. Warden Pickett said, "We will keep an eye on them. Maybe we can catch them at their hunting game."

Harland Pickett, Baudette game warden. Picture was taken in 1949 before wardens were issued uniforms

There were six men in that station wagon. They spent some time in a grocery store. Then they went into the number one municipal liquor establishment. Along about dusk, they came out and went to a restaurant.

Around 7:30 p.m., they came out of the eating establishment and got into their station wagon. It was now pitch dark. They had forty miles to go to Waskish, down Highway 72, where there are only a few farmers. It is through mostly state land and the big bog.

We followed them out of town for about four miles with our headlights on. Pickett was driving his patrol car, and I was the passenger. We turned off on a small gravel road, turned our headlights off and came back out on to Highway 72. The station wagon was about a mile ahead of us. Harland used his sneak light and we drove pretty fast. The station wagon had slowed down and we could see a strange light out onto the west side. We could not see a spotlight coming out of the vehicle, which we thought was really strange. We followed this vehicle for about six or seven miles. We were down near the county line. We were about an eighth of a mile behind them when the vehicle made a turn to the east right in the middle of the highway. Harland said, "They must see a deer on the east side of the road". Then the station wagon backed up, and then forward. Obviously, we guessed wrong. They were in the process of turning around. They must have seen something back a ways and were merely taking a precaution not to shoot the first time they spotted a deer.

We were too close to them to be able to turn around and get out of there without them seeing us.

Harland then said, "Get ready. I'm going to have to stop them for a check." In those days we had to catch the people with the gun loaded and uncased.

Harland raced to close the distance between the two vehicles and just as their headlights came on to us, Harland snapped on his headlights and red lights.

There was obviously no scrambling in this vehicle. The men just sat there while we ran to their vehicle, opened their door, and announced we were game wardens.

Here is what we found. Two men were sitting quietly in the front seat. Resting on the top of the back of the front seat was a 30/06-bolt action rifle in a case and no shells in either the chamber or magazine. The two men in the second seat each had three or four loaded rounds in their pockets. Then there were two men seated on a seat in the trunk space facing backward.

In rummaging around under the passenger sitting in the front seat, Harland pulled out a piece of stovepipe about ten or twelve inches long with a spotlight inside of it. He immediately called my attention to this piece of equipment. No wonder we didn't see the flash of light on the face as it was being shined around.

There was absolutely nothing wrong with what these men were doing. However, it was obvious to us that we had met some hunting chiselers that made a serious preparation for hunting deer illegally before they even left home.

I did inquire as to the name of the driver. He was from Minnesota, and now I knew a name. We then told the men they could go.

With that they turned around again and headed south towards Waskish.

Harland took me back to Baudette to get my patrol car and I returned to Waskish. I walked down to the resort and I could see the station wagon along side the cabin.

The next day, they loaded up their deer and pulled out. I would have to wait until next year.

As I thought over what had transpired, I came to the conclusions about how these men worked. If and when they spotted a deer, they continued on past it, and then turned around and went back to the deer or past it again to see if there were any witnesses anywhere. The two men in the second seat were probably their best shooters. They would shove one cartridge in the chamber, shoot the deer, and then they would all get out of there as fast as possible. They would return the following day, locate the carcass, dress it out, and haul it back to camp. It was a well thought-out plan and it would take a lot of luck for a warden to be in the right place at the right time to intercept them and make an arrest that would hold up in court.

To me these were the most unsportsmanlike people on the face of the earth.

Chapter 8/ RECOGNIZANCE RELEASE

Late one summer day in the afternoon, I went up to Ditch 14, which is the trail into Rocky Point Resort and to various accesses on the north side of Upper Red Lake. About four miles in on the Ditch 14 grade, I met a pickup truck with a camper mounted on the back. They were pulling a trailer with a boat on it. I assumed they had been fishing so I blocked the road and got out of my patrol car.

As I walked up to the vehicle, I could see there were a man and woman sitting in the cab. The man was driving and when he rolled his window down, I told him I was the local game warden and I would like to check their fishing license and their fish.

The man got out of the truck, took his billfold out, and handed me a resident combination angling license. The license looked okay so I asked where the fish were. He pointed to the back and said they are in the boat. I checked that out and there were twelve walleyes in a pail in the boat. I then asked if there were any in the camper and he said no. I told him I wanted to get in there to check, and he told me it was quite difficult to get into the back because it required letting the back gate down before you could open the doors to the camper. I assured him I could do it and when I was satisfied there were no fish in there, I would close it up like it was. I got into the camper refrigerator and found lots of fish all filleted out. There were fifty-two fillets so that meant twenty-six walleyes over the limit. I took the fillets and put them in a plastic bag and seized them for the state.

The man was very friendly and admitted to trying to take too many fish. He was so cooperative that I told him normally we were supposed to charge all the individuals involved with all the overage. I told him I would charge him with thirteen fish over the limit and his wife with thirteen fish over.

Having the combination license in my possession, I was able to make out the summons for the man and one for the woman. Also, each would have a seizure slip for thirteen walleyes over plus the six that they could have taken had they not been caught cheating.

I read and showed the summons to the man. Then I told him that because he was a resident, he had the option of signing the summons that he would appear for court in Kelliher on the date I put on the summons, or he could post bail. If he failed to comply with one of the two options, I would have to arrest him and put him in jail.

He was almost eager to sign the summons and I gave him his copy. We had been doing all this business in the back of the pickup. I then opened the driver's side door and addressed myself to the woman occupant. I told her who I was and that I had found that she and her husband had taken and possessed twenty-six walleyes over the legal limit. I showed her the copy of the summons and seizure receipts and explained to her the options she had.

She asked me if her husband had signed those summons. I told him he had. She fairly exploded. She called him a stupid s.o.b, a dumb bastard, and then it got worse. I've heard old boatswain mates in the Navy curse, but they sounded like angels along side this old gal. Her husband peeked around the corner and told his wife, "I think you should sign the summons."

She really tore into him. She asked him when he was ever going to learn to check with her before signing his name to anything. Then she told me there is no way I would make her sign those summons. I told her that was her option. She hollered, "See you didn't have to sign those papers."

I then went around to the passenger side, opened up the door, pulled some hand cuffs out of my back pocket, ordered her out of the car, and told her in a nice pleasant way, "Lady, you are going to jail."

She just sat there and gasped. I could see a faint smile on her husband's face. He was standing on the other side of the pickup. She finally caught her breath and said, "Give me your pen and where do I sign?"

Chapter 9/ A SOUR HUNTING TRIP

One fall day in 1961, Gill Keeler, the game warden at Little Fork, called me and asked if I would like to come over to Little Fork and hunt some sharptail grouse. He told me of a farmer in his district so pleased with an arrest that Gill had made of some local shiners that he wanted to show his appreciation. He had a huge farm of 640 acres and that year there was a big increase in the number of sharptail. There were three of us in on that work party that night. Gill Keeler of Little Fork, Ray Appleby of Orr and myself that were invited.

A day and time was set to meet at a cafe downstairs from where Gill lived. Ray Appleby told Gill he had two big black Labrador dogs that loved to hunt sharptail and he hadn't had time to get out hunting with them yet that fall. "Would it be okay to bring them along?" They were confined to a kennel up by the bunkhouse in back of Ray's house. Gill thought that having the dogs along might be a good idea, so he told Ray to bring them along.

We all met at the cafe, had lunch and laid out our plans for this hunt. Ray suggested that he would drive his vehicle with the dogs because they were pretty enthusiastic jumping all over the inside of Ray's vehicle. Gill and I approved and we drove out in a separate vehicle.

Gill drove because neither Ray nor I knew just where this farm was. Gill said that when we get there, he wanted to introduce us to this farmer who was so generous as to let us hunt on his property.

When we came to this farmer's road and turned off the county road, Ray, who was behind us, honked his horn and signaled us to pull over and stop. We did so and walked back to Ray's vehicle. The farmer's road was close to a half a mile long. We could see a nice, well-maintained set of buildings. The two-story residence was to the left of the end of the road. A huge barn was in back of the house and a small long building with lots of little windows was dead ahead of this farm road.

Ray said he would like to let his dogs out to let off a little steam. They seemed to sense we were going hunting and they were hot to go. Ray opened the door and the dogs came out and started to run around the vehicles. They had to stop and sniff at every bush and tried to leave their mark, urinating on every tree.

Then it happened. We don't know if those two dogs smelled or heard something, but they started towards those farm buildings on a dead run. Ray started to bellow and holler at them to come back. He finally found his whistle and blew on that. All of this was to no avail. Those dogs had been attracted by something. They were just two big black Labradors in an apparent race to see who would get to that farmhouse first.

When they hit that farmyard, we were in our cars racing down that road. We saw the big attraction—chickens. There were chickens everywhere, running and flying for their lives, and those dogs were grabbing them. There were feathers flying all over the yard. It was bedlam. Some of the chickens ran into that long low building with all the windows and the dogs saw that. The dogs shot into that little opening the chickens used and those chickens were trying to get out. Some of them did manage to break the glass and get out. Those chickens were making so much noise that I don't think the dogs could hear Ray bellowing or the whistle. The whole thing was one huge disaster—there were dead and crippled chickens everywhere and two of the happiest, craziest black labs. Their mouths were full of feathers and they were covered with blood.

That was the scene when the farmer and his wife came running out of the house. It was unbelievable. Ray finally got hold of the dogs and he was so mad he was hitting and kicking the dogs. The dogs finally got the message and started to cower down around Ray.

The chickens were still clucking and running off. The dogs were shaking. I think they wanted more chickens, but I'm sure they had had enough of Ray's big boot.

The dogs were put in Ray's vehicle. Introductions were made. It was an embarrassing situation. We started picking up the dead chickens and trying to catch the cripples. A price was put on the dead chickens and it seems to me it took all the money the three of us had to pay for them. The cripples were killed and as I remember the farmer said they would clean them and process them for their freezer.

I can't remember what was done about the broken windows but I would guess Gill spent some time out at that farm replacing broken glass.

That was the end of our sharptail hunt.

Chapter 10/ LEO'S SETTLERS FROM OHIO

Leo Manthei, the warden at Blackduck, called me one day in late August to ask me to go to Blackduck.

I arrived at Leo's residence around 11:00 a.m. He told me a rather weird story that had been related to him. It seems that two men from the Forestry Department had been cruising an area south and east of Blackduck when they came upon a small log cabin with three male occupants. The foresters were reasonably sure this building had been put up since April of that year when these forestry men had last cruised this area. Also, they were under the impression that all of this land was federal or state land. They thought these new settlers may have purchased the land or otherwise acquired this land and the Forestry Department had not been made privy of this transaction.

Immediately on returning to their headquarters in Blackduck, the forestry personnel made a search of all land transactions and found no private acquisition of land anywhere near this new log cabin. So the forestry personnel alerted Leo and he in turn told me. Leo showed me a township map with a pencil drawing of a dirt car or truck trail that ended at an 'X' where the cabin in question was.

So now Leo and I have to investigate this situation. We drove out on a county road. At the approximate area shown on the map, we located vehicle tracks through the bush. We finally came to an area where we were reluctant to drive our patrol car for fear of getting stuck. We began to assume a four-wheel drive vehicle had been used to crawl back into this area.

So we locked up our vehicle and continued on foot. We came to an area where we were going down a slight grade and across a small, wet area. Then as we started up the grade on the other side of this small gully, we looked up and there was the little log cabin. We were approaching the west side of the building. There was a door and a bench that three men were sitting on. The sun was shining on them and in their eyes, and they failed to see us for a couple of minutes.

Suddenly all three of them snapped erect. One man ran into the shack through the door then out another door directly across this shack on the east wall. Both Leo and I broke into a run. Leo went through the shack doors just like the one occupant. The other two stopped inside when I came in. The shack was about ten feet by fifteen with a kind of an open-end loft on one end. The floor was dirt. There were firearms all over the place— shotguns and rifles. Over in the southeast corner was a small workbench and shelves full of reloading equipment—lots of powder, primers, and pellets.

On the dirt floor was a unit made up of boards about three feet by three feet. I lifted that up and found a square hole in the ground about two feet deep. There were packages in there. I took one out and found it to be about a three-pound chunk of meat. There were some deer hairs on the meat and the meat was starting to smell rancid.

I made the statement, "That's venison." Then I asked these two men for some identification and they submitted their drivers' licenses. They were from Ohio! I couldn't believe what we had gotten into. These two men started to get a little belligerent but I straightened them out on what we had on them and suggested they could have a lot more problems.

I asked the two men what gun they used to kill that deer. One man said, "My twenty-two."

The only twenty-two they had was a twenty-two two-fifty, a real fast, high-powered gun. So I seized that.

About this time Leo came back with the runner. We started to check their billfolds. They were married men with children that just decided to take a wild fling and take off like old time settlers and live off the land.

We found partridge feathers, a bear, and beaver skins in tubs with some kind of preservative. They had failed to acquire non-resident hunting licenses. Not that it would have made any difference because no hunting season was open.

Leo charged them with taking one deer in closed season. We carried out some of the packages of meat for evidence. We also seized the one rifle.

I believe Leo charged them in Justice of the Peace Court and they all pled guilty and each paid a fine of $300 and costs. I never did hear if Leo did anything about their cutting down trees on state land and building their log shack.

I did run into one of them in a store in Blackduck about two weeks later. I was amazed and I confronted him with "What are you still doing in Minnesota?"

He just came back with, "Look, you guys caught us, we pled guilty and each paid a $305 fine. What more do you want?"

I never did ask Leo why they were still there and where they were staying.

Chapter 11/ DEER HUNTERS FROM GULLY

It was November 16 of 1961. The deer season with firearms had been open since Saturday at sunrise. I was stationed at Waskish, Minnesota, and I was up to my armpits with deer hunters all day long and a few of them at night. I could use some help, however, that was the status of all the other wardens. If I got in a real desperate situation, I could always call Leo Manthei or Harland Pickett.

On this day in November, Jerry Liemandt, my brother-in-law, stopped at my station and offered to give me a hand if we would put him up and feed him for a few days. He had taken the job as Chief Coordinator of the Firearm Safety Training Program in the State of Minnesota.

He said he had been up to Warroad doling out supplies and assisting Warden Markovich. Jerry was an old hand at working nights on deer shining so I really welcomed his expertise. Jerry's office was in the State Capitol complex however, he lived out by Lake Minnetonka.

He was really on his way home when he had decided to stop by to see how I was getting along. That evening my wife packed a double size lunch and two thermoses of coffee.

I had become aware of a group of deer hunters that were camped at Shorty Hillman's Resort and I had become aware of their tactics. They seemed to prefer cruising Highway 72 and Old Highway 72 that runs north and south through Waskish.

They used a dark color Chevrolet, a seven-passenger station wagon.

Jerry Liemandt, Bill's brother-in-law and Chief Warden for Minnesota when he retired

I decided on this night with Jerry, we would set up in the approach to the old C.C. Camp about five miles south of Waskish. It was a mild night. There were a couple of inches of snow on the ground. The highway was clear. However, the gravel roads and logging trails were packed snow—icy, and slippery. We started our surveillance at about 7:00 p.m. Over the next four hours we had three or four vehicles pass us at or near the maximum speed limit—not your typical hunting outfit. A little after 11:00 p.m., a car came from the west on Old Highway 72. It stopped at the stop sign and then continued east across Highway 72 down County Road Number 110.

I told Jerry we could possibly have a hunter in this vehicle because no one lived east of Highway 72. So we came out of our hiding place onto Highway 72 and turned south to County Road 110. All of this was without lights. When we came to County Road 110, looking east we could see the taillights of the vehicle. It appeared to be moving rather slowly so I turned east to follow it. The car was about a half a mile ahead of us. I drove as fast as I dared to without lights on a snow packed road that was full of ruts and was slippery.

We got up to within two hundred yards when the vehicle turned to the left on to an old logging trail. We were moving along about forty miles per hour when I realized he was backing up, apparently to turn around. I slammed on my brakes and we slid on that packed snow. Just as this car came about to head west, we stopped almost colliding with this vehicle. We immediately got out of the patrol car and ran to this vehicle. There was only one man in the car, but it immediately became obvious to us something was amiss. There was a spotlight in the back seat with a long wire up to and under the dash. Also, one back window was open.

This had all of the characteristics of a night hunters' vehicle that had dropped off one or more passengers to dress out or move a deer. With that in mind, we started to interrogate the driver. He told us he was a part of a group of four that had a hunting camp of tents set up by the wood dam on the Little Tamarac River. He said he got confused and realized he was on the wrong road back to their camp. That's why he was turning around.

I told Jerry I would almost bet that a deer may have been killed on the Tweeten Fields, which are located on the west side of old Highway 72.

This young man said there was no way he would be a party to any illegal deer hunting. He said they were all from Gully and Gonvick and anyone that lived in that country really frowned on hunting deer at night or in closed season.

I told Jerry I would ride back with the man in his vehicle and that he should follow us in the state vehicle. I carefully explained to Jerry we would go back west from where this car came from and then we would come to a pretty good-sized sweeping curve to the south. The fields on the right hand side would be the possible area this fellow had dropped off his passengers.

At this disclosure, Jerry said, "You know this country and roads better than I do. I'll get in the back seat and after this driver has negotiated this curve to the south, I will have him drive slowly and maybe his buddies will step out."

Then he said, "You stay close behind us without lights so when and if these guys show themselves you will be right there to back me up." With that, Jerry crawled into the back seat. Both of us were well aware this could be risky because the empty gun case was reason enough to believe they had at least one rifle with them. Also, we would be outnumbered.

With that, we started west. The car in question with my brother-in-law in it with their lights on and me in the state patrol vehicle following about thirty yards behind with my lights off. It was a black overcast night, no moon. About the time we crossed Highway 72, I heard Leo Manthei, the warden at Blackduck, check in on his radio.

I called him immediately and requested him to come up where we would probably be. I told him to come up the old Highway 72 from Kelliher. He was about thirty miles away so it would be some time before he got to where we were.

About the time I was finishing giving Leo the directions, we were into the big sweeping curve and I realized the car I was following increased the speed and all of a sudden I didn't know where the road was. I slowed down so I wouldn't go in the ditch. I could see the lights of the car Jerry was in going down the straight away south. At that instant, my right front wheel went over the edge and I could feel the car come down on the frame onto that ridge on the topside of the curve. Immediately I put the car in reverse and I didn't move.

I jumped out to see what kind of a mess I was in. The car actually rocked sideways on this high ridge. One glance down the road and I could see the brake lights come on the vehicle Jerry was in. They were at least a quarter of a mile away.

I took a quick look in the front of the car and I thought maybe I could drive the car ahead down on the grass and I could get enough momentum generated to get back up on to the black top. Also, there was a judicial ditch at the bottom and about thirty feet ahead where it came under the road in about a four-foot culvert. I know I made a request to the Lord to give me some help and with that I put her in low and with a lot of body English I went down the bank and then I cranked her to the left and I shot back on to the black top.

I could see in the back window of the car ahead that was stopped a light from a flashlight (Jerry's) flashing left and right. I fairly shot down that road and I snapped on my lights. Let me tell you, I was thankful to the nth degree.

I pulled up behind the car. Everyone was inside. Jerry said, "When the two men came in the back seat, I wrapped one arm around each of them and hollered, 'Game Warden'." There he sat and I wasn't there so he started waving his light out the back window—what a mess and it could have been a disaster.

We all got out of our cars and either Jerry or I looked down in the ditch and there was no deer. I noticed a knife in a holster on one of the men. I reached over and jerked it out. There was a little blood and some deer hairs on the blade.

We both got quite insistent asking where the deer was but they stuck to their story — no deer. I told them there were more wardens coming up from the south and when they got there, I would go home and get my dog, bring him back, and I would have that deer in minutes. They finally figured they were caught up so they took us further south about a hundred yards and there down in the ditch was a nice buck and a doe.

About that time, Leo showed up. He had someone with him, but I don't remember who it was. We loaded the deer up onto the trunk of my patrol car. We decided to haul the four hunters to Blackduck to put them in jail until morning when we would haul them to Bemidji to run them through court.

I asked these men, "Is there someone else out in your camp?"

They said, "No."

I then asked, "Are there guns or other things of value at your camp?"

They said, "We have guns and a few other items."

I told them, "If you would like us to, we will go out and remove these items from your camp and lock them in the trunk of the state car until the next day when we see you."

They said, "We would be pleased if you would do that."

The next morning I called the county attorney to see if I could get a shining charge against the four men. I told him exactly what happened and that it was so black out the night before you couldn't possibly see without a light to shoot. He asked me, "Did either one of you see them cast the rays of light on that field?"

I told him, "No we didn't actually see them cast the light."

He said, "All you can charge them with is 'Take one deer in closed hours' which is a misdemeanor with a maximum fine of $100."

I told him, "We can do better than that in the Justice of the Peace Court."

So we went to Blackduck and took them to Kelliher before Justice of the Peace Clara Quale. I wrote each man with two summonses, to wit, "Take one buck deer in closed hours and take one doe deer in closed hours".

That way each man paid $200 and because there were two violations we voided their deer licenses and snapped their tags and sent them on their way.

Chapter 12/ 'VENISON FOR SALE'

This is kind of a long story and I'm not going to take a stand for or against Bill Kues' claim against the State of Minnesota. I am, however, opposed to his method of getting attention.

The Waskish station was vacant and had been for two years when I was sent up to work with Warden Harland Pickett at Baudette in the fall of 1960. There was a state log house and several log out buildings located on the Tamarac River, which drained into Upper Red Lake about a quarter of a mile downstream. I became quite interested in bidding on this station. I then checked and found out that Warden Al Markovich of Warroad was the last man at the Waskish station. He let me know in no uncertain terms that I was crazy to bid on the Waskish station. He told me, "Those people in that community don't want a game warden there."

So, for the two years, it had sat vacant. It was divided up in 1/3 parcels with Warden Pickett absorbing the north part, Warden Manthei absorbing the southwest part, and Warden Claude absorbing the southeast part.

In the southeast part, Warden Claude inherited a feisty old character, Bill Kues. Bill Kues was having a battle with the State of Minnesota. Bill claimed that the State of Minnesota made an agreement with a group of commercial fishermen during World War I asking them to take less money for their fish per pound. The money the fishermen did not receive would be given to the fishermen after the war as a bonus. When the war ended, the Indian fishermen got the bonus but the white fishermen did not. Bill kept track of the amount of money and claimed the state owed him $90,500. Bill Kues claimed that if the law to return his money to him did not exist, then there was no law in Minnesota and he planned to operate as if no laws existed. Now, Bill didn't just carry out his battle with Minnesota in the hinterlands of the state. No sir, he carried his battle right to the Commissioner of Conservation, the Minnesota Legislature and the Governor. At one time, he went to St. Paul and personally and physically occupied the Commissioner of Conservation Office and chair for two days. Apparently, the commissioner found something to do in other places of the state and he allowed Bill to occupy his chair.

Bill Kues often got good publicity from newspapers and was able to have papers print articles about his fight with the State of Minnesota. He was shooting deer illegally and advertising that he had venison for sale. Selling game was also illegal.

The following editorial cartoon by Fearing ran in the <u>St. Paul Dispatch</u> and was later copied in the <u>Kelliher Independent</u>. The cartoon is printed courtesy of the <u>St. Paul Pioneer Press</u>.

At any rate, this is where I came into the picture. After all, I was 43 years old and I was expendable and I'm sure the head office thought that maybe I could remove this thorn in the side of the department. At the time when I bid on this station, I had never heard of Bill Kues.

On January 16, 1961, I was to report to Supervisor Tarte at Bemidji and then to go on to Waskish to take up residence in the state house. My wife and children wanted to stay in our home in Edina until the school year was out in June.

Forester Roger Anderson and Bill with a moose in front of the forestry building at Waskish

When I arrived at the Waskish residence, I found the furnace had been removed. The water heater had been removed, but that didn't matter because there was no water. The district forest ranger, Roger Anderson, who lived in a state house about a hundred yards north of the warden residence, took compassion on me and allowed me to move into one room of the forestry log office building.

It was during these later winter months and early spring months that I started to hear bits and pieces about this Bill Kues.

My first contact was when he sent me a post card in March of 1961 that he had caught a fox.

Dear Bill!
I got a Fox so
I wish you com
over with your
Bonty Papers I
would bring em
in to Warkish, but
the Fox smels over
strong I am libel
to stink the hole
Warkish out ef
Roger Anderson got
a few trees to spare
bring some out W Kues

In those days, the state paid a bounty of three dollars for a fox. Bill didn't have a car and he lived about five miles north and east of Waskish, so I gathered up my bounty book and drove up to Bill's home. It wasn't much of a house. It was one room with tarpaper on the outside. He did have one electric light hanging from the rafters. He had a wife, Rosie, who had the mentality of a five year old. The story was that Bill's father-in-law gave Bill one hundred dollars to marry her. I can neither prove nor disprove that rumor, but it seems reasonable.

Home of Bill and Rosie Kues

Now Bill Kues was one powerful man. He stood about five foot ten, but he must have weighed about two hundred fifty pounds and there was not an ounce of fat on him. He had big bones, broad shoulders, and lots of muscles. Newspaper articles about Bill's battles said Bill was 85 years old but actually, he was around 70 years old when I first moved to Waskish.

Bill had quite a guttural brogue. He obviously was not a native, so I engaged him in a little conversation. He told me he had hired on a merchant ship as a seaman to escape being conscripted for the German army. He said the ship made port in a western seaport, I think in Washington State. This occurred in 1914. It was there he heard about land being given away in northern Minnesota. He settled on a 160-acre tract on the east side of Ditch 30, about a mile north of Upper Red Lake. There he learned the English language and he learned to read and write. His writing, though, was phonetic as you will note in his writing.

Bill went into a lot of detail telling me about his commercial fishing on Upper Red Lake, about various laws that permitted these homesteaders to fish during World War I, how they sold their fish through the Indian fisheries at Redby, and about the bonus the Indians got but the white men never received. He showed me reams of letters from representatives and senators as to what these various legislators were going to do to correct the inequity between the Indian fishermen and the white fishermen. All this is the basis for my story. There were a number of other white commercial fishermen or their offspring living in and around Waskish that were interested in Bill Kues getting a settlement with the State of Minnesota. In the event Bill got some money, they too would benefit because paying off Bill would set a precedent. These other people were not so bold. However, they would coax Bill on and he, being a full-blooded, bull-headed German, enjoyed being in the local spotlight. All of the white fishermen involved, as a group, retained the services of a lawyer from Bemidji known as Whitney Tarutus.

On one of Bill Kues' trips to St. Paul, in May or June of 1961, Bill managed to bull his way into the governor's office and the information that finally trickled down to me was that he told the governor or his staff that if he didn't get his money, he would go home and shoot a deer and sell it. If that didn't get their attention, he would shoot a moose and sell it, and if that didn't get their attention, he would shoot a game warden. That got my attention.

On July 25, 1961, I received a letter from Bill that he had venison for sale and that he had put a sign up on a fence post "Vension for Sale".

I called my supervisor, Dick Tarte, and told him this latest attempt by Bill Kues. Supervisor Tarte told me not to do anything until he contacted the county attorney and the probation officer. A few days later, when I went by the Kues' farm, I tore the "Vension for Sale" sign down and took it with me. Eventually, I turned it over to Supervisor Tarte.

On August 23, 1961, I stopped at the Kues' farm to bounty a fox and at that time, I asked Bill if, in fact, he really had killed a deer. He said yes and that he had shot it on his field one morning about ten days ago.

On September 5, 1961, while passing the Kues' farm, I saw a fresh deer hide hanging on the fence next to a new "Vension for Sale" sign. Again, I notified my supervisor and he told me not to do anything until he got back to me.

On September 14, Supervisor Tarte told me to come to Bemidji the next day and secure a search warrant from Judge Reed of Probate Court.

On September 15 at 9 a.m., I was in Judge Reed's office to receive the warrant to search Bill Kues' home, outbuildings, and land for deer or parts there of. If I found such contraband, I was to return to Judge Reed with the evidence and the person who had the contraband in possession.

Otto Herman, Rosie and Bill Kues in front of refrigerator with illegal venison seized with the search warrant

I contacted Warden Manthei and Warden Richards to meet me at my office in Waskish at 11 a.m. We met and proceeded to Bill Kues' farm where we made our search and found deer meat in about five pound chunks. We also took the deer hide and the "Venison for Sale" sign. I also took Bill Kues. Then Bill and I, with the contraband, returned to Bemidji to Judge Reed's chambers to return the search warrant and make my report to the court.

Bill Kues, Judge Reed and myself sat down at a table in the judge's chambers. The judge then produced a complaint form that was submitted to me to read. It was a standard form charging William Kues of having deer meat in possession in closed season in violation of the appropriate statutes. The judge asked me to swear to the complaint then sign it, after which Judge Reed read the complaint to Bill and asked him if this was a true statement. Bill Kues agreed that it was. Then the judge asked if Bill would enter a plea and Bill said he was guilty but he wanted a jury trial so everyone could hear why he had done this. At this point, the judge told Bill he had best seek council. So Bill said, "Get me the liar."

"The liar?" the judge said. "You mean lawyer. Whom do you want?"

"I want the liar. You know—the liar, Tarutus." Kues said.

The judge had a hard time containing himself for a few minutes. Then he announced this hearing would be continued to an unknown future date when Bill Kues would have time to seek council from his attorney, Mr. Tarutus. The judge then instructed me to take Bill home and that I should retain possession of the contraband in my deep freezer.

I was notified to pick up Bill Kues and have him in Judge Reed's chambers on September 20. When Bill and I arrived at the judge's chambers, we found Bill's attorney, Mr. Whitney Tarutus, waiting for us. After some consultation between the lawyer and his client, we all took our places around the table. Again Judge Reed read the complaint and Bill's attorney entered a plea of not guilty by reason of temporary insanity and delusion. The attorney requested a twelve-man jury with the trial to come up as early as possible in the upcoming term of District Court.

On September 30, 1961 at 4:30 p.m., I turned over one package of the meat that I had taken from Bill Kues' deep freeze to my supervisor, Dick Tarte. Tarte, in turn, was to take it to St. Paul for examination by the Minnesota Bureau of Criminal Apprehension Laboratory to test the meat to be sure it was, in fact, deer meat. The evidence was received at the laboratory from Chief Warden F.W. Johnson at 10:00 a.m. on October 2, 1961.

After many repeated continuances, starting with October 10, 1961, the county set up a trial date in District Court room in Bemidji on January 24, 1962.

On January 18, 1962, I received a letter from Paul Kief, the assistant county attorney, that I should check with Bill Kues to be sure he had transportation to Bemidji and if not I should bring him down. The trial started with the selection of a 12-person jury and eventually Warden Richards and I were called upon to testify to the facts concerning said meat in possession (believed to be deer meat). Then Mr. Fong, from the Bureau of Criminal Apprehension, was called upon to testify to the fact that the meat was from an animal in the deer family. Also there was a lot of concern on the defense attorney's part that the package could have gotten mixed up. The state had to satisfy him as to the continuity of possession in the transfer from my possession to Mr. Fong in St. Paul at the B.C.A.

At this point the judge declared a short recess. The jurors were escorted to the jury room by the bailiffs, and Mr. Fong sat down on a bench in the lobby accompanied by the county attorneys and the wardens. Out of the courtroom Bill Kues came and went directly up to Mr. Fong and said, "Could you tell if it was a buck or a doe?"

Mr. Fong responded, "No."

"Well, for your information, it was a buck," said Bill Kues loud enough for almost anyone in the courthouse to hear. Fortunately the jurors' door was closed. The bailiffs, who were with the jurors, said they did not hear Bill's outburst and it was their belief the jurors did not hear it.

After about a half hour, the court reconvened and the attorney for the defense now called for Bill Kues to testify in his own defense. He was sworn in, but before he could say anything, the judge stopped the trial because of the original plea Tarutus had submitted that Bill was mentally incompetent. The judge ordered me to escort Bill Kues to the Upper Mississippi Mental Health Clinic to be evaluated by Doctor Reed and his assistant. The two doctors spent about two hours with Bill Kues and then Doctor Reed and Bill Kues returned to the courtroom with me.

Doctor Reed was sworn in and he took the stand. I don't remember the exact terminology he used, but he made it clear in no uncertain terms that when Bill Kues really got to thinking about his problem with the state, he could easily kill people and it would not bother him in the least.

At this point, the trial was put on hold. The jurors were released, however, they were instructed not to discuss the case and that they would be called back within ninety days to complete the trial. In the meantime, the judge ordered that Bill be sent to the state mental institution at Fergus Falls for further evaluation. The District Court judge at that time had the authority to detain a person for up to ninety days in one of the state mental institutions for further study.

About two and a half months later, I was notified of a mental hearing trial date for Bill Kues by the Beltrami County attorney's office. I was told I should be in attendance, but I probably would not be called on to testify.

On the day of the trial, I was in the Beltrami County court house in Bemidji. I was rather surprised to see almost everyone from Konig and Waskish Township in the courthouse. I was told that Bill's attorney, Whitney Tarutus, had subpoenaed almost everyone from Waskish and the surrounding country.

A new jury was selected and impaneled and the trial got under way. Bill Kues was seated at a table with his attorney, W. Tarutus. Bill was obviously pleased to see the big turn out of his friends and neighbors on his behalf.

At the prosecution table was the county attorney and two doctors from the state mental institution at Fergus Falls. The doctors were sworn in and they took their turn at being interrogated by the county attorney and the defending attorney. Each of the doctors had a briefcase crammed with sheets of paper summarizing their observation of Bill Kues. Both doctors had similar findings and they corroborated Doctor Reed's findings made on January 16, 1961. There seemed to be no question that Bill's next move, if he were released, would be to kill a moose and attempt to sell it and if that didn't get some response, he would kill a game warden and he would have no remorse. After all, Bill felt it was the state's fault. The State of Minnesota drove him to it.

On an occasion the summer before, I had an opportunity to talk to Bill, man to man, about his statement he had made to the governor about eventually killing a game warden. He answered, "I'm getting older. Forty years have gone by and the State of Minnesota tries to ignore me." Then he went on. "I like you, but I have no transportation. You are the handiest game warden. So, yes, I guess it will have to be you."

Upon completion of the testimony from the doctors, Bill Kues' attorney, Tarutus, called one after another of the people from Waskish to testify as to Bill Kues' mental condition. To a man, they stated Bill Kues did not have a mental problem.

There was one incident in the testimony that especially stood out in my recollection of the events and that was when Milton Babin was called to testify. Now I will have to give you a little background on Mr. Babin.

Mr. Babin and his family came into the Waskish area (or to

be more exact, the township of Popple Island) from the vicinity of Chicago where he had been employed as a night watchman. He, too, came to this area because of the free land and all he had to do was prove up on it for five years. In his possessions he had a law book from the State of Illinois, which I believe, had some bearing on his being chosen by his neighbors to be their justice of the peace. If he ever doled out any judicial opinions on Popple Island, there is no record of it.

Now we have a situation where Mr. Babin is in a genuine courtroom with a judge in a black robe, bailiffs, court reporter, attorneys, and the American flag. He has been called upon to testify. When he responded to the clerk of court when asked if he would tell the truth, anyone on the second floor of that courthouse could hear him say, "I do." He then took his seat in the witness box. When Tarutus questioned Mr. Babin as to his name and where he lived, it became obvious that he was hard of hearing. Mr. Tarutus repeated his queries several times before getting an answer. Also, Mr. Babin would cup his hand behind his ear to try to improve his hearing.

Tarutus was tiring of yelling his questions to Mr. Babin, so he decided to ask the one and final question, "Do you think Bill Kues is crazy?"

"What's that you say, young feller?" Mr. Babin asked, as he again cupped his ear. Mr. Tarutus repeated his question at which time Mr. Babin came out of the witness box, down to the defense attorney's table, and again asked, "What's that you say?"

Mr. Tarutus repeated his question, "Do you think Bill Kues is crazy?"

Mr. Babin straightened up as tall as he could, he looked all around the court room. His gaze stopped and he stared at the two doctors, who happened to be sitting in front of me. Mr. Babin said loud and clear for the whole world to hear, "If Bill Kues is crazy, so am I!"

At this point, I overheard one of these doctors whisper to

his partner, "We didn't get them all."

The other doctor whispered back, "We'd better send a Greyhound bus up there."

The trial finally came to an end with the jury concurring that they thought Bill Kues should be committed to a mental institution for the rest of his life.

Eventually, he was released and he spent his last years with his wife in the nursing home in Kelliher, Minnesota.

I can assure you, my wife was thankful.

Chapter 13/ ENTRAPMENT

It was the second week in August 1961. I was stationed in Waskish, Minnesota. I had been here for eight months. I received a telephone call from my former employer, Bill Groth of St. Paul Linoleum and Carpet. I had been an installer of floor covering and eventually they had made me the dispatcher of the installers. I was paid about $10,000 a year. I quit to take a job as a game warden for about $4,000 a year. A lot of people thought I was a candidate for a mental institution.

Bill wanted to know if I could do an installation for them. The job was a new school building at Red Lake on the Red Lake Indian Reservation. I told Bill I had about two weeks of accumulated leave coming, and also I could use the extra money. We had a boy in high school and we had a daughter in college at Bemidji. However, I would have to get permission from my supervisor, Dick Tarte. I told him I would call Supervisor Tarte and see if I could take my leave at that time.

I called Supervisor Tarte and told him what had been offered to me. He said, "Willie, do you have many tourists around Waskish and are the walleyes biting?" I told him the resorts were about 30% filled and the fishing had slowed down considerably. I assured him I would have all car-killed deer picked up in the evening, and I would be home at Waskish on the weekends to check weekend fishermen. My wife would be home to take any calls or messages.

So he said "How long will it take you"? I told him there were eight classrooms, one long corridor and two apartments for new schoolteachers in another building. A total of about 12,000 square feet of floor covering and eight linoleum counter tops. I told him if everything was ready it should take me about eight, eight-hour days. He said, "OK but send me a written request for the days you want off."

I thanked him and I called Bill Groth back and told him the supervisor said I could take my accumulated leave. So Bill said, "Wonderful, we'll send you the plans, color schedule and the patterns." Then he said the general contractor had called the shop and asked for an installer to be on the job site the following Monday.

My wife and I were elated. We would be able to pick up about an additional $500 plus my salary as a game warden.

So, the following Monday, I loaded up my toolbox, tile cutter, and roller. My wife packed me a lunch and a thermos of coffee. I still had three or four old shirts that said "St. Paul Linoleum" on the back and my name "Bill" on the shirt pocket. I took Patricia's Ford sedan and left for the new Red Lake school about fifty miles away. I got to the job site about 7:30 a.m. which surprised the superintendent for the general contractor. He asked, "What time did you leave St. Paul?" I told him about 2 o'clock that morning. The last thing I wanted to be known was that I was a game warden for the State of Minnesota. I would be about as popular as a rabid skunk at a ladies' tea party.

He asked how long I thought it would take me to finish the job, and I said a wild guess, if nothing goes wrong, would be eight or nine days, providing he would see to it I got spaces free of other workmen. He assured me he would cooperate. He wanted to wind this job up.

So, I started in cleaning out about four classrooms when in came a Mr. Roger Jourdain. He was wild. He was the head muckity muck on the reservation. He told me I had to hire one Indian for every white man on the floor-covering job. I told him I didn't need a helper. He really exploded after that. He said it was in the contract and I was not to go to work until I hired an Indian. I asked to see the contract and he showed it to me. Also the super on the job confirmed it. I told both of them, "I don't see any Indians with the carpenters, painters, or plumbers." They assured me they were around somewhere. I told them I would have to call St. Paul and check on that.

It turned out it was on the specs, but the estimator didn't tell Bill or Howard, the owners, when he submitted the bid. Maybe that was the reason he was the low bidder. Bill asked if I thought it was compulsory. I told him this Roger Jourdain is king here on the reservation and he said I don't work if I don't hire an Indian. I asked Roger Jourdain if he had any Indians who knew how to lay floors. He told me, "I've got a man out in the car for you to hire." So, I told him to send him in.

The man came in, and looked like a fairly decent person. So, I had him fill out 1040 papers and told him I was authorized to pay him apprenticeship wages, which was always 50% of a journeyman's wages. He agreed that was fair. So, I took the man up to the room I was cleaning out. I gave him my broom after I showed him how to use it. I left him in the room sweeping. He acted as though he thought the chore was beneath him.

I took my two-wheeler and went down to the room to check the quantity of boxes of tile and the colors. Everything checked out OK, and so I loaded up the two-wheeler with some adhesive to stack out in the hall in front of the various rooms.

I looked into the room where my Indian was, and he was gone, the floor unswept. I asked one of the tradesmen on the job if he had seen him. His response was he was probably with the rest of the Indians and he didn't know where they were.

At noon the workmen gathered out on a concrete platform

on the north end of the building to eat their lunch so I joined them. Also, here was my helper along with several other Indians. I asked where he went and why he didn't tell me he was leaving. He told me he went home to pack his lunch.

After we got done with lunch, all the Indians got in a couple of cars and left. I asked one of the painters, "What goes on around here?"

He just said, "That's the way it is around here." Also he warned me not to deduct any money from their check or I would not find things too pleasant. He said this is just like another nation and Uncle Sam foots the bill.

I hadn't planned on any help so I didn't miss him. The Indians always seemed to show up at 8 a.m. Then they came every day and ate lunch and they always came back at quitting time at 4:30 p.m.

On Thursday, a fair sized Indian approached me. Told me he was the assistant principal in the grade school. He wanted to know if I wanted to buy a moose and take it home with me. I told him, "No, I don't want to buy a moose and anyway I wasn't going home until the next evening." It was warm and the meat would be spoiled.

Then the fellow said, "We haven't killed the moose yet. They plan to go hunting tomorrow and they are sure they can get one for you."

I said, "No way," and also, "it is against the law." He assured me it was not against the law for them to kill any moose or deer anywhere any time on the reservation.

I then asked what would it cost me. He said twenty-five cents a pound dressed out, and they would cut off the hooves and head. Again I told him, "No way and if I got caught hauling a moose, I would be arrested and the police would seize my car."

Then this fellow said, "We will deliver it to your house for twenty- five cents a pound."

Then I said, "I live in St. Paul."

He said, "I know that, just give us your address and telephone number."

I told this man, "I'll think this over this weekend and also I have to check with my wife. I'll let you know Monday when I come back." That's the way we parted.

That evening when I got home to Waskish, I told my wife the offer and that I was going to call Supervisor Tarte and see if he wanted me to set this up. I called him up and told him the whole story. I let him know I did nothing to start this offer, but I was sure I could arrange it and he could have some wardens down around the cities intercept these Indians with the moose. The super said, "Let me think this over and I will get right back to you." He didn't call back that evening.

He did call the next day and told Patricia to tell me, "Don't make any deals with the Indians regarding the moose. It would be entrapment."

Chapter 14/ WINTER FISH HOUSE

This incident started on March 1, 1962, on Upper Red Lake. As of this date all fish shelters and debris are supposed to be removed from the ice of Minnesota public waters. So I, as the local game warden, was out on the lake to be sure this law had been complied with. I came upon several shelters still out on the ice. The name and address is required to be attached to the outside of the house. I was able to write the summons for the violation and either present it to them in person or mail it to them.

Eventually, down along the south side of the lake, I came across a fair size fish shelter that was about eight foot by eight foot and seven foot high. The door was open and there was about a foot of ice on the floor. The last fisherman to open the fish holes had chiseled at least one hole open, and as the area was heavily laden with snow, the water gushed into the house until the water reached its pressure level.

Then the fisherman, instead of blocking his house up above the water table, chose to abandon the shelter and leave it. He apparently knew it was against the law because the name and address had been removed from the outside. The shelter license was removed from the inside. Also, the stove and all the fishing gear—stools, chisels, scoopers, etc.—had been removed.

Now, I'm getting a little mad about the situation. If I can't find out to whom this shelter belongs and get him in court and subsequently make him go out and dig his house out and remove it, I've inherited the job of removing it before the ice breaks up.

The more I thought of it, the madder I got. I started an inch-by-inch search of the walls and roof, inside and out, for any clue as to the owner. I noticed a hole on the side about the size of a baseball that was covered over by something on the outside. The owner had used a piece of cardboard stapled to the outside wall to cover the hole. I pulled off this cardboard and on the other side were a name and a mailing address to someone at Red Lake on the Indian reservation.

Now, I know if it's an Indian there is no way I will get him off the reservation to respond to a summons. However, I had to find out. As I had established a good relationship with the Red Lake police, I went down to the Red Lake police station and looked up Sergeant Smith. He knew everything and everybody on the reservation. He told me the man I was looking for was a white man and was a schoolteacher at the Red Lake school.

The next stop then was the Red Lake school. I met a white lady who was the principal. She knew this person when I mentioned the name. However, he hadn't taught there for some time. She thought she heard that he had found an opening in the school at Deer River. I thanked her and urged her not to inform this man I was looking for him. She agreed to this.

The following morning I drove to Deer River, approximately seventy-five miles from Waskish. This was to be a long shot. The name found on the piece of cardboard could be from someone else other than the owner of the house. I would have to be very careful when I met this man. However, I had to know.

I found the school in Deer River, entered it, and went to the office. The lady behind the counter said they had a teacher by that name. He taught high school English. She also informed me of his classroom number and that he had a class but that would be over in ten minutes.

I located his classroom and knocked on the door. A man opened the door and I asked him, "Are you Mr.."

He said, "Yes, I am."

I then asked him, "Would you step out in the hall? I have a couple of questions to ask you."

He told me, "I'm in the process of giving a test and can't leave the room."

By this time every student in the room was staring at the two of us. I then said quite loudly, "I'm sure you can trust your students. They all look honest to me. They won't cheat."

With that, he decided to step out in the hall and closed the door. I told him, "My name is Bill Callies," and I held out my hand for a handshake. I went on and told him, "I live at Waskish, Minnesota, and I am the game warden there. Part of my district is Upper Red Lake. On the first day of March all fish houses on the ice of public waters are supposed to be removed." Then I started to say, "I went out on the ice of Red Lake to see if—"

At that moment he interrupted me and said, "I have a fish house shelter on the ice of Red Lake and I plan to go up there this coming weekend with a couple of friends and remove it."

I had the right person—what a feeling of satisfaction. I told him, "Go back into your class and I'll make out the summons after you release your class." I scheduled him into Justice of the Peace Clara Quale's court that following Saturday, at 9:00 a.m.

Three men appeared in her court at the prescribed time. The violation was read to the schoolteacher. He pled guilty so the judge assessed a fine of $75 or thirty days in the county jail. That was a lot of money in those days; the normal fine was $15.

It took the combined effort of all three men to come up with the $75. Then the judge told them, "If you go out to the lake and dig out and remove every bit of the shelter, I will refund $50."

Then the judge turned to me and said, "I want you to be there at 12 o'clock noon to see that my order is carried out." She went on to say, "I don't want even one nail left out there." Then she went on to tell these men, "In prior years, before Bill Callies came here, there were fish houses and parts of fish houses floating around in the lake after the ice broke up. It was a menace and a nuisance to watercraft, swimmers, and cabin owners. I am one of them and from now on, it will not be tolerated."

The men worked like beavers chopping, digging, and hauling that house onto their trailer. They got the $50 back.

Unlike the fish house in the story, this fish house was left on Red Lake

Chapter 15/ GILES KISNER

One evening in late summer, my wife Patricia and I were sitting in the kitchen watching a pair of flying squirrels. They were sitting in our bird feeder that we had hanging just outside our kitchen window and eating sunflower seeds as fast as they could shuck them out. These animals are nocturnal. They have black bulging eyes and beautiful gray fur. It was pitch dark outside. These animals were regular visitors about this time of the evening. They had little or no fear of us sitting in a lighted kitchen within three feet of them.

Suddenly they jumped on the logs of our house, out of our sight, and were gone. About this same moment, we could hear the sound of a motor and a pair of weak headlights turned into our driveway. It was a man on an orange colored tractor. I got up, turned on a yard light, and met this person at the back door.

It was Giles Kisner. He was a beef farmer that lived about four miles south of Waskish on the east side of Highway 72 in Beltrami County. His face looked like it had been in a meat grinder. I invited him in and at the same time asked him, "What happened to you?"

He just said, "Leland and I have been at it again." Leland is Giles' number two son. The two of them had been bachelors for some time. Giles' wife had passed away. Giles had two other sons and one daughter—long gone from the nest.

Giles' house had neither inside plumbing nor electricity. He just didn't consider those things a necessity. At that time, Leland was about twenty-five years old. He was a big, powerful young man, but a little short on the mental side.

It seems Giles was not inclined to be an early riser. In fact, sometimes he didn't get up until past noon, but he liked to work late in the evening sometimes until midnight. This aggravated

Leland and they had many arguments and fights about this before.

When Giles threatened to have Leland committed to a mental institution, Leland would beat him to it. He would commit himself in and that way he could commit himself out. When the state psychiatrist would evaluate him, he would usually end up in the criminally insane unit at St. Peter, Minnesota.

Giles was told many times by members in the county that he should commit Leland but he was reluctant to do it. After all, where could Giles find a strong, young man to work for nothing?

This time, however, it seemed Giles just couldn't take another beating like he had just been subjected to. I told him, "I will not go down and pick up Leland but I will call Sheriff Tom Tolman and have him come and pick up Leland. I will assist the sheriff. However I am sure the sheriff will want you to sign the commitment papers tomorrow. Otherwise I doubt if the sheriff will make the sixty-mile trip from Bemidji to Waskish."

Giles told me, "Call Sheriff Tolman and I'll sign the commitment papers." I got on the phone and called Tolman. I told him the whole story and that Giles would go through with the papers. I told him to come to the state house and I would go with him to Kisner's.

In the meantime, Patricia got up some food for Giles. She also helped him clean up the dried blood on his hands and face and stuck on a few bandages.

About an hour later, Sheriff Tom Tolman and one of his deputies showed up at our state house. Giles restated the whole situation while Patricia kept busy filling coffee cups. Finally the sheriff was satisfied about how we would handle picking up Leland.

Giles was to ride with me in the state patrol car. The sheriff and his deputy were in the county sheriff's car. When we got to Kisner's, I was told to stay in my car while Giles and the sheriff went in to call Leland out. From where I was, I could see the light from the sheriff's flashlight playing around the rooms of the house on the first floor. Also, I could hear the sheriff's voice demanding that Leland come down from there.

About ten minutes later, the sheriff came out to me and said, "Leland is up in the loft. There are no windows. The stairway is almost as steep as a ladder. There are guns in the living room but I'm not sure if Leland has one with him."

Leland finally hollered down, "I'll surrender to the game warden," meaning me.

The sheriff asked me, "Go in and try to talk him into coming down."

I went into the house with my five-cell flashlight. I called out to Leland who I was and then asked him to come down and get this over with. He apparently sat down on the floor in the loft because I saw his two shoes come down on the top step. The two of us talked nicely and quietly for maybe ten minutes then real slowly the shoes turned around and Leland backed down the steps.

He jumped the last three steps and then fairly shot across the room to where several guns were leaning against the wall. It made me just freeze but it wasn't the guns he was after. It was a big brown manila envelope he scooped up off this old table right next to the guns.

We went out to the cars. I had planned to go home, however, Leland wanted to ride with me. So I followed the sheriff the twelve miles into Kelliher. The sheriff stopped in front of the school and motioned me in behind him.

He came back to my car and told Leland there was no sense in making me drive him all the way down to Bemidji. Then I would have sixty miles to go back home. Leland agreed to go with the sheriff until the sheriff pulled out some cuffs. Leland took some offense at that, so I told Leland that if he would behave himself, the sheriff would not cuff him. The sheriff relented and agreed to this so Leland got into the sheriff's car and headed for Bemidji.

Chapter 16/ ON DULL, DRY DAYS

There would be days later in the summer when it seemed no one was violating the Game and Fish Laws. Leo and I would meet in Kelliher for coffee and complain to each other about how we couldn't make a pinch anywhere. We were desperate. However, for sure, we couldn't do our job sitting in a cafe.

So, we decided to head for the reservation. We would see if we could catch someone who had bought some fish from one of the Indian fishermen, not from the Indian fisheries at Redby. Buying from the fisheries would be a legal transaction and they would have a receipt from the fisheries.

There was a place on the east side of Lower Red Lake and on the east side of the blacktop road that came from Ponemah that was on the Red Lake Reservation that I could maneuver my patrol car through the brush and end up looking north at the road due to a small jog in the road. (I was always quite concerned that if a bunch of young bucks caught me in there, I would probably come out about fifth best.) Unless I was seen driving into that jog, there was little chance of my being seen when the leaves are on.

Leo would usually sit on a place on the north side of State Highway 1 where it comes off the reservation.

There we would sit, wait, and watch. We had constant contact with each other by way of our two-way radios.

Every time I saw a car coming from the north, I would check it out with the aid of my binoculars. Most of the cars were native people. When a car came towards me with white men in it, I would alert Leo. Sometimes, I would be able to read the license number.

When the car had passed my entrance point, I would come out on the black top and follow it, providing there were no Indians there to see me. I would usually be a half-a-mile behind the car at first, but I would get close enough to know if the driver turned east on Highway Number 1 or crossed Highway Number 1 heading south towards Nebish. This was the information Leo was waiting for. Usually they turned east. If they went south, Leo had a way, by hard driving, to get ahead of them. I always stayed behind at least a quarter-of-a-mile until I got off the reservation.

Then I would gain on the car but would stay back until I saw Leo cruising in front of the car. Then we would close in, give the driver the red lights, stop the car on the shoulder, identify ourselves, and have the driver open the trunk. Every time we did this we found fish—lots of fish.

This area was a part of Leo's district so he made out the summons, seizure receipts, got the person before the judge, and made out the arrest reports. He usually put me down as an assist.

One time, Leo called me and said he got a tip that Albert White from Ponemah was going to the Twin Cities with a load of fish. He would be leaving about noon with his family in a maroon colored four-door Oldsmobile. We got down in the area about 11:00 a.m. and hung around until about 1:00 p.m. before we decided he either didn't go or he left the reservation by some other route. So we drove onto the reservation past Albert's house and his car was gone. Leo and I were each in our own car. Leo suggested we drive into a trail off the Jerome Road where the Indians fillet out thousands of pounds of walleyes. You have to see it to realize the quantities of fish these Indians sell illegally. There are trails throughout the bush around the perimeter made by bear coming in to feed on the heads, guts, etc.

I was ahead of Leo when we came out to the Jerome Road. I looked to my left and there was a maroon Oldsmobile getting gas at the one hand-powered pump in front of Jerome's Little Store. I grabbed my mike and said, "Leo back up," and so did I. We got back out of sight of the Jerome Road then I told Leo, "I saw a maroon four-door car at the gas pump."

Leo suggested that he would go back to Highway Number 1, then east to a county road, and then north to intercept him. I was to wait until the maroon Oldsmobile pulled out and follow him at a fair distance so as not to alarm him but keep a running report as to his location.

That's the plan. Leo pulled out and turned west, then south to Highway Number 1, then east. About this time, Albert came out of the store, got in his car and started east on the Joe Jerome Road. I followed him about a half-a-mile behind him. About three miles down the road, he spotted me because he started driving faster. When he came to County Road 23, he turned south instead of going east on County Road 34. I called Leo and told him, "He has me spotted and we are driving pretty fast on 23."

Leo Manthei having the nursing home administrator sign to accept a gift of confiscated fish

Leo called back and said, "I will be heading north on County Road 23." He said he would put his car crosswise in the road just south of the last turn to the south. We had him boxed in only he didn't know it until he made that last turn south and saw Leo's car.

I was real close behind him. He would hit the brakes, then go ahead, then hit the brakes again. He didn't know whether to let me take him or let Leo take him.

We got him stopped. He had eight plastic bread sacks of filleted walleye pike. There were twenty-five fish in each one for a total of two hundred walleye pike.

Chapter 17/ LITTLE ALCAN HIGHWAY

It was November 10, 1962—the first weekend of the Minnesota firearm deer season. My supervisor, Dick Tarte, had sent a man up to assist me to check hunters. His name was Jack Backer. He was new with the game warden department but the Minnesota State Fisheries had employed him. I think he had made a lateral transfer, but I don't remember if he was on probation or not at that time.

Also, there was my son, Fred, who had built for himself a deer stand about twelve miles southeast of Waskish.

The three of us along with my wife had planned to get up about 5 a.m. My wife was going to make breakfast for us. She had made up three big lunches for us to take along in case we ended up a long way from home around noon.

Our day really started at 3:45 a.m. when the phone rang. I got up and answered it. It was one of the deputy sheriffs of Beltrami County down in Bemidji. Some party had called them a few minutes before to locate some deer hunters at the Kansas City Resort. It seems there was a death in one of the deer hunter's family and they wanted him notified. The deputy put in a long distance call to the Kansas City Resort and no one answered. That is why the deputy called me and asked if I would try to call the resort. If I got no response would I go down to this resort, locate the specific person, give him the telephone number, and tell him to call it on receipt of this information?

The Kansas City Resort is located on the southeast part of Upper Red Lake. The only way you can get there by car is to drive south of Waskish about two miles. The trail that goes off to the southwest is well marked on Highway 72 with a big sign, "The Little Alcan Highway to Kansas City Resort".

This trail, for two and a half miles, is strictly a one-car, dirt road. At various places there are small turnouts for passing cars going in the opposite direction.

The first thing I did after receiving this call was to call the Kansas City Resort. I let it ring many times, but it was finally obvious Elmer Tuttle wasn't going to get out of bed to answer his phone.

I decided to wake up my whole crew and start the day an hour earlier. My wife was already up and dressed so she started making a big breakfast. Everyone got up and dressed and came down to breakfast. With Fred in the back seat with his rifle and lunch, and Backer in the front seat, we left the town of Waskish to head for the Kansas City Resort.

It was dark as it could possibly be, overcast, and the temperature was in the twenties. I always had hopes of catching a night hunter, so, I only drove with the aid of my sneak light. There were no cars out on Highway 72. Then we turned down The Little Alcan Highway.

About half way down the trail, we could see the glow of headlights coming toward us. The road had several small curves at the particular place where I stopped the patrol car. I told Jack and Fred I would wait ahead on the road about fifty feet which would be about where the oncoming car would realize the road ahead was blocked. I would check them to see if they were the party I was to give the message to.

When the vehicle came around the curve and saw our patrol car blocking the trail, it stopped within a few feet of where I was standing. When I opened the driver's door, I saw movement of someone trying to hide an uncased firearm. I immediately retrieved the firearm and opened the action to find it was fully loaded in both barrel and magazine. I laid the firearm on top of the car and then asked if any of the occupants were the party wanted for the death message. They were not. I then asked the driver for his deer license or driver's license. He submitted something to me. His name was Wilmert Arndt. I checked my watch and it was just 5 a.m. I told the men that it was at least an hour and a half until legal shooting time. I told the driver he was in trouble for transporting a loaded, uncased firearm in a motor vehicle. I also advised them if they had seen a deer and shot at it they would all be in trouble, big time.

At this time, I saw another set of lights coming toward us. I told this group to just hold still while I checked this second car to see if any of the occupants were the one wanted for the death message.

I opened the driver's car door and again saw an uncased gun in the back seat with two men. They were in the middle of trying to get it in a case. I pulled the gun and case out and I also found the gun loaded. Again, I got either his driver's license or deer license for identification. I then asked if any of these men were the person wanted for the death message. They were not. I then advised the driver, Ervie Roemhildt, that he was in violation of transporting a loaded, uncased firearm. I stuffed his identification into my pocket because I saw another set of headlights coming through the bush. I laid the gun in the gun case on the roof of the vehicle, told the occupants I would take care of them as soon as I checked this third car. I looked at my watch and noticed it was 5:10 a.m.

The third vehicle proved to be a station wagon and again there was an uncased and loaded firearm. I asked if any of the occupants were the person I was looking for to be notified of the death message. They were not. The driver of the car was James Roemhildt. All of these people were from near Elysian. Also, I knew the Roemhildts; they were shirttail relation on my dad's side of the family. None of them knew me. However, they would recognize my name on the summons.

When I moved to stop this third vehicle, I saw Backer come bouncing out of the patrol car.

We wrote up the summons and seizure slips, and gave copies to each of the violators. I told the men I would leave the guns with the justice of the peace in Kelliher. After they had been in her court and paid their fines, they could submit their copy of the seizure slip and she would return their firearms.

Over the years, I was to catch other members of this group from Waterville, Elysian, and LeCenter. The last one was when I caught Lee O'Malloy from LeCenter on November 19, 1972, transporting an untagged deer up on Pine Island. He wanted to know how much longer I was going to stay at the Waskish station.

Well, we did finally locate the party that had a death in the family. Elmer Tuttle, the resorter, said the phone rings off and on all night and he just quits answering it when he goes to bed.

I took Fred to where his deer stand was and then Jack and I went to work checking hunters.

Chapter 18/ THE LAST DAY

It was the last day of the deer season, November 17, 1963. I had had it with the "Big Deer Hunter Sportsman". It seemed everyone had to get a deer and they didn't care how. I was so tired and fed up with lost hunters and violators. It was sundown and I was going home to my wife and son. I wasn't going to work another night.

My wife had promised Fred, our son, that he could invite his football coach to our house for a good home-cooked meal. I, too, was looking forward to a nice quiet dinner at home and pleasant, peaceful relaxation afterwards. My wife, Patricia, had gone all out. She had cooked Fred's favorite food—ruffed grouse, wild rice with mushrooms, low-bush cranberries, blueberry pie and all the fixings with it. It was a magnificent dinner.

It was about 5:45 p.m. It was pitch dark outside but so bright and beautiful inside—warm and cozy. I began to relax. I had survived another deer season. Life wasn't so bad after all.

We all sat down to the table and I looked at this young schoolteacher staring at all this food. I'm sure he hadn't seen a meal like this for a long time. We all pitched in eating, talking, and even laughing and then the phone rang. Patricia said, "I'll get it. You're not going out tonight. I'll take care of it."

Patricia said, "Hello," and then she listened. She looked up at me and she said, "It's Jim Petrowske. Someone shot right in front of his house on Highway 72 on the south end of Waskish."

Jim was a close friend and he hated night hunters. I knew I had to go. Patricia just told Jim, "He is on the way," as I went out the door.

I jumped in the patrol car and took off fast through town. There, sitting on the highway was an old car and a man was standing in the back with a five gallon gas can pouring gas into the car. There was another man outside the car.

To say the least, I was mad. I told them I was a game warden and I opened the car door. There was an empty 30-06 shell on the floor of the back seat. I picked it up and I could feel some warmth in the shell. I turned on these two men and said, "Where is the deer that you just shot."

The response was, "We didn't shoot any deer."

About this time, Jim came across the ditch from his home

on the east side of the road. I asked him if this was the car the shot seemed to come from. He allowed it was and it hadn't moved since the shot.

I then said, "I'll bet they killed that little fawn that had been coming out to the west side of the road ditch to graze every evening."

I pointed to about where I usually saw the deer, and I asked Jim to go see if the deer was there. Jim took off with one of my flashlights and within a minute he hollered, "Here is the deer shot right in the head."

I went to the fellow putting the gas in and I asked, "Who did this car used to belong to?"

He said, "It's my car."

"Not any more," I told him. Then I asked, "Which gun did you use to kill that little deer?"

All the guns were cased. The man along side the car said, "This one," and handed me one of the gun cases.

I pulled the gun part way out of the case, shoved it back into the case and told him, "You lie to me one more time and I will lock you in jail until next spring."

He grabbed another case, then shoved it in my hands and said, "I'm sorry officer, this is the right one." This gun was a Remington semi-automatic with a scope—at least this gun was a 30-06 to match the warm shell.

I went around to the back of the car and the man filling the car was dribbling gas all over on the highway and bawling like a baby. He started to plead with me to let them keep the car. It wasn't much but it was evidently all he had.

I had Jim drive the car into his yard. I got the deer licenses from these men plus their drivers' licenses. I asked Jim if he would jerk the entrails out of the little deer. Then I took the men to Kelliher. I had cooled off some by then. I showed them the bear cage in the fire hall where I was going to lock them up. Instead, I told them that if they had the money, I would let them stay in the old hotel in Kelliher until the following morning.

The following morning, I went down to the hotel and picked them up. I told them the night before I had intended to take them to Bemidji and charge them with shining which carries a fine of up to one thousand dollars each and/or up to one year in jail. However, in the morning I felt a little compassionate. I would take them before the justice of the peace in Kelliher. I would reduce the complaint to a misdemeanor. It would be "Take one deer in closed hours". The maximum fine a justice of the peace could impose would be one hundred dollars and five dollars costs and/or up to ninety days in jail. I told them if they conducted themselves like gentlemen, they probably would get off with just the fine and costs—one hundred and five dollars. Also, I would release the car but I would confiscate the gun.

They both thanked me for considering the lesser route. They promised they would never do a stupid thing like that again.

Chapter 19/ HANK WISTROM

One summer day, I was checking fishermen on the south part of Upper Red Lake. I came across a limb of a tree bobbing in the waves. I could tell by the way it was bobbing it was secured to something on one end.

When I was a young punk I used to go with John Slatinski, a commercial fisherman on Namakan Lake, as a helper. On a few occasions, John wanted to set his nets on the Canadian side of Namakan. We would go to shore and pick out a fair size limb or small log which he would tie a line to on one end with the other end tied to the net so that we could locate the net the next time we clerked it. He used to refer to these markers as his Canadian booyah, strictly illegal.

I was sure there was a net down under that piece of a limb

so I did not touch the stick. I just kept on proceeding in an easterly direction checking fishermen and watercraft. I was hopeful that whoever may have a net out there wasn't watching me from shore. I may have hesitated my boat or turned my head just a bit towards the stick. If there was a net down there and whoever set it had any suspicion that I was alerted, the owner would abandon the net.

Eventually, I got back home and told my wife what I had come across and my suspicions. I thought it might be a good idea to get down in that area where I could watch to see if someone would come to clerk the suspected net.

My wife packed me a huge lunch. I packed in my sleeping bag, mosquitoe dope, and drove to the area just at dusk by way of an old logging trail. I got close enough to the lake so I could see a boat out on the water near the suspected net from my patrol car. I did take my binoculars and walked down through the bush to check to see if that piece of limb was still there. It took me about fifteen minutes of intense looking, but I did locate the stick. So I settled down for some watchful waiting. A couple of times during that night I dozed off so when I came to, I would take my binoculars and slip down through the brush to check on that stick. There was about a half moon and the wind had gone down. Each time, I was able to locate the stick. Eventually, the sun came up and still no one showed up to check the suspected net.

I was able to call the dispatcher at Thief River Falls to call my wife that I was okay and still waiting and watching.

Early that evening I got a call on my radio that Harland Pickett, my neighboring warden from Baudette, was at my residence. My wife had told him where I was and what I was up to. Harland asked if there was anything he could do to help. I told him I could use some more food and something to drink. So my wife packed up some more grub and Harland started to come to try and find me with the food and drink.

It was getting quite dark again and I was in the process of

talking Harland into my stakeout site. Harland was about a half a mile away when I saw a dark object out on the water near the suspected net. Then I could see a small lantern light at the dark object.

I called Harland on the radio and told him to hold wherever he was. I thought my suspected net fisherman was in a rowboat near the net site. I told him I was going to leave my patrol car and walk to an area about an eighth of a mile west of me where there was a summer home owned by a doctor from North Dakota. I knew he had a nice fourteen-foot wooden rowboat turned upside down on the beach in front of his cabin.

I slipped through the brush to this cabin site and there I saw an old vehicle parked on a trail on the west side of the cabin. Also, when I looked to the beach, the boat was missing. I sat down in the brush along side the path that led from the cabin to the beach. Eventually I could hear the creak of oars and the splash as the dark shadow of a boat and two people in it coming into shore.

I sat real still as the boat was pulled up on the beach. A huge tub was lifted out of the boat. Then the boat was turned over. The two people picked up the tub (one on either side) and they came walking toward me.

When they were about fifteen feet from me, I stood up and shone my light on them. It was Hank Wistrom and his stepdaughter, a grown woman.

They dropped the tub and Hank just groaned, "Not the G... D... game warden."

I told Hank, "You got it right and you folks are under arrest for taking walleyed pike with a gill net." With the aid of my flashlight, I made out the summons and seizure receipt and set up a court date before Justice of the Peace Clara Quale. I did not charge the stepdaughter, as I knew Hank was a struggling farmer over next to the Indian reservation boundary and he could ill afford two fines.

When Hank came into court he pled guilty and was fined

thirty dollars or thirty days in the county jail. Hank told the justice he'd take the thirty days and she would have to send the Beltrami County Social Services to go out and feed and clothe his family for the thirty days he was in jail.

The judge said that was okay while she started to fill in the blank spaces on the commitment papers in her old typewriter. Then she said, "But first, I will make out a search warrant to check your deep freeze and root cellar to see how much and what kind of food you have on hand."

That was too much for Hank. He whipped out his pocket book and paid the court thirty dollars.

I would have liked to have served a search warrant. I'm reasonably sure I would have found all kinds of illegal game and fish.

Chapter 20/ FOUR BROTHERLY FISH HOGS

This problem started one day when I saw four men going upstream on the Tamarac River past my residence and office. They were in a sixteen-foot model "K" Alumacraft. I thought I had seen them coming back from Upper Red Lake earlier that day. The boat was from the Great Northern Resort owned and operated by Charlie Renwanz.

I thought this might be a good opportunity to check their fishing licenses and the number of fish in their possession. They had about a mile to go on the river to the resort. I thought if I took my patrol car, I would possibly arrive at the resort about the same time. I missed by a few seconds. They had already passed under the bridge that I had to go over. Their boat was slowed almost to a stop as they turned into the dock at the third or last cabin to the south on the east side of the river.

One of the men in the front end of the boat apparently saw me crossing the bridge and started pointing and waving his arms. Then two of the men started throwing fish back in the river. I had to drive south about 200 feet and in between the second and third cabin. I bailed out of the car and screamed, "Stop throwing those fish out of your boat and get that boat into this dock, now!"

Waskish warden residence and office

They did just that. There were lots of fish in the boat. However, I used an oar and pushed the boat out into the river. I used their dip net and scooped up three walleyes that were belly up. The way they were throwing the fish back, there must have been at least a dozen that came to when they hit the water and escaped.

That was all right because I was sure there must be around forty fish in the boat. They could legally have twenty-four.

I came back to the dock and asked for and collected their

angling licenses. All four were brothers. I heard someone in the background say something about "Gestapo Tactics".

I counted all the fish in the boat and there were thirty-nine which is fifteen more than they are allowed. Then, I walked into their cabin and I found twelve fillets in their refrigerator which would amount to six more walleyes. I then asked, "How many fish do you have in Renwanz's deep freezers out in his garage?"

They said, "I have no idea."

I went over to Renwanz's house and found the house empty. I then went to the garage where Charlie cleans, wraps, and freezes his guests' fish. The garage was locked, so, I sat down in the patrol car and filled in most of the blank spaces on the summons. I put their names on the seizure slip but left the quantity blank as I was sure I would get a good load out of the deep freezers.

I sat there in the patrol car waiting for Charlie and his wife to come home to unlock the garage. I thought Charlie might demand a search warrant although I knew I had the right to inspect his deep freezers in the garage—not in his home.

I called the dispatcher at Thief River Falls to get a hold of Leo Manthei, the warden from Blackduck. The dispatcher made several calls but Leo wasn't at home nor in his patrol car. If I could have contacted him, I would have had him pick up a search warrant from his justice of the peace for all of Renwanz's resort.

I thought I probably won't get more than a $100.00 fine from the local justice of the peace no matter how many fish I took from these men.

I wrote up the seizure slip, had the men sign them, and gave them their copies. The men appeared before Justice of the Peace Mary Rytter. I think they were all fined about $100 each.

While I was in the process of writing the summons, another of Renwanz's guests came over to see what I was doing there. When I told him I was waiting for the Renwanzs, he told me they had gone to Bemidji to have some skin cancer taken off

Charlie's face and he thought they were staying in Bemidji overnight. So, I gave up waiting.

Sometime later, I received copies of letters from the St. Paul office. These people had sent in a list of complaints. As I understand, these were some important people. The rumor was that one worked for the federal government and the other one was some church official.

Mary Rytter

Their big problem was they got caught.

I've got to give these four brothers "A" for effort but "zero minus zero" for sportsmanship and good citizenship.

Chapter 21/ *WOOD TICKS, ETC.*

On the second day, which just happened to be a Sunday, of the walleye pike season in 1964, a young man drove into the driveway of the warden station at Waskish, Minnesota. He introduced himself as a former resident but now a landowner on the south side of County Aid Road 110. He told me his dad was the homesteader to the property and he was born and raised on the land. His dad had long since passed away and he had inherited the old homestead.

The old house and a couple of sheds were still on the property but were in a sad state of repair. However, he still used the buildings when he came up to Red Lake to hunt and fish.

His problem was an old, old ongoing condition on the southwest part of their hay meadow—beaver! He claimed that a judicial ditch that flows from east to west plus a small spur judicial ditch that flows from north to south was plugged up by beaver dams. I asked him, "Have you seen the dams?"

He answered, "No. Not since I left the old homestead and moved to the cities."

However, many years ago when they put up hay and found that part of their hay meadow under water, they checked the judicial ditch and found beaver dams. Again this year in a walking patrol of his property, he found the southwest part of his hay meadow under water and made a request of me to remove the beaver and their dams.

I asked, "Why? Are you planning on putting up hay this fall?"

He responded, "No. I am not planning on putting up hay, but, Giles Kisner, my closest neighbor to the north asked me if he could cut and have the hay on this meadow."

Giles had a small herd of beef and was concerned that he might not have enough hay on his own property plus what he could find along side the road ditches.

I told this young man I would look into it that coming week and do what I could.

One day in the following week I happened to hear the state pilot, John Parker, talking on our state radio. I called him and asked, "Are you reasonably close to Waskish and can you spare a half hour of your time?"

He responded, "No problem, I'll be at the Waskish grass strip in ten minutes."

John picked me up and gave me a quick trip up this judicial

ditch. I could see I had over a mile hike ahead of me but it was all dry so I wouldn't have to walk with hip boots on. It was even dry on the down side of the dam. John dropped me off at the airport and I thanked him for the knowledge I had gained.

I went home and rigged up a trigger charge and along with a half dozen extra sticks of dynamite in my packsack. I drove down to where the judicial ditch passed under Highway 72 through a culvert.

From my observation with Parker, I wouldn't have to wear those rubber hip boots. I could make the trip with my eight-inch leather boots. So I struck out east on the grade on the north side of the ditch. There were popple trees with up to fifteen-inch diameter trunks plus dried weeds up to two feet tall. I had good walking so I was making good time. About half way in, I had to make a stop to drain my bladder. I looked down at my trousers and they were covered with wood ticks. You couldn't even see the cloth from my knees down and above the knees there were at least two hundred ticks on each leg up to my crotch. I almost panicked. I tried to brush them off. They didn't brush off. Then I could see the high weeds were full of ticks.

I whirled around and took off for the black top. When I got back out on the black top I used my knife to scrape the ticks off my trousers. I must have had over a thousand ticks crawling around on the black top.

Now, I decided I would have to wear my rubber hip boots after all. So I finally got myself cleaned of the ticks and put on the hip boots. I walked back to the dam, punched a couple of holes in the dam with a small pole I pulled out of the dam and dropped all my dynamite in the holes. I lit the fuse on the trigger unit and dropped that down one of the holes and I took off. A minute or so later, she blew and that water started pouring through the big opening.

I got back to the patrol car. No wood ticks could hang on to the rubber boots. I removed the boots and headed for home. I met my wife and told her what I had gotten into. She made me go down in the basement and remove all my clothes. We searched all over my body and in my clothing. We found about twenty more ticks on me but mostly in my clothing.

Officers from five states at a sport show in Kansas City.
Left to Right: Callies, Emerson (IA), Wright (MO), Craig (NE),
Elder (KS)

Patricia made kind of a threat to me if she would find any in bed that night. It did seem in the tick season we would occasionally find a few in bed with us.

This station was famous for mosquitoes, moose flies, and black flies. In fact, you name the bug, we had them.

In March of 1971, I was sent to the sport show. It was a ten-day show. My duties at the Minnesota booth included being dressed in my class "A" uniform and try to answer any question put to me relative to game and fish laws.

One man came up to me and asked, "Do you have any bugs or insects in Minnesota?"

This was certainly an unexpected question, but I responded with, "Mister, you just tell me what kind of bug you're looking for and I will tell you when and where you will find them at their peak. We have all kinds."

He came back with, "You are just honest enough. I think we will plan on a visit to Minnesota."

Chapter 22/ SHORTY CASTLE

One fall day in 1964, Harland Pickett, my neighbor warden to the north, called me at Waskish to tell me he wanted me to work with him that night down in the southeast part of Lake of the Woods County. He suggested I meet him at an abandoned farm on the west side of Highway 72 just south of the county road that leads into the Pine Island Forest area. He said he would meet me around seven p.m. which would be about sundown.

Shorty Castle and his wife lived on the south side of this road and another piece of property on this road was owned by LeClaire from Sauk Center. LeClaires would come up to their shack in the fall to hunt.

I met Harland that evening as planned. He told me to leave my car on the backside of the old farm buildings where no one could see it from the road. We pulled out onto the blacktop of Highway 72, cut a small branch off a spruce tree to brush out our tracks into the abandoned farm, then headed north on 72 to the gravel road that went east six miles to the county line and the start of a huge wilderness area known as Pine Island.

About two and a half miles in on this road, Harland turned north on a trail back to an abandoned farm. The trail was so soft I was sure we were going to get stuck but we made it. Harland pulled his patrol car into a spruce clump so it could not be seen from the road. Then we walked back out to the county road about an eighth of a mile. There we stood watching for any illegal activity. At this time, Harland told me he had received a letter from Shorty Castle that there had been some shining going on along this road. Shorty said in his letter that he was afraid someone would shoot one of his cows in his pasture on the south side of the road. He went on to say he had no telephone so he used this letter to alert Harland. He also said when Harland came down in this area that he should park his car in his yard.

The Indians from the Red Lake Reservation had a huge area over on Pine Island known as "The Indian Pines". It was Shorty's theory that it was probably Indians coming from the reservation on their way to the Indian Pines doing the shining.

We stood on the road for about two hours when we saw a pair of headlights show up on Shorty Castle's road. The lights turned west coming towards us. The vehicle was about three-quarters of a mile east of us. It came about a quarter of a mile then it turned so the headlights were shining north into the woods, or if there was a field down there, out onto the field. Then the car completed its turn around and ended up facing east. We saw the brake lights come on. Almost immediately, we could see a spotlight shining to the north from the driver's side of the vehicle. Then came a shot from a high-powered rifle. The door on the driver's side came open and a person with a small flashlight came out of the door and disappeared to the north.

Harland made a remark, "It looks like we're in business." Then he said, "You stay here and watch what happens. I'll go get the patrol car." Harland was gone about fifteen minutes. In the meantime, I saw the person with the small flashlight come back to the car and the car started moving east.

Harland pulled up to the county road without lights and I told him what had happened. We could see the car's taillights and the glow of headlights shining on the trees on either side of the road.

We started after this car as fast as we dared driving with no lights. This car was driving slowly so within about a mile and a half, we were able to catch up to it. We could see by their lights that there were two people in the car. Just about the time we were about a hundred yards behind them, a doe came out of the bush on the south side of the road. It passed about a hundred feet in front of the car we were following, and then it went north across the road into a stand of popple trees. The brake lights came on, a hand-held spotlight came out on the driver's side of the car and the light was on the deer. The deer was walking in a northwesterly direction. We could see the deer as it moved through the popple. The deer never stopped to give the shiners a good shot. The deer kept moving and finally disappeared into some thick brush.

The spotlight was turned off. Then the car started to move on to the east for about a mile where you come to a "T" in the road and that is the county line. The car turned south about twenty feet and then started to back up. Harland told me, "Get him."

I bailed out of our car on a fast run to the passenger side of the car. I grabbed the door handle and jerked the door open. There was a boy passenger about twelve years old. The driver was looking out to his left while backing up. The kid yelled, "Jesus Christ! Where did you come from?" as I went across him to grab the rifle that was uncased in between the man and the boy. The spotlight was plugged into the cigarette lighter and was resting between the legs of the driver. An empty 30-30 shell was rolling around on the floor.

The driver didn't seem to realize I was there until I turned off the key and pulled it out. Then I yelled at him, "Get out of the car and get up in front of your headlights." The kid was just paralyzed.

The driver started to get out of the car when Harland showed up on the driver's side exclaiming, "Shorty, not you!"

So after a few minutes, everyone calmed down. Harland checked the rifle and it had one shell in the chamber and one or two in the magazine. So Harland told Shorty we would be charging him with shining. Harland took Shorty in the patrol car and I drove Shorty's car with the kid back to their home. Harland made out a summons on Shorty and a seizure tag for the car, rifle, spotlight, loaded and empty shell.

Harland instructed Shorty to be in Baudette at the courthouse by nine a.m. the following morning to be bound over for District Court. He was to be charged with a gross misdemeanor.

Then Shorty said, "If you take my car, I won't be able to get to town. It's over twenty miles." So Harland said we would leave the car for him to use. Then Harland asked him if he had a deer out on that field where he shot.

He just said, "There is no deer out there." In the meantime, I was going through the car we had seized and I came across a six-inch hunting knife with dried blood and deer hair on it but it was old, a couple of weeks or a month. I walked over to Harland where he was talking with Shorty and offered the knife on my open palm to Harland. Shorty snatched the knife. I grabbed his wrist and the next thing I knew, we were tumbling end over end down through the high weeds. I managed to hold his wrist with the knife and I finally got his other arm and pinned him down and sat on him. He was a small person but very muscular.

Then Shorty said, "Do you guys know what you are doing with me?"

I told him, "Yes. We are charging you with deer shining." At this point, he had enough movement in his hand to give a mighty flip of the knife out into the tall weeds and we never did find it.

Then Shorty said, "You guys are sending me back to prison." I knew nothing of his prior life so he told me he was sent up for life for getting two fourteen year old girls pregnant that the county had turned over to his wife to care for. He had served about four years and was let out on probation providing he not violate any laws.

Harland and I checked the field where Shorty shot and could not find anything. Harland took me back to my car and I returned to Waskish. I was told to be in Baudette the following morning at nine a.m. to get Shorty bound over to District Court.

The following morning I was in Baudette around eight o'clock. I stopped in at Tom's Cafe for breakfast. I was amazed.

It seemed the whole town knew we had caught Shorty. Everyone that spoke to me thanked me and hoped Shorty would get the most weird punishments I ever heard of.

In municipal court, Harland testified to what we saw and heard. Shorty elected to add to the story in his own defense. He admitted to shooting, but he said it was at a timber wolf that he thought might bother his cattle. Timber wolves weren't protected then.

The Municipal Court bound him over to a gross misdemeanor to be tried in District Court sometime in the future.

I went back to Waskish. About a month or six weeks later, I was told Shorty applied for and got a change of venue. The county attorney was a bit upset because he would have to go to some other county seat to try the case. However, he was confident he could get the story across to any jury anywhere and get a guilty conviction.

The trial was moved to International Falls in March of the year following the arrest. Shorty Castle said he had no money to hire an attorney, so the court at the Falls appointed a defense attorney.

On the day of the trial, the county attorney from Lake of the Woods, Harland Pickett, and myself met at the county court house in the Falls. A twelve-person jury was selected.

Harland testified to what he had heard and seen. I was called to testify to what I saw and heard. Then Shorty got on the stand. He said he was at home when he also heard a shot. He went out to investigate and he took his rifle along for protection. He said he couldn't find the culprit that shot because they turned out their lights and he was using his spotlight to search the fields for the intruder. He also told about writing the letter to Pickett about his concern of someone shooting his cows. Harland had brought up the letter. So when we showed up, he assumed we were down by his place looking for possible cow shooters.

The son was put on the stand and he was confused. Every question that was put to him he would look at his mother in the audience and she would give an affirmative or negative nod. The judge caught this and he severely chastised the mother. However, that didn't stop her and I can't remember if they took the boy off the stand or removed her from the courtroom. At any rate, they retired the jury to the juror's room for deliberation. The bailiff commented to me that they wouldn't be out long. They will be back after the first ballot with a guilty verdict.

The jury didn't come back for over three hours and when they did, they found Shorty Castle not guilty. We were all stunned—the bailiff, the court reporter, even the judge. The judge did say afterwards to us that you can never be sure what a jury will do.

About two months later, the county attorney met one of the jurors and asked her where we had made our mistake. She was somewhat reluctant but finally said the first ballot was eleven to one to convict. So they talked it over and the second ballot was eleven to one to convict and so it went on through a half a dozen votes. However, they finally came down to one man that always voted not guilty. When accused of it, he said he had no intention of changing his vote. He told the other eleven if they ever wanted to go home they would have to change their vote. He also told the other jurors that this problem occurred in Lake of the Woods County and it was really none of their business.

So the lady told the county attorney, we were told to come back with a guilty or a not guilty plea. A hung jury would not be accepted. So we found Shorty Castle not guilty.

Chapter 23/ MINK TRAPPERS

About five o'clock in the afternoon on November 14, 1964, I received a call from a gentleman who asked me to stop by his house as soon as possible. He had some information that he thought I might be interested in.

I told him, "I'll leave my house immediately."

Somewhere on the road, I met this man in his automobile. He said, "A party came to my house right after I called you and I don't want them to see me talking to you."

(For the reader's information, the firearm season for taking deer had opened on November 7, 1964. The season had been open for one week. The season for trapping mink opened at sunrise on this day of November 14, 1964.)

Someone was on the Loman Road in Pine Island to hunt deer. A trapper named Oscar Osmundson from Bemidji was there in a school bus. On the right side of the rear of the bus, a wire was stretched and there were mink pelts hanging on stretchers suspended on this wire line. He said there were over thirty skins hanging. Then the next evening when he came back from hunting, he found Oscar's partner skinning out ten more mink and the smell from the animals was terrible. The deer hunter also told my informer that there was a jeep truck by the school bus.

I contacted my supervisor, Dick Tarte, who was with Leo Manthei, my neighboring warden from Blackduck, on my car radio. I told them, "I have some information that is good but the timing is bad. Where can I meet you, the both of you?"

We met on the scenic highway south of Blackduck at approximately 8:00 p.m. I spilled out the whole story as it was given to me.

My supervisor, Dick Tarte, suggested, "Go to Big Falls and

contact Warden Richards and tell him what you have told me. Then maybe the two of you can locate these trappers and check them out."

When I got to Big Falls, I found Warden Keeler and a Koochiching County Deputy Sheriff visiting with Warden Richards. I spilled the whole story out to the three men. Warden Richards said, "I'll go with you and help you search for the school bus."

At the same time Warden Keeler said, "The deputy and I are going down into the Dent Table country to snoop around for illegal deer hunters."

Warden Richards and I started out for the Pine Island country west of Big Falls. About twenty-five miles in, we passed the old abandoned ranger station and came to the Fiero Truck Trail. We turned north on the Fiero Trail because Richards who had been in this country most of his life suggested we would probably find them up in the Black River country.

We drove north at least fifteen miles to a 'Y' in the road. We took the right hand trail, as that is the one to Loman. Eventually, we came upon a hunting camp that had a school bus and a jeep truck. There was also a late model car with a North Dakota license on it. We suspected this could be the trapper's camp.

I got out of my patrol car and went over to see if I could wake the occupants and find out if this was the Osmundson camp. It was around midnight. I had my five-cell flashlight lit and in my hand. I pounded on the front door of the bus and finally through the glass, I could see someone rise up and come to the door.

I shined the light on my Minnesota warden shoulder patch and on my face. Then I announced that I was a Minnesota State Game Warden and that I was looking for a Mr. Oscar Osmundson.

At that bit of information the door was opened from the

inside and the man standing there said, "I'm Oscar Osmundson."

At that time, I called out to Richards, "This is the right place." I stepped up on to the first step until Richards got there.

While standing on the bus steps, I shined my light around the bus and located a bunch of mink pelts hanging on a wire on stretch boards in the back of the bus. Richards moved in front of me and he also saw the pelts hanging in the back of the bus.

Due to the fact the mink season opened that morning and a legal trapper would be spending the opening day setting his traps and that mink are normally nocturnal animals, it is hardly feasible that they would have any legal pelts in their possession at the time we entered the bus.

Warden Richards made the statement, "You guys are at it a little early."

To which Mr. Osmundson remarked, "If you're caught you are caught."

To which Warden Richards said, "It's nice to do business with gentlemen."

Mr. Osmundson came back with, "If you are caught fair and square, there is nothing to cry about."

Mr. Osmundson's partner who was sitting up on his bunk in his underwear said, "Not by a damn sight. I'm getting a lawyer."

We checked the fur and there were only nine mink and two rats so we asked the men, "Where are the rest of the furs?"

To which the men claimed, "I don't know."

At this time Richards advised me, "We're in Keeler's district and we should call him to come over here."

About an hour later, Warden Keeler and Deputy Jim Gilbert showed up. We made a diligent search around the bus for the rest of the pelts but could find none. I had known others to roll up illegal fur in tarpaper and hang them next to the trunk of a heavily branched spruce tree. They're even hard to locate in the daylight.

We all decided we would have to stay there the rest of the night or take these men to International Falls and lock them up until we could get back there in the daylight to search.

Warden Richards joined Warden Keeler and the deputy sheriff to escort Osmundson and his partner Myles Williams into International Falls to detain them until we could make a good search of the area.

Richards, Keeler, and I met at the campsite at sunrise but we found nothing. Now we would have to go with what we had, nine mink skins and two rat skins. The violation occurred in Koochiching County in Warden Keeler's district so it behooved him to contact the county attorney and make out a formal complaint.

The two trappers were allowed to return to their campsite about noon on the 15th of November.

About a week later, Warden Keeler contacted me and said he had a severe problem. The prosecuting county attorney was only standing in for the duly elected county attorney and he had a severe drinking problem. He told Keeler to drop the case and return the evidence to Osmundson and Williams. The only way he would proceed with the case would be to have my informants come in and make a statement, and in the event of a trial, they would have to testify.

I told Keeler that just isn't going to happen. I had assured my informer that I would not disclose him. Keeler said he had already told the acting county attorney that. We were pretty sure we were all washed up and would have to return the evidence.

END OF THIS CASE? — WRONG!

On December 4, 1965, I received a notice of wrongfully doing from Oscar Osmundson with Whitney Tarutus as the plaintiff's attorney. Further checking disclosed that Wardens Richard and Keeler received similar notices served on them by the sheriff of Koochiching County.

The three of us advised the Attorney General of the State of Minnesota of this action.

The three of us were advised that we were to be in Bemidji on December 28, 1965 at 1:30 p.m. for the purpose of taking a deposition. We were each being sued for $5,000.00. Linus J. Hammond, the Assistant Attorney General from the State of Minnesota, would be representing us.

For some reason, unknown to us the Attorney Whitney Tarutus canceled the date for the deposition and no alternate date had been set. We assumed maybe Oscar Osmundson had a change of heart and that would be the end of the case.

WRONG!

On April 19, 1966, the three of us game wardens were advised by our Supervisor Tarte that we were to be in the county attorney's office on April 27, 1966 for the purpose of taking depositions. Mr. Linus Hammond would be representing us.

We all met at the county attorney's office and Oscar Osmundson, Wardens Richards and Keeler, and I each gave a deposition. We were all examined and cross examined by Whitney Tarutus and Linus Hammond and it was all duly recorded by a court reporter.

Upon completion and off the record, Tarutus told Linus Hammond, "When you get back to St. Paul, if you would just make arrangements to send Mr. Osmundson $3,000.00, we can call the case closed."

Mr. Linus Hammond responded with, "Mr. Tarutus, you are not suing the State of Minnesota, you are suing those three game wardens. Between these three game wardens, they haven't got a pot to piss in." This seemed to put an end to this incident.

We were all of the opinion, if originally the substitute county attorney of Koochiching County had had any backbone, this case would be history, win or lose.

END OF THE OSMUNDSON CASE? WRONG!

On October 20, 1966, Warden Richards and Supervisor Tarte approached Myles Williams, the trapping partner of Oscar Osmundson, who gave a written statement completely exonerating all three game wardens of any wrong doing on November 14-15, 1964, in regards to the bus, the fur, Oscar Osmundson, and Myles Williams.

FINAL END OF THE OSMUNDSON CASE? WRONG!

Later on J. C. Richards retired from the Conservation Department as a game warden with over 35 years of service.

On April 28, 1968 Game Warden Gill Keeler was killed in an automobile accident while on duty.

On May 22, 1968, I received a notice to the effect Oscar Osmundson, through his Attorney Whitney Tarutus was suing J. C. Richards and myself in District Court in International Falls. Trial was to begin on July 29, 1968. It would be a twelve-person jury trial. Depositions by Warden Keeler and J. C. Richards were sent to Special Assistant Attorney General Laurence Anderson.

On a Sunday afternoon about three weeks before the trial date, my wife received a call from an attorney in St. Paul. He said he was Gordon Moosbrugger from the Attorney General's Office. He wanted to advise us that the State of Minnesota and the Attorney General's Office would not be defending me and he suggested that we should hire our own attorney.

When I got home, my wife was ready to explode. I, too, could not believe what was happening. I called our supervisor, Dick Tarte. He told me he would check on that in the morning.

The next evening, Tarte called me and said he was down in St. Paul that morning and everything was straightened out. The attorney general's office was going to defend me.

The attorney from St. Paul contacted me and asked me to meet him in a motel in International Falls to go over all the details.

Finally, on July 29, 1968, a twelve-person jury was selected and the trial started. It lasted two days. At one time Tarutus knew he was losing and he homed in on me. Actually I think he was putting on a show for his client. Judge Murphy finally had enough. He banged down his gavel and ordered the two attorneys into his chambers. The three men were in there about twenty minutes. Whitney Tarutus was a different man when they came back.

The state attorney told me later he never heard anyone get their ass ate out like what Tarutus just experienced in the judge's chambers.

The case went to the jury. They were out about an hour. Osmundson lost.

END OF THE PROBLEM? NOT YET...

On September 16, 1968, I received a letter from State Attorney Laurence Anderson that he appeared in District Court in Grand Rapids in opposition to Tarutus motion for judgment not withstanding the jury verdict or for a new trial.

Judge Murphy signed an order denying both of Tarutus' motions. Tarutus had thirty days to appeal.

Apparently, Osmundson finally got the message or he ran out of money.

THE END.

P.S. By the way, in a round about way, we found out that Myles William's son picked up thirty-one stretched and dried mink skins sometime on that Saturday, November 14, 1964. Osmundson and Williams were up in Pine Island under the guise of hunting deer but were there getting a head start on legal mink trappers.

Chapter 24/ LOCAL SHEEP FARMERS

It was the latter part of August, 1965 when I received a call from Hilmer Leonhardt. Hilmer raised sheep and cattle on a large farm up in Konig Township of Beltrami County.

Hilmer had little use for any member of the Department of Natural Resources. He was inclined to put up with the Forestry Department so that he could buy stumpage in the winter providing he could find piece cutters to do the cutting and stacking of the pulp sticks.

However, this complaint call was to me because he had lost some sheep to wolves. He insisted I come up and walk with him out into his pasture to personally view the destruction. He wanted to know how he could recover his loss from the State of Minnesota. He also wanted me to get busy and trap or shoot the wolves.

I told Hilmer that the state had no funds for him to collect for his loss. I made the suggestion that if he had insurance on his livestock, he could be reimbursed for his loss.

I said, "I know you have some traps capable of holding a timber wolf or a coyote. If you catch a timber wolf or a coyote, I can make out the bounty papers and you will recover some of your loss." (The bounty at that time was $35.00 for a timber wolf and $15.00 for a coyote.)

Hilmer in his haughty way said, "I have a better idea. You come up here and I'll let you trap the wolves. Then you can make out the bounty papers in my name and that way I will recover some of my loss."

I said, "Hilmer, it doesn't work that way. If I trap the wolves, nobody collects any bounty. I am a salaried employee of the Department of Natural Resources and I will set up some traps but no one collects any money."

I never did hear any more from Hilmer so I assumed the wolves or coyotes only made a one time visit to his stock.

Several months later I was discussing a similar situation with a neighboring farmer. I brought up the subject of Hilmer Leonhardt's loss. However, I said I had never heard from Hilmer since then.

This neighboring farmer then said, "Apparently, you didn't hear what happened? Hilmer set several traps out around those rock piles in his pasture. The next day when he went out to check his traps he found one dead sheep, one crippled sheep, and both of Hilmer's dogs were in the traps, their mouths full of sheep wool."

Chapter 25/ GOOSE HUNTERS

It was a beautiful day in late September. The small game hunting season was open. The local hunters were very active hunting partridge and sharp-tailed grouse in this area of northern Beltrami County.

J. C. Richards, the patriarch of game wardens in our region, came over to Waskish and suggested we go check sharp-tail grouse hunters and at the same time, we could take our shotguns along and possibly harvest a bird or two for ourselves.

Sharp-tail grouse like open fields with clover surrounded by groves of popple trees near swamp areas where there are low-bush cranberries and lingen berries.

I told Ces we could go west and south of Kelliher, then over into the Saum area. This is partly in Leo Manthei's district. Leo is the warden from Blackduck. There are a number of abandoned farms as you go west of Kelliher over to the Red Lake Indian Reservation.

On this fall day in 1965, we drove to Kelliher on Highway 72 then west of Kelliher on Old Highway 72 for three miles to a gravel road going south. About two miles south, we came across a car parked on the east side of the road facing north. The car was empty but there was an empty gun case lying on the front seat.

I told Ces something is about to happen if it already hasn't happened. Ces said, "Come on and get back in the car. You are overly suspicious." Instead I grabbed the binoculars, climbed on top of our car, and looked to the east. There was a six or seven foot rise in the field east of the parked car, but by standing on top of the car and using the binoculars, I had a good view of the field east and south of us.

Almost directly east of us and about an eighth-of-a-mile out on the field was a stand of timber that was on the north edge of the field. Also, I could see a small red tractor coming out from some farm buildings south of us about a half-a-mile. With the aid of my binoculars, I could see the tractor operator had an uncased gun laying crossways on his lap. Also, I was aware there was a fair, northwest wind blowing.

I hollered at Ces that something was about to happen but I didn't know what. I told Ces about the uncased gun on the tractor operator's lap. The tractor was going in a northeast direction from the farm buildings. I could see the tractor was moving at a fast pace. Then I saw the driver raise the gun out of his lap by the pistol grip with one hand while the other hand controlled the wheel.

At about that instant, I saw a flock of geese rising off the ground. They had to fly into the wind to get air-borne quickly which brought them closer to the tractor. The tractor operator let go of the wheel and started shooting at the geese. He fired five shots and I never saw a goose fall. The geese swung to the south towards a big pile of field rocks. A man stood and started shooting. I don't remember how many shots he fired, but the geese swung north towards the woods. When they passed over the trees, someone started shooting again at the geese. In all that shooting, I didn't see one goose fall or appear to be hit. A common mistake made by many hunters that usually hunt ducks is that the geese look so big the gunners think they are in range when they are not.

At any rate, I jumped down from the roof of the car, got in behind the wheel and told Ces to hang on.

I drove south to the farm buildings' approach road, up that road through the farm yard, past the out buildings and out onto the field where the tractor had gone minutes before. We caught them flat-footed. E. C. Bastien was on the tractor with his shotgun in his hands.

O. H. Bastien was coming from the woods. He was about halfway between the woods and the tractor and young Frenzel was about halfway from the rock pile where he had been shooting.

Bastien told us we were trespassing on his land and they had a right to shoot anything on their own land and they didn't even have to have a license.

I granted him that he didn't have to have a small game license to hunt small game on his own land in season. However, I told him I witnessed him shooting at that flock of geese. The goose season wasn't open. Also, he didn't have a federal duck stamp. He was shooting at migratory waterfowl from a motor propelled vehicle and his gun was not plugged.

At this, Ces spoke up and said, "Boys you're just wrong too many ways." We gathered up their guns, wrote up the complaints, made out the seizure slips, and gave each man their copy after they signed the summons to appear in Justice of the Peace Court in Kelliher.

There had been a change in the justice of the peace just prior to this incident. The postmaster in Kelliher had elected to take retirement late that summer.

Mrs. Clara Quale was the elected justice of the peace in Kelliher and she owned and operated the local newspaper that she and her assistant put out once a week. Mrs. Quale was a strong outspoken Democrat and as these postmaster jobs were by political appointment, and Mrs. Quale had let her representative know she wanted this position, she got it. However, she had to relinquish her job as the justice of the peace.

Oliver Latteral was the president of the local bank and mayor of Kelliher and he inherited any other undesirable position and title in the community. So he had agreed to finish out Mrs. Quale's term as the local justice of the peace. Oliver was a businessman and he knew everyone in the community and he was reluctant to penalize anyone. However, I showed him the Beltrami County bail schedule. I told him all the judges and the JP's assessed the fines the same as the monetary amount on the bail schedule. I also told him, at his discretion, he could fine the violator more and/or reprimand them to the county jail for up to ninety days after they plead guilty or were found guilty.

The Bastiens and Frenzel came into the bank on their assigned day and hour. Oliver Latterell read the complaint on each of them, which was "Attempt to take wild geese in closed season in violation of state and federal laws".

All of them pled guilty. I told the judge just what they had done and that in spite of all the shooting, not one goose came down out of that flock.

The judge looked at the bail schedule and for this violation the schedule called for $50.00 fine and $3.00 cost each. Then he showed this schedule to the violators. He told them, "I'm supposed to fine you $50.00 but I'll cut that in half, make it $25.00 each—that ought to be fair enough. I'm going fifty, fifty with you."

I did however, seize and confiscate their guns.

A couple of days later, Leo showed up with a long face. He told me I sure screwed up his ability to hunt partridge and sharp-tail grouse on the Bastien's farm. I told Leo the only reason they let you hunt there is so they know exactly where you are and then, too, you become obligated to them.

Chapter 26/ ILLEGAL FISH SALE

It was November 8, 1965. I had requested help from Harland Pickett, the warden at Baudette, on some anticipated night hunting. Before Harland had arrived at my home and office in Waskish, Leo Manthei, the warden at Blackduck, had called with a pretty forceful request for help south of Saum on the east side of the Red Lake Indian Reservation. I told Leo I had Pickett coming down to help me. He just said, "Good, I need a lot of help. Meet me down around Saum as soon as you can get there."

When Harland showed up, I told him I had just promised Leo we would go down and help him out for a while. Harland didn't care too much for Leo and he was a bit upset about giving him any help. Finally, he said he would go along with me.

Harland got in my patrol car. We drove south to Kelliher then turned west on the Old Highway 72 then onto County Aid Road 34, so we ended up south of Saum. I called Leo on the radio and told him where we were. He told us to go north to a certain farmer on the east side of the road. I asked Leo where he was and he said, "The pie house." That's a retired farmer that lives directly across the road from Arnold Wolden who owns and operates Wolden's Store at Saum.

Harland said to me, "What's Leo doing at the pie house?"

I told him, "Probably getting something to eat and also he catches up on everything that's going on down in the Saum area."

Harland came back with, "I'll bet we are going to be doing Leo's work while he's sitting in there eating."

Knowing Leo I said, "That's probably a pretty accurate statement."

The next thing we knew Leo was on the radio. He was

talking rather quiet and huffing and puffing throughout the conversation. He said while he was sitting at the table he saw the light come on in the front of Wolden's Store. The farm lady said, "That's odd. Slim never reopens the store after hours."

Leo left the table and went out into the dark to investigate. He crept up behind some trees where he had a good view. There was a car parked in front of the store. Then two men came out of the store, one of them was Slim Wolden and the other was Carl Falk, the county commissioner. They had a large carton between them that they loaded into the trunk of the car. Carl lifted the top and commented, "Those are sure some beautiful whitefish." With that he pulled out his wallet, took out several bills, and gave them to Slim Wolden.

Leo went on to say, "The two men are standing there in front of the store talking. When they leave I will tell you which way they are going." Then he announced, "Carl is headed south right to you."

I told Harland, "I don't want to stop him out in front of this farmer's place. We will drive south to where the Joe Jerome Road goes off to the west, we'll block him there."

So we left this farmyard without lights. We got down to the Joe Jerome Road and waited. When Falk got there we gave him the red light, blocked the road, had him open the trunk. There were about twenty real nice, fresh, four-pound whitefish. I asked Carl Falk if he had an angling license and a netting license. Then I told him we had a witness who watched him buy these fish from Slim Wolden. We made out a summons for buying whitefish illegally and a seizure slip for the box of fish we took from him. Then we released him on his own recognizance to appear the next day in the Justice of the Peace Court in Kelliher.

We went back, met Leo, and all three of us went to Slim Wolden's house immediately behind his store. There was a light on in one upstairs window.

We went up on the porch and pounded on the door. After a

few minutes, a light came on downstairs and Mrs. Wolden opened the door. We told her we wanted to see Slim Wolden. She said, "He is in bed for the night."

We responded, "He hasn't been there very long." She called him down.

Then we told him we caught Carl Falk with the whitefish and that we had a witness who saw him pay Wolden money.

At that moment the phone rang and we could hear Mrs. Wolden answer it. She listened a few moments, and then she told the caller, "They're here now."

Slim couldn't seem to believe what was happening so we took him out to the patrol car, opened the trunk, and showed him the box of fish.

Carl Falk and Slim Wolden appeared the next day before Justice of the Peace Oliver Latterell, and they each paid a $25.00 fine and $4.00 in costs.

Chapter 27/ IN THE DAYS WE HAD COOPERATION

It was the 30th day of October 1966. The Indian police at the Red Lake Reservation called my supervisor Richard Tarte in Bemidji to say that a car with three male Indians (not registered Red Lake Band Indians) may have left the reservation with a deer or parts of a deer in the trunk. They had the license number and make of the vehicle.

They wondered, "Would supervisor Tarte alert his men and the state police to watch for this vehicle, intercept it, and search it?" They thought these men were from Minneapolis and might be going east or south from the reservation.

Tarte contacted me, gave me the circumstances, the license number, and the color and make of the car. He told me he had also alerted Gus Clemenson, the warden at Bemidji. Warden

Manthei of Blackduck was not available.

So I drove south on Highway 72 through Kelliher and Shooks, turned west on State Highway 1 when I came to the Busy Corner where Highways 1 and 72 separate. I found a place where I could watch for cars coming from the reservation.

Within ten minutes, I spotted the car coming from the west on Highway Number 1. I caught up to it and pulled it over, took the keys out of the vehicle, and opened the trunk. There were parts of a deer and some fish in the trunk so I charged all three men with possession of deer meat in closed season.

All three men lived in the same place in Minneapolis, an area known by Minneapolis police as the Minneapolis Indian Reservation.

I hauled the men to Kelliher before Justice of the Peace Clara Quale. Casey, the man who owned the car, was fined $100.00 and costs or ninety days in jail. He said he was broke so he was committed to ninety days in the county jail.

Slinker was fined $70.00 and costs. He paid his fine.

Dickinson was fined $55.00 and cost. He paid his fine.
Supervisor Tarte advised the Red Lake Indian police that the men had been caught and charged in the Justice of the Peace Court, pled guilty, and paid their fine or were put in jail.

Chapter 28/ EXPLOSIVES

One night in the spring of 1967, I had stationed myself back in the brush just off the Old Highway 72 where it crosses Shotley Brook. The stream was full of walleyes going up to spawn. From my hiding place, I could see if any vehicles came from the north or south or down a dirt trail that ran east and west connecting the new and Old Highway 72.

There were logging trails off this dirt road that led down to Shotley Brook. If a car came down this old dirt road, I would be able to see their vehicle lights.

I had called and talked to Leo Manthei earlier so he was out and on watch some place down near Blackduck. We were usually able to call each other by our car radios if we needed assistance.

Around 11:00 p.m., I heard a single loud explosion to the east of where I was sitting. I couldn't believe what I heard. It sounded like about one stick of dynamite. No one lived within three miles of where I guessed that sound came from. Also, I did not see or hear any kind of a vehicle. I was reluctant to leave where I was because I felt I had the best place to observe anything that moved.

I called Leo on my radio and told him I heard an explosion that sounded like dynamite. Then I asked him to come up and take over my observation post so I could take a hike down along Shotley Brook east of me. Leo answered me and I got the feeling he was reluctant to drive thirty miles on a questionable venture. When I got a little more insistent he responded with, "What you heard was an aircraft that broke the sound barrier." He went on to say, "An airplane flew over where I was sitting on the Blackduck River and I heard a big boom when it broke the sound barrier just a few minutes before you called. The aircraft was heading north in your direction."

I knew right then he was putting out a bunch of bull putty. He just didn't want to come!

So I drove east, positioned my car across one of those old logging roads and took a hike down to Shotley Brook. I could neither hear nor see any activity so I checked another trail further east—no results. I was beginning to think maybe I had dozed off and dreamt the whole thing. I know I was pooped out. Even Patricia, my wife, was giving me hell for burning the candle at both ends.

Finally, about 2:00 a.m., I gave it up and went home to bed.

I woke up about 8:00 the next morning. I told Patricia my weird experience the night before when we were having breakfast. I was berated for depending on Leo. We both knew he would rather play golf, shoot ducks, or catch fish than to sit and watch for something to happen. Leo had a low priority on patience.

After breakfast, I just had to go back down to Shotley Brook and try to figure out if I was dreaming or if something illegal had happened.

I parked my state car, put on a pair of hip boots, and with a dip net in hand I started to follow the shoreline up stream from where I had been sitting the night before. Within a quarter-of-a-mile, I saw two or three dead fish on the bottom in a quiet stretch of water in about three or four feet of water. Using a piece of a downed dead tree, I worried those dead fish into shallower water where I was able to scoop them up with my net.

Using my jack knife, I made a cut along side the dorsal fin. I found the flesh of the fish loosened from the backbone. I was right—I had heard an explosive! I continued on up stream and came across more fish lying on the bottom.

Finally, about a mile and a half up stream there were no more dead fish. I did run across some boot tracks but I could not find for sure where these thieves came in or went out. There was one place where there were some car tracks but they looked old.

The only other way someone could get in there was on an old ditch grade south of Shotley Brook or by a small boat or canoe. Also, there was the possibility a car was driven in from the new Highway 72 without lights.

About a week later, I stopped into Grone's Cafe in Kelliher for breakfast. I sat down in a booth and overheard a conversation about someone in the group coming home with over a tub full of walleyes.

When their group passed my booth to pay up, one fellow got a real startled look on his face when he saw me.

Chapter 29/ *A BOW LICENSE FOR DEER*

This incident occurred on October 15, 1967. I was stationed at Waskish. I had a man by the name of Robert Olson sent to me as a trainee. He was about half way through his probation period. I was having some problems with beaver building dams in the road ditches along side of Highway 72, north of Waskish. This was a common, ongoing problem for eighteen miles on either side of Highway 72.

Anytime a beaver tried to take up residence and build a dam or a lodge along this stretch of highway, I would be notified immediately by Ole Roe or Pete Halvorson, the Minnesota highway maintenance men assigned to this area. They hated beaver, and they were always afraid the beaver would take to burrowing under the highway, which could be a catastrophe.

I had been alerted by these men that a beaver had moved into the east side ditch about seven miles north of Waskish.

As this was a part of our chores, to remove beaver and their dams, I took my trainee the day before to this site to show him how to live trap a beaver. The beaver hadn't started a dam good enough to make a set by the dam. I located several places where the beaver was coming up out of the ditch into the bush to gather limbs.

Normally I like to make a water set, but in this ditch at that time, a beaver's thrashing around would make the trap sink into about four feet of water, and he would drown. So I elected to make a dry set back from the ditch. These are harder to make. If the beaver smells or feels anything under foot before he hits the trigger, he will back off. I had located and set the live trap where I thought I might catch this beaver. Nothing is for sure no matter how careful you are.

A series of pictures showing Bill setting a beaver live trap:

Now we come to the day in question. I was going to take the trainee and go check the beaver live trap when we heard by the state radio that my area supervisor was en route to Waskish to check on me and how I was getting along with this current trainee.

So we waited at the Waskish office and residence for his appearance. This was Lester Borning, who was stationed at Thief River Falls about a hundred and twenty five miles west of Waskish.

When he arrived at the house, we had coffee. Then the three of us went up Highway 72 to check the beaver trap. I was fortunate this time; the beaver was caught in the trap. I had my camera along so I asked Lester Borning and Robert Olson to crouch down on either side of the live trap and I took their picture.

Supervisor Les Borning and Trainee Olson with beaver

We came back to the station and my wife told me Roger Anderson, the local forest ranger, wanted to see me. It was urgent.

So while Supervisor Lester Borning was checking out the trainee, Robert Olson, I went over to Roger's office. He said that morning he went up to his garden which was located on Irv Davidson's property, about three miles north of Waskish on the west side of Highway 72, to finish up some cultivating he had been working on the evening before until it got so dark he couldn't see.

When he arrived there, he found a fresh deer gut pile on the edge of his garden and about ten feet from the gut pile was a Minnesota resident deer license and tag to take deer with a bow and arrow. The bow season was open. However, this deer had to have been taken at night and obviously was transported without the tag—that's two things wrong—and I would guess it had been shot.

Of course the license showed the name and address of the possible culprit. I came back to my office and residence and told and showed my supervisor what Roger had come across. To say the least, I was mad. It is kind of a personal affront to have someone come into my district and kill a deer and get away with it.

The man's address was Fosston, Minnesota, about ninety miles from Waskish. I told my supervisor I wanted to go and find this insolent person and get him into court.

Supervisor Lester Borning said, "We will call Carl Johnson, the warden at Fosston, and have him go and interrogate this person."

I told Lester Borning, "Tell Carl Johnson that he should not tell this person how we know he was here in the Waskish area." I was worried about Carl Johnson doing that.

Lester Borning insisted, "I think Carl Johnson is capable of performing this task."

There wasn't much I could do so I let Lester Borning call Carl Johnson. He gave the name and address of the party shown on the deer bow license. He told Carl we found this gut pile of a deer that had been killed last night. Also, he was to find out if this party had a partner and to check out the vehicles they had up here in Waskish for evidence—blood, hair. Then call us back as soon he finished checking.

About an hour later, Carl Johnson called back and said he checked this party. He worked in a Phillips 66 gas station. He checked this man's station wagon, said he went over the vehicle with a fine-toothed comb—nothing. He did say the party admitted he and another man (a plumbing contractor in Fosston) were in the Waskish area hunting partridge over the weekend but they didn't kill any deer.

Lester Borning knew I was upset and he commented, "It's all over now. If they do have some venison they will get rid of it." He went on to comment that you couldn't win them all.

Around noon Lester Borning left, heading south on Highway 72, leaving Robert Olson and myself at the Waskish station. I was really upset that those no good bastards came in my district and killed a deer.

I sat there and stewed about that for about ten minutes and then I told Robert Olson, "I'm going to call Lester Borning on my car radio and get permission to go to Fosston." I did that.

Lester Borning said, "I'm just coming into Kelliher and I will meet you at the Corner Cafe. I am sure the whole mess was cleaned up and it will take you an hour and a half to get there."

I met Lester Borning at Kelliher and again he said it was a waste of time and money. However, he could see how insistent I was. He finally gave in reluctantly, but said, "I'm going down there with you and try to keep you out of trouble." We drove two cars because afterwards Lester Borning would be going back to Thief River Falls and we would be coming back to Waskish.

As soon as we got in our cars, I got on the radio and I called the dispatcher to have him call Jack Backer in Bagley and Carl Johnson in Fosston with instructions that each was to go by the houses of the two possible deer hunters and keep them under surveillance until we got there. If they saw anyone come out of either house with boxes or packages to stop and hold them on the spot until I got there. This was done. Carl Johnson watched the gas station employee's house and Jack Backer watched the plumber's house.

When we got into Fosston, I called Carl Johnson to get directions to the gas station. We drove there with both vehicles. To tell the truth I was beginning to wonder what I was doing there. I walked into the station with Lester Borning and Robert Olson behind me. There were several people in the station and I asked who was the party I was looking for. One man claimed the name. I told him to go to the next room, which was the grease pit.

I then told him, "I want you to know I'm no nice guy like Carl Johnson. I came down here to get that deer you two bastards killed up north of Waskish and I'm not leaving town until I get it."

The man started to shake and I knew I was on the right trail. However, he stuck to his story, "We did not kill a deer." I threatened him with mayhem. He was scared but he wouldn't fess up.

So I told him, "We will go after your partner."

Lester Borning was good. He didn't slow me down. He said we would all ride out to this job site the plumber was working on. I went in and got him, but when I saw the other workmen around I suggested he come out to the patrol car. He sat in the front seat with Borning. I was in the back seat with Robert Olson. I let this man know that I was positive he and his partner had killed a deer the night before north of Waskish; I wanted that deer and I wasn't going to leave Fosston without it. He was definitely upset but he stuck to his story—no deer. So I told him to get out of the car. I was done with him.

I told Lester Borning to take me back to the garage and it was then that we got a break. When I checked with Carl Johnson and Jack Backer, Backer had witnessed a woman carrying many packages that had white paper wrappings to another house across the back way. This could be the venison.

When we got back to the garage, I got this man back in the grease pit. I told him I was fed up with their stalling. I let him know, "There are wardens watching your house and your partner's house, and one of the wardens witnessed the movement of a lot of packages from the plumber's house to a neighbor's house. Now I am going to the courthouse to get search warrants for your house, your partner's house, your neighbor's house and any other place I think that meat might be. And because you two have been screwing me around, when I get you in court I'm going to recommend the judge fine each of you the maximum—$1,000 and a year in jail—plus I'm going to get your station wagon for transporting that deer."

This guy's legs were getting pretty wobbly and he asked, "Can I take a minute to make a telephone call?"

I allowed, "You can go in the office and do that."

While he was making the call, Supervisor Lester Borning came out to the grease pit. He had over heard me talking to this fellow. He told me, "You are coming down on him too hard and I would like to intercede."

I told him, "Be my guest."

Lester Borning stopped him on his way back to me. I could see Lester Borning pointing to his supervisor's badge. There was a lot of talk between the two of them. Then Lester Borning came out to me and said they are giving up. He said, "I had a hard time to convince him that I had any control over you. I told him several times I was your supervisor and that I had control over you."

The man kept saying to Lester Borning, "If we give up the deer, he will take over and we will be looking at jail time and the loss of the station wagon."

Lester Borning finally convinced him to turn the meat over to Carl Johnson. Carl Johnson would charge him in that county with "Take one deer in close season". The maximum fine on a misdemeanor would be $100 and/or ninety day in jail for each of them. He would tell Carl Johnson to recommend no jail time to the court.

Also, he assured this man he would get this ugly old white-haired man out of town.

I thought we did pretty good to finally have them cough up the deer. Then I told Lester Borning to tell this man I would go along with his recommendation providing they turn the gun over to Carl Johnson and that he confiscates it.

With that Lester Borning told me to get on the radio and tell Carl Johnson the whole story and that he should take over seizing the deer, the gun, and run the men through court.

I would like to have taken these men back to Beltrami County for processing but you have to give a little sometime.

Chapter 30/ JOHN OLSON—WHITE FISH

On the 23rd of October 1967, I was out on Upper Red Lake checking whitefish gill-netters. The season had been open a few days for the taking of white fish with the aid of a gill net. In those days, you could use two one hundred foot by three foot nets. Each net license cost $1. The fishermen also had to have a current resident angling license. One of the main restrictions was that no part of the net could be set in water over six feet deep. Also, each net had to have a metal tag with the owner's name and address and the net had to be marked by a buoy or flag two feet above the water.

On this day I checked many fishermen and their nets and licenses. I finally worked my way down to the southeast part of Upper Red Lake. This was an area a lot of the locals and cabin owners used to set their nets. Somehow I happened to look way out on the lake and I thought I saw something flutter. It looked to be almost a mile away. No one would even think to set nets that far out. I checked all the nets just north of the Kansas City Resort for about a mile.

Again, I looked way out on the lake. I could see nothing. However, being a person that is curious, I thought as long as I was there and I had the time and my employer, the state, furnished the gasoline for the motor, why not check out that glimpse of a flutter? I thought I would probably find out it was a seagull or some trash.

So I headed out that way and lo and behold there were net marker flags everywhere. It looked like a dozen. Two of the nets belonged to John Olson, a resident of Waskish. He had lived in Waskish for most of his life. I was told on many occasions that when he was a young, handsome man, he had his way with the ladies and the grape. However, before I showed up in Waskish, the Lord got hold of him and straightened him out. John and God had their own laws that superseded the state's laws. I noticed the names on the other nets were of Scandinavian descent. Most of them had cottages on land that John had sold them.

John probably knew from years of experience where the whitefish would travel enroute to their favorite spawning grounds and he would intercept them.

I was quite certain these netting fishermen would be out there the following morning at sunrise to clerk their nets. So I contacted Leo Manthei of Blackduck to come up and give me some assistance seizing the nets, the fish and the fishermen. Somehow, Gus Clemenson, the warden at Bemidji, got in on making an assist. He wanted to know if he came up to help maybe he could get a fish or two to take home to eat. I told him we could possibly arrange that if there were lots of fish in the nets.

Leo and Gus were to be at Waskish at least a half hour before sunrise.

The next morning, October 24, there was a real boomer of a northwest wind blowing. There were big waves and white caps.

Leo and Gus had taken a trip into the campgrounds and got a good look at those waves rolling in. It was raw cold. We all had waterproof gear and life jackets. It was then that Gus announced that no way was he going out on that lake. Then he let me know that even if the lake were calm, he wouldn't go out on that big S.O.B. of a lake.

Upper Red Lake waves and whitecaps

I asked him why he volunteered to come along to help. His answer was to get some fish.

The state had an 18-foot Crestliner aluminum boat and an old thirty-five horse Johnson outboard motor that I intended to use to pick up and haul the nets in.

So Leo and I started out. When we got down in the area, we held off about a mile waiting for the netters to show up. We began to realize these netters were apparently reluctant to go out on the lake because they failed to show up, or possibly, they knew I had located their nets and were not coming out.

I told Leo I had measured the water the day before when the lake was calm. The nets were set in nine to ten feet of water. Also, I had taken their names and addresses off the locator floats. I told Leo, "Let's just go ahead and put the nets into our boat and then go look up John Olson and his friends. We'll tell them what we have done, check their licenses, give them a copy of the seizure tags, and schedule them into Justice of the Peace Court."

We had a wild old time pulling those nets, weights, and fish into the boat. It was almost impossible to maintain your balance and we had to be extra careful not to get the motor prop tangled in all the ropes and nets. The bottom of the boat was slippery with flopping fish. Both of us were exhausted. The boat was so loaded it just plowed through the water. We were wet right down to our under clothes in spite of the rain gear. The boat had about six inches of water so we had to open the drain plug. The spray from the waves sent water spraying into our faces and into the boat about as fast as it was draining out. Our biggest worry was that the old Johnson motor would shut down on us.

About eleven o'clock, we finally turned into the Tamarac River and calm waters. We pulled up to the state dock and started the chore of untangling nets, salvaging the fish, and recording the owner's names and addresses. All Gus Clemenson could say was, "You guys are crazy." It was just a job that had to be done. We made out summons and seizure tags. Gus, I think, got a couple of whitefish before we started our count.

Then we went down to John Olson and had him sign his summons and seizure receipt. There was a time and date he was to appear before Justice Quale or he could go earlier and post bail.

We asked for and got directions as to where we would find the other people that we had the names for. We looked them up, explained and showed them the law in the synopsis although I'm positive they knew what they were doing wrong. They signed their promise to appear and the seizure receipts.

Eventually, I checked with the justice of the peace. She advised me they had all been in—pled guilty, paid their fine, and left. John Olson showed some dissatisfaction at this old gray-headed upstart moving into Waskish and telling him what he could or couldn't do.

About a week later, I walked into John in Gabby's store. He doubled up his right fist and shook it under my nose and he said, "You took my nets and you took my fish and you made me pay a fine and I'll never forget it."

Chapter 31/ GOOD INFORMATION

On October 6th in 1969, I received some information about a David Mohstad and a Steven Reandeau. I was told that they had recently killed deer and it was before the deer season.

I didn't know this David Mohstad or Steven Reandeau. I was told Mohstad just retired from the Navy and lived on a farm across the road from his folks. Reandeau and his girlfriend were up visiting his father who had just acquired a farm on the northwest corner of County Aid Road 108 and the road that goes to the public access.

I went to my home and office in Waskish, and told my wife the information I had just received. Then I called Leo Manthei at Blackduck to meet me at the Justice of the Peace Clara Quale's office, at 8:00 a.m. the next day.

At 8:00 a.m. Warden Manthei and I met at the justice of the peace's office at the Kelliher Independent. I told her what had transpired and that I wanted search warrants for the two farms. I gave her the descriptions. Justice Quale thought I probably had enough evidence to make the search.

First Leo and I, in my car, started to locate Reandeau. We drove to Clifford Reandeau's farm. We were told they didn't have any deer meat, so we showed the old fellow the search warrant. Then he admitted there was the skeleton of a deer in the basement. We went inside and down in the basement was hanging all the bones of a doe deer. I asked the old man, "Where's the meat?"

He said, "By now it is probably in Sioux Falls, South

Dakota." Some of their relation took the meat the evening before and started for Sioux Falls so the meat wouldn't spoil. He told me his son Steven had brought it home the day before. Steven wasn't there so I made out a summons and a seizure slip for the bones. Steven was to appear the next morning at the justice of peace court in Kelliher at 8:00 a.m.

Then I told Leo, "You are going to have to wait here to see that Reandeau doesn't call Mohstad. I will go over to Mohstad's to find his deer and write him up. Then I will come back and pick you up."

Leo then told me, "Reandeau hasn't put in a phone yet."

I asked Leo, "Are you sure?"

Leo then told me, "When you were writing things up, I walked around the house and there weren't even any telephone wires leading into the house." Leo also advised me that Robert Wilhelm had heard us talking on the radio when we were on our way to meet in Kelliher. While I was inside writing Reandeau up, Wilhelm called and wanted to know what we had going. Leo was sitting in my patrol car so he told Wilhelm we had located one deer and next we were going to hit another farm. Leo invited Wilhelm to meet us on County Aid Road 108, north of the Saum Store. We met and Wilhelm crawled in the back seat and we started west on this dead-end road to find David Mohstad.

About a half mile down this road I saw a man with a packsack on his back and about a quarter of a mile north of a farmhouse on the north side of the road. He was walking exceptionally fast heading for the tall timber. I jumped on Leo, "See that man out there? I'll bet he has a load of venison in that packsack. Reandeau had to have a phone."

In those days there were ten families on each party line. You could have twenty parties listening in on a conversation if everyone was home. When we arrived at Dave Mohstad's farm, they were waiting for us—all smiles and friendly. I told Dave why we were there and showed him the search warrant. He assured me we would not find any venison.

Someone had told me that when old man Mohstad killed a deer illegally, it was brought home, dressed out, butchered, cooked, and cold packed within hours. There was a huge deep hole in the yard half full of water. I told Leo and Wilhelm to find some long handled tool and probe down in the hole and feel for fruit jars.

I went in the house and down in the basement. There was an area full of home preserved fruit jars. The shelves were packed except an area about three feet wide, two feet high and two feet deep. It was obvious. I turned to Dave and made the statement, "That's where you had the venison." Dave just stood there and smiled.

I went upstairs and walked through the house. I told Dave, "Stop playing games and bring out the venison so I don't have to tear your house apart. I have no intentions of leaving without the evidence." I had noticed a small space in the bathroom that had a homemade ladder up to a hole in the ceiling. I was reasonably sure that is where the jars had been moved to. I thought I would go back down in the basement and mess around and give Dave time to haul the jars of venison out in the open. Instead Dave followed me down in the basement so I put on a show of digging through pots and pans and lo and behold I found a pint jar of freshly packed venison.

My folks used to cold pack all kinds of game and I recognized this jar as venison. Dave left me and bounded up the steps and I could hear him complain to his wife. "How come you left that one jar in that old coffee pot?"

Her answer was, "I couldn't carry any more jars to you up in the attic and when I went back down in the basement the wardens were here. There was only one jar and I had to get rid of it quick so I stuck it in that old coffee pot."

I was up in the kitchen and I just said, "This one jar is enough evidence. You plan to be in the Justice of the Peace Court tomorrow morning at 8:00 a.m." I made out a summons,

"Did take and possess one deer in closed season". I told him, "The bail schedule calls for $300 plus $5 cost for the judge. You best have that with you or the justice of the peace will give you the alternative—ninety days in the county jail."

I went outside and told Leo and Bob, "He will be coming to the Justice of the Peace Court in the morning." All three of us signed the seizure card I attached to the jar. I told them I knew where the rest of the jars had been moved to. They would have time to think about some mighty expensive meat.

The following morning we all met at Mrs. Quale's office at the <u>Kelliher Independent</u>. They both pled guilty and the fine was $305.00 or ninety days in jail. Mohstad was able to pay the fine. Reandeau said it would take a couple of days to acquire that much money. The judge gave him twenty-four hours to come up with it. I was pretty sure we had a runner on our hands so I accompanied him out to his van. When I checked inside, I found deer hair and blood. I told Reandeau, "I really should be charging you with a gross misdemeanor, 'Transport an illegal big game animal', which carries a penalty of up to one thousand dollars and/or a year in jail and the loss of your van."

However, I said, "I will seize the van and give you a seizure receipt, and providing you pay up with the justice of the peace within twenty-four hours, I will let the original charge stand. I will lock the van in the Phillip 66 garage and I will leave the vehicle key with Mrs. Quale. She will give you the car key and authorize the release of the van when you pay the $305."

This Steven Reandeau kept babbling and talking about his fighting over in "NAM." I heard him say "NAM" over a hundred times. I was a bit suspicious of him and I told Leo as much. Leo said, "I think you are overly suspicious."

I told him, "Maybe so, but I am going to call the dispatcher at Thief River Falls and have him check with Fort Snelling in Minneapolis."

I called the dispatcher at Thief River Falls and told him I

was a bit suspicious about this Steven Reandeau. I gave him what information I had about him and asked him to check with Fort Snelling in Minneapolis or wherever it was feasible and advise us of this person.

About an hour later, the dispatcher called me back. He said this man is not A.W.O.L. He is a deserter and the army wants him right now. He went on to say this information comes from the Provost Martial at Fort Snelling. He went on to say this Steven Reandeau was a really slippery character. He advised us to put handcuffs and chains on him and lock him up in a good solid jail.

I told the dispatcher that we didn't have him physically but I was pretty sure I knew where he was and we could pick him up.

The response from Fort Snelling was to get at least a half dozen law enforcement people and try to pick him up immediately. I told the dispatcher I would get a hold of Leo as I was reasonably sure we could get him.

I put out a call for Leo to meet me in Kelliher as fast as he could get there. We met at the justice of the peace's house where I made a request to reuse the search warrant if necessary. The judge OK'd that.

It was around six o'clock in the evening when Leo and I got together. We left his car at the judge's house and Leo got in my patrol car. We headed out for the Reandeau farm hoping we would find Steven there. On the way there, I said to Leo, "You know how the driveway passes the Reandeau house on the north side." Leo agreed with me. I then told Leo, "I'll come almost to a stop as we come to the front porch. Then you should jump out of the car and go by the front door and watch for Steven. I will continue to the back of the house, get out and come up on the back porch. I will let the father know why we are here and go in the house and find Steven or maybe flush him out the front door."

Just as I rolled out of the car Steven came out the back door like a shot. All he had on was a pair of jeans and a pair of stockings. In about ten jumps, I had him and he submitted without a struggle. I called for Leo and he came running around the house. We got handcuffs on him and then he wanted to go back in the house to get his clothes. About then a blond woman came out on to the porch, all she had on was a brassiere and panties. She started to bawl and hug Steven and wanted to take him back in the house to get the rest of his clothes. I told her, "No way. You go in and get his clothes and bring them out here on the porch." We got Steven dressed and loaded in the patrol car and headed for Bemidji to lock him up in the county jail.

We called the dispatcher at Thief River Falls and told him we had Reandeau and were on our way to the county jail in Bemidji.

A few minutes later the dispatcher said the Provost Marshall or some military police would be on the way up to Bemidji to pick him up.

I told him to hold up a little. We had him in the Justice of the Peace Court this morning. He pled guilty to taking and possessing one white tailed deer in closed season. The judge gave him twenty-four hours to pay a $305.00 fine or go to jail for ninety days. I had seized the man's van until he either paid his fine or did his time in the county jail. After we got done with him, then the military could have him. That was not to the liking of the military but they had to admit, if it weren't for us they didn't even know where Steven Reandeau was.

The next day Steven Reandeau did not come up with the money, so he started serving his time in Tom Tolman's new county jail.

About three weeks later, I got word that Reandeau escaped the county jail. This was a big blow to the sheriff. He had considered his new jail escape proof.

I was later advised Reandeau had gotten into the recessed light box in the ceiling and punched out one or two of those nickel like slugs. Using these slugs, he started digging at the mortar that was used to hold the cement blocks in the wall behind his bunk. Eventually he was able to remove a couple of the blocks. The deputies figured he waited until about two or three a.m. He was able to squeeze through this opening ending up in the maintenance man's closet. From there, he was able to slip out through the garage door.

Upon hearing this, I went out to the Reandeau farm to advise Clifford, if he didn't know, that Steven had escaped from the county jail. The old man said he had no knowledge of this nor did he know where Steven might be.

When I left the house and got in my patrol car, a young man stepped out of some bushes along side the car. He handed me a piece of paper and told me he had no use for Steven. The address was a relative of Reandeau that lived in a suburb of Minneapolis, which was within walking distance of Fort Snelling. He told me he was pretty sure Reandeau would be found there.

I passed this information on to the dispatcher at Thief River Falls to relay it to the Provost Marshall at Fort Snelling. I was told the military police captured him. The sheriff did not want him back to finish his sentence. Everyone was satisfied to leave Steven Reandeau to let the military deal with him.

Chapter 32/ *WHITE BEAR LAKE HUNTERS*

It was November 8, of 1969. I was on general patrol on the first day of the deer season. I was checking hunters to see if they had a license, checking their firearms while transporting them in motor vehicles, and checking deer in camps and being transported that they were properly tagged.

I had a young man with me that my supervisor had sent up to me as trainee on probation. I was not too impressed with this young man. He did not seem to possess an aggressive curiosity that is a prime requirement for a game warden. I felt maybe after a while he would develop. I had a feeling he was concerned he would do something wrong and I would chastise him for it.

He was a college graduate and his studies were along the lines of game management or as a biologist. He took and passed the test for a game warden so he must have known he was getting into the law enforcement section of the Conservation Department. Time would tell.

We stopped in at Johnson's Resort northwest of Waskish on Upper Red Lake. There were no hunters in camp at the time. I got out of the patrol car and started walking around the resort cabins. In back of the buildings on the north side, I came upon a screened-in fish-cleaning shack. I could see there were three deer hanging in there. I went inside to check if they were properly tagged. None of the deer were tagged. They were all dressed out and I took a little smell in the body cavities. The buck and one doe had a smell that led me to believe they had been killed before that morning which would be before season.

I then contacted Mr. Johnson, the owner of the resort. I told him, "There are three untagged deer in your fish-cleaning shack. You have a problem, because, I will have to sign a complaint against you unless the deer belong to some of your guests. If the deer are your guests', you will have to tell me which cabin they are in."

He told me he had been down among his cabins and ran across the three untagged deer about a half an hour earlier. He went on to say he had made two calls to my office but the line was busy both times. He said, "It's got to be the hunters in the cabin closest to the lake on the south side. They came in with a deer around noon and had their lunch. To the best of my knowledge, no other hunters have brought any deer in."

I told Mr. Johnson, "I am going to go down and seize the deer. I will stay out of sight until this gang comes home at which time I will sort them out and write them up." I noticed my trainee seemed to be somewhat concerned to be involved in what I said I was going to do.

We drove the patrol car down by the fish-cleaning shack, hauled the three deer out, and piled them onto the trunk of the car. I got some rope out and tied them on good so they wouldn't fall off. Then I maneuvered the car around so it would be out of sight of the hunters when they drove in. I thought I might catch them transporting another untagged deer.

At about 6:00 p.m., the hunters came in—three men in a pickup and two men in a sedan. I checked their guns and they were all cased and unloaded. I asked to see their deer licenses and they all dug them out. I just stuck them in my pocket and told the men we would all go in their cabin. If we turned the lights on there, it would be easier to read them.

On checking the licenses, I noticed one was made out to a woman from White Bear Lake. I said I have a license here made out to a Mrs. Hammond. It was issued at a sporting goods store in White Bear Lake, Minnesota.

At this disclosure, one of the men spoke up and said, "I gave you the wrong license. Here is my license." He pulled a second license out of his billfold. The second license was made out to Richard Hammond Jr. and signed by him as the issuer of the license.

I then asked him, "Do you own the sporting goods store in White Bear Lake?"

He acknowledged, "Yes, I do."

I then said, "You, of all people, know you can't possess another person's deer hunting license unless the party is in the immediate group."

To this he said, "That is my wife's license. She left here about noon to go back to White Bear Lake to oversee the employees in our sporting goods store. I forgot to give her the license when she left here."

I told him, "I am going to check your story out."

Then I said, "The main reason I'm here is there are three

untagged deer in the fish-cleaning shack. Two of them, I'm reasonably sure were killed before the season was opened. The other one, I believe, was killed today. The resorter said your group brought one in about noon. As no other deer hunters in camp have taken any deer, I can only assume all three of those deer belong to your group. All I want is the three men that those deer belong to. Give me their names."

At this, Richard Hammond spoke up and said, "Those deer don't belong to us. You can't hang somebody else's problems on to us."

I then told them, "I have enough evidence to tie you to those three deer and if the three people that are responsible for those deer won't speak up, I'll charge five of you with possession of three untagged deer in camp." I went on to say, "I can charge all five of you on this violation for only one deer, and had I come across the deer being transported untagged in a motor vehicle, all the occupants of the vehicle would be charged with a gross misdemeanor. The vehicle would be seized and the occupants would be subject to up to $1,000 fine and/or up to a year in jail."

"I'm offering to charge just the three persons for the three deer with a misdemeanor with a probable fine of $100 and/or ninety days in jail. Make up your minds gentlemen, I'll give you five minutes."

For one man, Mr. Warren Beaverfield Jr., that was too much. He spoke up and said, "One of those deer is mine, one belongs to Raymond Hammond Jr. and the third one belongs to Ronald Will."

With that, I made out the three summons and the three seizure receipts. I told the three men, "You will ride in the patrol car with my assistant and me. The other two men will follow in your sedan automobile. We will all stop at my office where I will call the Justice of the Peace Clara Quale in Kelliher and tell her that I will want her to open court in the Municipal Building that evening and get this mess cleaned up."

We all drove to my residence where I left my assistant in charge of these men while I went in to call the justice of the peace to arrange for court.

After I talked to the judge, I called the telephone operator and obtained the telephone number of the White Bear Lake Sporting Goods Store and Richard Hammond Jr.'s home number.

I called and finally got hold of Mrs. Hammond. I asked her, "Can I speak to Mr. Hammond?"

She told me, "He is at some resort near Waskish hunting deer."

I asked her, "Do you know the name of the resort?"

She said, "No."

I then asked, "Were you at the resort this morning?"

She said, "No. I had to stay and operate the store." She was curious so I explained some of the problems.

When I came back out to the car, I told Mr. Hammond that I had talked to his wife and she denied being in Waskish. So I told him I'm going to give you an "A" for effort along with another summons for having your wife's license in your possession.

At the Municipal Building, I wrote up this last summons. Justice Court was held and all the protocol was run through. Raymond Hammond Jr. plead guilty to both counts and was fined $100 and costs on each one. Ronald Will plead guilty to the untagged deer and was fined $100 and costs. Warren Beaverfield Jr. plead guilty. I spoke up and asked the court if a little leniency could be accorded him because he had spoken up admitting his guilt and putting the finger on the other two violators. The judge fined him $100 and costs. However, she suspended $50.

I returned the two licenses to the two men who supposedly were not involved in the violation. I then snapped the tag on the other four licenses and then seized and voided the licenses. The five men got in their sedan and left a little wiser and their pocket books a little lighter.

I don't think Mr. Richard Hammond Jr. really got the message. He left the courtroom with a cocky attitude.

My trainee, all through court, stood facing away from the court proceeding. A couple of times he actually faced the wall. When I asked him what his problem was, he told me he felt sorry for those men and he thought if I would have just let the men go out and tag the deer it would have made better relations between the sportsmen and the Conservation Department.

Eight days later, I was driving the patrol car accompanied by my trainee up on Ditch 14 when we met a pickup truck with three men in it. When we got right up to them, I turned on my red light. I blocked the road with the patrol car and bailed out fast, running to the pickup. I could hear the truck operator holler, "Here come the little game wardens, run, run, run, check the guns."

The truck driver was Richard Hammond Jr. The other two men were the ones I had returned their licenses to. All the time, Mr. Hammond was chirping, "Check the guns, check the guns." One of the rifles was an 1886 Winchester Rifle 33 W.C.F. caliber. I pulled the gun out of the case and opened the action. There in the action was a shiny, brass 33 caliber bullet—loaded.

At that disclosure, Mr. Hammond started to give his passenger a tongue lashing for failing to unload his rifle. I then told Hammond, "This is your pickup, and you're the driver so you are the person that is liable for transporting a loaded firearm." He couldn't believe it when I made out the summons in his name for "Transporting a loaded rifle".

He found the justice of the peace, plead guilty, paid a fine of $50. Mr. Hammond, if his money holds out, may eventually take some time out and learn the game and fish laws that good sportsmen follow.

Chapter 33/ FOUR YOUNG MEN WITH PROBLEMS

It was the fourth day of the deer season in the late 1960's. I had been working nights around the Upper Red Lake area. There was a huge area between Highways 72 and 71 and Highway Number 11 that was known locally as Pine Island. No one at that time lived in this area. Even the Pine Island Ranger Station had been abandoned. The area had been heavily logged over in the late 1950's and early 1960's. It was full of old abandoned logging roads and ditch grades. I thought maybe this would be a good area to work this night. I might catch a night hunter looking for a deer.

After dinner that evening, my wife packed me a big lunch and a thermos of coffee. I started out north and east of Waskish into "No Man's Land". About 35 miles from Waskish, I came to a huge open area where the state had cleared and removed the stumps and leveled the ground somewhat. It was cleared well enough so a tail dragger airplane could use it as an emergency landing strip.

I parked my patrol car on one of the many trails that led off from this grass strip and took up my post watch sitting on the hood of my patrol car. By sitting outside the car a person can get a better direction on the location if a shot is fired.

Sometime after midnight, when I had eaten my lunch, I saw a glow of a strong light against the low overcast clouds. The light seemed to be moving back and forth and getting brighter. I had reason to believe whoever was doing the shining was coming in my general direction. Because of the brightness and boldness of the light, I thought it could be Red Lake Indians.

There is an area north of where I was sitting known as The Indian Pines. This land is part of the Red Lake Indian

Reservation, and in that area the Indians can do anything they want to do any time. However, they were not allowed to violate Minnesota or federal game laws in the area where I was.

As the light seemed to be working its way towards me, I thought it would be prudent to hold still and see what transpired. The only problem was I was starting to get the shakes. I had a problem that way from when I was a little kid down in Iowa. The anticipation of what was going to happen was almost too much for my nervous system. However, when I would start to act and become physical, the shakes would leave me. I was always thankful for that.

Eventually, I was able to make out, through the brush and trees, the headlights of the vehicle. I also caught glimpses of a hand-held light, so I knew the occupants of this car were shining.

In those days, we used to have to catch the occupants in the car with a loaded, uncased firearm capable of killing a big game animal. In other words, when you blocked the shining car, you had to move very fast to get to their vehicle before they could unload the gun and get it sacked up in a gun case.

The car came out onto this big opening and the headlights and hand-held light played out all over the field. There were no deer out on the opening at that particular moment. They drove the full length of the field—south to north. In the northwest corner, they drove off the field on an old logging trail that had seen active use by the partridge hunters.

I got in my patrol car and drove as fast as possible to the trail they left the field on. Occasionally, I had to use my sneak light. I had to use the sneak light on the logging trail. I could see their light up ahead. Fortunately they were driving slowly, searching the woods and openings with their hand-held light. I finally got to where I could see their vehicle dead ahead.

I turned out my sneak light and maneuvered up where I could drive by their lights. I was about a 100 yards behind them. Now, I could also see with the glow of their lights that there were four people in the vehicle. A few minutes later, their brake lights came on and I thought that they may have seen a deer. I had my window rolled down to hear if they shot. Then their back-up lights came on and I realized they were at a dead end.

I drove my car ahead as quickly as possible and when I was within about 15 yards, I stopped my patrol car and jumped out. My car had the trail blocked. Just as their car came about and they could see my car blocking the trail, I was jerking their car door open and screaming, "Game Warden. Get out of the car and up in front of your headlights." The four young white men just seemed paralyzed.

There were two loaded, uncased big game rifles in the hands of the two men in the back seat. I reached in and took the guns out of their hands. Then I reached over and turned off the motor and pocketed the keys. These young men just seemed stunned. I told them again, "Out of the car and stand in front of the headlights." They finally started to move and do as I told them. I took the guns to the patrol car, turned on my headlights, and gathered up my summons book, seizure tags, and statement book. Then I asked for their deer hunting licenses. Two of the men had deer licenses. The other two only had small game licenses.

Whoever the party was that sold them the licenses had used the machine where the information came off by inserting their driver's license. The print was very poor so I told the men to break out their driver's licenses. The youngest was nineteen years old. The oldest was twenty-two according to the driver's license. So, I wrote them all up and charged them with deer shining which was a gross misdemeanor. I made out seizure slips for the two rifles, the spotlight, and the car. I told these men three of them would ride with me and the fourth would drive their car to my headquarters in Waskish. Then, I would have to take the four men to International Falls and put them in jail. Later on that day, they would appear in Municipal Court to be bound over for District Court. Then the Municipal Judge might set bail that they could post and they could get out of jail. Otherwise, they would stay in jail until the date set for District Court. One of these young men started to bawl. So, I told them, "You young fellows have to pay the price. If you want to play, you've got to pay."

Then this one lad said, "We're all juveniles."

I responded, "Not according to your driver's licenses." Then they pulled out their driver's licenses and showed me how by using a razor blade they could shave off the raised numbers and letters and maneuver them around to change their birth dates. By getting under the headlight, I thought I could detect a little discrepancy in their glue job.

I told them I would still put them in jail for the night and let the court sort it out the next day.

It turned out they were all juveniles. Their parents had to come up from the metropolitan area and vouch for their kids.

They had to appear in juvenile court on the shining charge, which ended up with a bawling out from the judge.

However, their driver's licenses were turned over to the Minnesota State Patrol. What they did with them I never heard.

Chapter 34/ FOLLOW ME

The incident occurred on January 22, 1969. I was in the state patrol car driving out on the ice of Upper Red Lake checking fishermen. The dispatcher at Thief River Falls called and told me my wife had called and asked to have me return to my headquarters. It was not an emergency but it was necessary that I return.

So with that, I drove off the ice at the closest exit and headed for Waskish.

When I came to the circle driveway around the warden headquarters, there were two vehicles in the driveway. The one in front was empty. The second vehicle was a Cadillac with one man sitting behind the wheel.

When he saw me pull up behind him and get out of the patrol car, he got out of his car. I asked him, "What can I do for you?"

"That's what I'd like to know," he said. "I was minding my own business out on the lake fishing walleye pike when this ugly man came over to me and shouted, 'I'm the man, follow me'."

I said to this fellow, "He must be in the house. I'll get to the bottom of this." I left him and went into the house to find Bob Gregg, the warden from Deer River, drinking coffee with my wife.

I asked Bob what this fellow did. Bob said, "I think that guy owns a restaurant and wants to serve walleye pike for the next month. Tell him to open up his trunk."

I went back out and told the fellow, "Open your trunk."

He said, "Do you have a court order or a search warrant? Who was the guy that told me to follow him?"

I told him, "That was Bob Gregg, the warden from Deer River. Open the trunk!"

He opened the trunk and there were 17 walleyes.

I took him down to the justice of the peace in Kelliher and it cost him a $50.00 fine and $5.00 in costs, and he lost all of the fish.

So, Bob Gregg got an assist on his day off.

Chapter 35/ THE GREAT WHITE HUNTERS

I don't remember what year this was but I do know it was the night before the deer season. It was in the late 60s or early 70s.

My neighboring warden, Leo Manthei, from Blackduck had asked me to come down and work with him that night. He wanted to check an area just east of the Red Lake Indian Reservation on Highway #1.

Leo Manthei, the warden at Blackduck

There was a huge area on the south side of Highway #1 that had been acquired by some Texas cattlemen for pasturing some of their beef. The north side of the road was, for the most part, state land and heavily wooded. There were a couple of small families on the north side of Highway #1 in about a six-mile stretch.

Someone had told Leo the Indians had come out on this uninhabited stretch of road and shined and shot deer. We knew the Indians sold a lot of deer to the great white hunters.

Leo thought we might catch some of the members of the Red Lake Band hunting deer off the reservation.

So here I am sitting with Leo down in the ditch along side of Highway #1 waiting for something to happen. Our car was back in the bush out of sight but one of us could get to it quickly if we needed it.

A few cars passed us going either east or west but not driving slowly or running a spotlight—just travelers.

Sometime around 2:00 a.m. a big new Cadillac sedan came off the reservation headed east doing about fifteen or twenty miles per hour and passed us. We scrunched down so they wouldn't see us. About a mile east of us, we saw the brake light come on. The vehicle turned around and came back toward us. We thought they might have seen a deer with their headlights. The car passed us and went back onto the reservation.

About fifteen minutes later, what appeared to be the same car did the same thing as before and back onto the reservation. This really aroused our imagination so we decided if it came back again we would stop it to see what was going on. We could see there were four men in the vehicle as it passed.

Some time passed, maybe a half-an-hour. That same vehicle came and passed us again. One of us got the patrol car running and down to the approach. The other got in the ditch about where the car would be forced to stop when the patrol car was driven out onto the highway with all the lights flashing. We got the car stopped and then Leo and I were made privy to the dumbest people south of the Canadian border.

These men were from St. Paul. They were dark skinned. I guessed they were Greeks or Italians. They were connected to the restaurant business.

They had come up north to hunt deer. They all had deer licenses. The evening before they had checked with people in Bemidji as to where to hunt and where to get a good meal. It was suggested to them to go west on Highway #2 to Jack's Bar and Cafe.

That was their next stop. At this bar they saw some Indians from the Red Lake Indian Reservation. They engaged them in small talk, and bought the Indians a few drinks. They all had dinner together and then these men inquired as to where they should go to hunt deer.

I don't know what kind of agreements were made, but these men were invited up to the reservation to meet some of the local young ladies. At any rate, these Indians told these men they would go out and hunt and get their deer for them. However, the Indians said that they didn't have any guns.

The Indians suggested if these men would loan a couple of their guns to them, they would go shoot their deer for them. One of the great white hunters offered to loan each of the four Indians a gun.

It seems the young ladies got tired of these men and wanted to go to bed to sleep so they more or less turned them out.

They were hanging close to where the four Indians had left them so they could get their deer and their guns back when the four Indians men came back from hunting.

I don't know if he heard me or believed me. I just told one man, "You will never see those Indian men or your guns again." With that, we turned them loose to their dream world and got out of there.

I often wondered whatever happened. All those Indian men would only need one gun to hunt the way they do on the reservation.

Chapter 36/ THE LARGEST ILLEGAL FISH BUYER IN MINNESOTA

In the last part of the sixties, I became aware that McCarthy Bodin Fisheries in International Falls was the recipient of huge amounts of illegal walleye pike from the Red Lake Band of fishermen. On several occasions, I called Marv Smith, the Game Warden at International Falls, to watch for Red Lake Indians selling fish at McCarthy Bodin's. He seemed to feel I didn't know what I was talking about.

Marv's son was gill netting rough fish on a helper's license and was doing most of his fishing in Namakan Lake. My folks at this time were living in their home on Twin Alligator Island on Namakan Lake.

One day when my dad was going into International Falls for supplies, he met Marv's son, Mike Smith, with a load of rough fish at the public dock on the Ash River waiting for a ride to McCarthy Bodin's to sell his fish. My dad told Mike he would haul him into International Falls to the fish buyer. When the two of them arrived at the fisheries, they found a number of Indians with boxes of walleye pike. My dad commented to one of the Indians, "Those look like Red Lake walleyes."

The Indian responded with, "That's where they came from."

After Mike sold his fish, dad took him home to Marv Smith's home. My dad told me at a later date of the entire affair, not knowing that it was an illegal transaction.

Leo Manthei and I would catch an occasional car or truckload of fish going through Kelliher enroute to International Falls to be sold illegally.

The normal give away that would alert us to stop the vehicle was when you would see only two Indians in the vehicle but the back end of the vehicle would be so depressed it was almost dragging on the ground. You could be positive the vehicle was loaded with fish. They would usually be headed to the Falls between 10 a.m. and 12 noon, right after they came off the lake and emptied their gill nets.

This whole operation was illegal, and both the buyer and the Indians knew it. Consequently the buyer usually paid about half of what the fish were worth. The Indian fisherman made a quick, one-time cash sale.

Eventually, I made another call to Marv Smith to alert him to Indians selling fish to McCarthy Bodin. Again, he claimed that was not being done. I told him to check with his son Mike and ask him about it when he stopped at McCarthy Bodin's to sell his rough fish. Marv said Mike was home at the time and I could hear him call to Mike to question him about Red Lake Indians selling walleye pike.

I could hear Mike's response when he answered, "Almost every time I stop at McCarthy Bodin's to sell my fish there are Indians in there selling boxes of walleyes."

Marv's response to me was, "I guess, I don't know what's going on in my own town."

Chapter 37/ SCHOOL TEACHERS' FISH RUN

It was in April of 1970. It occurred in Pickett's district, Baudette.

Harland called me early on a Friday and told me he had a lot of northern running in some of the judicial ditches. He told me to come to Baudette just after sundown, around 7:00 p.m.

On my arrival at his home, he told me he had been given some complaints by a reliable source that there had been illegal spearing on two different ditches that drained into Bostic Creek then into Four Mile Bay and Lake of the Woods.

I left my patrol car and got into Harland's state car and we headed out northwest of Baudette. After we left the black top, Harland turned off his lights and we preceded with the aid of his sneak light. We were on a poor gravel road for three or four miles then he turned on to a ditch grade. I hated those ditch grades because in those days they were, at best, a lousy place to be driving an automobile. We finally backed into a brushy area where the car was pretty well hidden. However from this place, we could see a huge area.

As I remember, it was a black night, slightly overcast. I didn't actually know where we were—there were no farms, buildings, or yard lights. Every time Harland got me up in this area, I was always afraid it would rain and we would never drive out of there.

A long towards midnight, Harland said maybe the information he had gotten was a one-time operation. However, we would stay until at least 2:00 a.m. in the event it was some of the drinking crowd. The saloons and nightclubs closed at 1:00 a.m. That meant, at the best, if nothing happened, it would be 4:00 a.m. before I would get home to Waskish.

It was shortly after midnight —we had cleaned up the brown bags our wives had made up for us. Off to the east, we could see the glow of some vehicle lights. Harland suggested maybe we were in business or it could be a couple of lovers.

Eventually, we realized there were two cars coming. They came to within a mile of us, when they made a turn around at an approach to a field. The two vehicles went back east about a quarter-of-a-mile then we saw brake lights come on.

With the aid of our binoculars we could see a number of people get out of the cars and with the aid of their flashlights they went down into the ditch. We were unable to see for sure what they were doing. Harland suggested maybe they had a fish trap in the ditch.

At any rate, we realized we were at a disadvantage where we were. The ditch grades are not wide enough to be able to pass those parked cars and block their escape should these people try that on us. Harland told me he thought there was a trail where he could get around and be facing or blocking these cars. I wasn't too keen on that, remembering the time we went off the grade with Harland driving and damn near rolled over into the ditch. At least that time, there were some huge popple trees that we chained his come-along to and after two hours we got back up on the grade. That wasn't the only time Harland put his vehicle in jeopardy. However, I won't bore you with those other incidents now.

I then suggested, "Why not take the bull by the horns? I'll walk down there and get up close enough to see what they are doing. I'll take my flashlight. I'll give you two winks if you should come down there slowly and quietly with just your sneak light on. If I give you three winks, turn on your lights and come as fast as you can. If no lights from my flash, it's of no concern to us."

So away I went. I got to the parked cars and these people were so involved in what they were doing they did not know I was there. They were spearing little northern, about a pound to a pound and a half. It was obvious from the voices that there were some female people in the group. I gave two winks twice with my flashlight.

I was almost in between the two parked cars when some male voice called a woman's name to bring another gunnysack. This party came up to the trunk of the car and picked up a sack. When she saw me, she didn't put her flashlight on me she just said, "Come on help me pick up some of the fish."

I heard another woman's voice say, "Isn't this fun?"

I followed the party with the sack and finally took it and held it open while different ones stuck those little northern that they picked up flopping around in the weeds.

Eventually, Harland was standing there turning his flashlight on the people spearing and gathering fish. Then he started calling out names. Then he hollered, "Game Wardens!"

There was sudden silence and then Harland ordered all of them up on to the road. It was a pretty silent group standing there. Then Harland said to me, "These are a big part of our Baudette school teachers."

He just admonished them by saying, "You people know better than to pull a stunt like this." He got all their names. We, Harland and I, loaded up two gunny sacks of fish into the patrol car. As I remember, Harland set up a time and a meeting place for later on in the day when he would do the paperwork.

With that, we all got in our cars and headed back to town. I transferred to my patrol car and went home to Waskish.

I never did inquire what the fines were or whatever happened after I left. To say the least, there could be some severe fall-out. Harland had said on our way back into town they were all good, dedicated teachers and he would talk this over with the county attorney and the judge.

Chapter 38/ FISHERMAN LITTERER

Mrs. Clara Quale was the justice of the peace in the northern part of Beltrami County. She lived in Kelliher with her husband Sig. They had a nice little cabin on Upper Red Lake. She operated a weekly newspaper. Every Saturday and Sunday they spent at their cabin fishing, hunting, mowing grass, and manicuring their seventy-five-feet of sand beach.

One day after the opening of the fishing season, she complained of a fisherman with a woman and a boy anchored out in front of their cabin fishing. The man would sit in the back on the motor and would drink out of cans and then lean over, fill the can with water, and let it sink to the bottom. He had been coming every weekend, and she guessed he had drowned at least a case (24) of cans every weekend.

On this day of June 7, 1970, I came across a man from Bemidji angling with too many lines. This was on a Sunday. I told the man the justice of the peace had a summer home on Red Lake and if he agreed to it, I would transport him in the state boat to the justice of the peace cabin where he could post bail and be done with his problem. His two partner fishermen could continue to fish and I would bring him back when he had completed his business with the justice of the peace. The man agreed to this and transferred himself from their boat to the state boat.

When we landed the boat at Quale's cabin, Mrs. Quale met us at the shoreline. I offered her the copy for the judge for the man I had with me. She had a pair of binoculars that she gave me. Then she said, "Watch that boat anchored out in the lake. That is the party that has been putting his cans in the lake."

I sat down with the binoculars and kept a constant watch on this boat. The man sitting in the back was a big man drinking from a can. He would take a swallow or two then place the can in the transom of the boat.

All of the people in the boat were catching fish. When they would catch a larger fish, they would take one off the stringer, release it, and put the larger fish on the stringer. Then the man would take up the can and take another swallow and so it continued until the can was empty. Then he held the can in the water for about a minute and his hand came up empty.

That was enough for me. I pushed my boat out in the water, started the motor, and proceeded out to the boat to check the fisherman out. I pulled along side the boat, told them who I was, submitted identification and asked to see their angling licenses. The man handed me a resident combination angling license that covered him and his wife. The lad was obviously about ten or eleven years old. They could legally have eighteen walleye pike and that was what they had.

Then I told the man I had watched him from shore with a pair of binoculars and I saw him release a can into the lake. I also told him I had received several complaints from the cabin owners about him doing the same thing I had just witnessed. So I told him, "I will give you one option, you go down to the bottom of the lake and retrieve that can, take it home and throw it in your front yard or else I will write you up for littering in public waters."

He told me, "The lake is nine-feet deep where I am anchored and I can't swim." I wrote up a summons that he did deposit litter in Upper Red Lake, to wit one can. I set the court date for June 8th, which was a Monday. He was to appear at 7:30 p.m. before Justice of the Peace Clara Quale.

I then told him the justice of the peace was at her cabin and he could go in and post bail with her right now. He elected to do that. However, because he had a big runabout boat and would have a hard time getting the boat into shore, he elected to ride in with me.

When he started to transfer to my boat his son, who had a real foul mouth, started to curse at me. His dad and mother both told him to shut up.

When we got to shore, we went up to Quale's cabin. The judge told him to deposit $105.00 bail.

He jumped up from his chair and screamed, "For one damned can?" Then he settled down when Mrs. Quale gave him a tongue lashing like I never heard before without one swear word. She let him know the likes of him was not wanted around Red Lake.

He wrote out a check for $105.00 and said he would be back for court at the time on the summons.

I appeared at the Municipal Building the following evening only to find out he had gone to an attorney in Bemidji, and requested and got a change of venue to the Municipal Court in Bemidji. The justice of the peace had to mail the check to the attorney in Bemidji.

The man owned a furniture store in Bagley and to the best of my knowledge never appeared in any court to answer to the charge of littering. There was one blessing—I don't believe he ever came back to Red Lake.

Chapter 39/ *MARV SMITH BECOMES A HERO*

Early one day in September of 1970, Leo Manthei, the game warden at Blackduck, called me and said he got a tip from an Indian friend that a big load of fish was going from the reservation to International Falls. I met Leo at Kelliher and we discussed how we would try to intercept as many of these Indian fishermen as possible.

The Indians transporting the fish never traveled in a group.

Their vehicles would be strung out ten or fifteen minutes apart. However, it seemed that when they came off the reservation, they all would use the same road. In the past, we would let one or two pass and then about the third vehicle we would pounce on them as fast as possible, hopefully, while they were still in Beltrami County so we could get them before the Justice of the Peace Clara Quale. She would assess some strong fines and occasionally she would also include jail time for repeat offenders. She had the title of "Maximum Clara".

This particular day, we decided to monitor the Joe Jerome Road and the North Trail out of Ponemah Point. I ended up with watching the Joe Jerome Road and Leo the North Trail. Occasionally, they used Minnesota State Highway No. 1, but as there were only two of us, we chose the trails we thought thieves would most likely use.

Along about 9:30 a.m., the first vehicle with two passengers and the low-hanging back end came from the west on the Joe Jerome Road. I had a good pair of binoculars plus my spotting scope with me, which confirmed my suspicions that they were Red Lake residents and the vehicle appeared to have a load in the back. I alerted Manthei of this fact and that it would appear the fish would be coming out the Joe Jerome Road. Leo said he would hold where he was for about ten minutes to see if a second vehicle came out the Joe Jerome Road or the North Trail. Also, Leo asked if I was able to get the license number of the vehicle. I told him, "No."

He suggested, "Try and get the license number of any following vehicles."

Of course, we carried on this conversation by using our state radios. Obviously, any other state warden or highway patrolman that was reasonably close could hear our conversation. At any rate, K233, Don Claude, who was in the process of transferring from Northome to Big Fork, heard us and called asking, "What have you guys got going?"

I answered him and told him, "Leo had gotten a tip that

some fish were coming off the reservation."

Don complained that my conversation was breaking and would I relay the traffic through the dispatcher at Virginia. I switched channels to Virginia and repeated my answer. Don wanted to know if we needed help. I told the dispatcher to tell Don that so far only one car had come through but we were expecting more. Don then asked if we had any idea where they were going with the fish. I came back with that they were probably going up to McCarthy Bodin at the Falls. I then told the dispatcher to tell Don that Leo was enroute to the county line to intercept the first car and by that time I was hoping we would have two or three more cars between us to round up so that we could run them through the Justice of the Peace Court in Kelliher.

Don came back with, "Why don't you let them go through up to the Falls? Then we might be able to round all of them up."

I told the dispatcher I would like nothing better and then we could get the buyer and get his license cancelled for one year. However, Marv Smith doesn't believe McCarthy Bodin would buy illegal fish, so I, for one, would be reluctant to lose control of the situation—a bird in the hand is worth two in the bush.

Evidently, Marv was in his patrol car and heard the traffic between Leo, Don Claude, and I. Marv told the dispatcher he had heard the relayed traffic and he would work with us if we would let the Indian fishermen come through.

I checked with Leo because, basically, this was his pinch. He was somewhat reluctant because of Marv's past history regarding the fisheries at International Falls. If Marv would concentrate on charging the buyer so we could get his license cancelled, Leo would OK the new plan.

I called the dispatcher at Virginia and told him to tell Marv Smith to let the first Indian car come into the fisheries, sell their fish and leave. Then when the second car came, let them unload the fish and then move in on the buyer and seize his books, which will disclose the first sale, the poundage, and the amount of money. Marv agreed to that. We told him we would be along hopefully following the last car. Also, we told Don Claude to get up to the Falls and assist Marv.

As I remember, there were ten Indian cars that came past us that we assumed had fish. Leo and I parked one of our patrol cars, and we rode together heading for International Falls.

About the time we passed Little Fork, my son, Fred, who is a highway patrolman out of the Falls, called on his radio and commented on the parade of Indian cars coming into the Falls and Marv had them rounded up and took them to the court in South International Falls before Justice of the Peace Shirley Whitbeck. He then asked us if we knew the truck route, the short cut to South International Falls. I told him we had never heard of it. So he said he would wait for us out on the intersection of Highway 71 and Highway 11 and guide us through.

We met and followed Fred on the truck route. About half way on the way, we passed two Indians parked on the side of the highway drinking from a bottle. I called to Fred to come back. We had a pinch for him. He came back and the three of us approached the car. They were drinking from a bottle of whiskey. So Fred wrote them up, seized the whiskey, and we continued on to the community building where Justice of the Peace Whitbeck was holding court.

Mr. Blake, the fish buyer of McCarthy Bodin, who was the holder of the Minnesota Fish Buyer's License #1, pled guilty to purchasing three hundred pounds of walleye pike from Simon Kingbird of Ponemah, Minnesota. I think the receipt showed he was paid $254.00.

Blake was fined $300.00 and the Indians that followed Simon Kingbird pled guilty to fish in possession with no valid license and were fined $50.00 or sixty days in jail. They all paid their fines. There were a bunch of surly Indians out in the parking lot off Eighteenth Street and First Avenue South. They were out their money and their fish.

I was surprised to see Matt Minerich, the area supervisor of that district, writing out the complaints plus Don Claude and Bob Wilhelm who was the new man moving into Northome.

I asked where Marv Smith was and they said he left supposedly trying to find someone to purchase the seized walleyes, which I was told, amounted to about three thousand pounds.

There was nothing more for Leo and I to do. We visited and had a cup of coffee with Fred. Leo and I requested a copy of the bill of sale for Simon Kingbird and it was given to us.

On the way back to Kelliher, we made plans for the next day to go over to the Red Lake Reservation to see if we could get Simon Kingbird and take him up to the Falls and run him through court.

Leo and I met the next day and drove to the police station at Red Lake. We looked up Sergeant Smith, with whom I'd had a fairly good working arrangement in the past. We showed him a copy of the bill of sale and told him what we would like to do. He was not impressed with our idea about arresting a fellow Indian. Then we told him there was a total of three thousand pounds of walleyes seized in this one caper and we suggested how much money the council lost. That seemed to put a different light on the situation. He told us to wait at the station until he had a chance to talk to some of the chiefs on the council.

Sergeant Smith came back about an hour later with a written order to the policeman at Ponemah to turn Simon Kingbird over to us. Leo and I drove up to Ponemah, found the policeman, and gave him the warrant for the pick up.

He let us know he wasn't too pleased with this chore and for sure he wouldn't turn Kingbird over to us on the reservation. He instructed us to go to the east entrance on State Highway 1 and wait for him outside of the reservation. We moved down there and waited. About a half-hour later, the Ponemah cop came with Kingbird in the police car. He stopped outside the entrance, pulled Kingbird out of his car, and gave him a shove toward us. We loaded him into the back of the patrol car, hauled him to the Falls, and ran him through the Justice of the Peace Court. He paid a $50.00 fine. He was still ahead $204.00. We left him in the Falls to find his way back to the reservation.

A few days later, we heard that the fish buyer's license was cancelled for one year, just like the law said it should be. However, now politics came into play. Our legislators that wrote the law and our invincible Commissioner Lierfallom thought it best to license another member of McCarthy Bodin so they could reopen the business, and it was done.

About three weeks later, two Indian fishermen from Red Lake were returning to the Red Lake Reservation from International Falls. They had gotten drunk and rolled their pickup on State Highway 71 and were killed. I can't prove it but I would bet a $100.00 that they had taken a load of walleyes to McCarthy Bodin's, sold them, got drunk, and unfortunately had this terminating accident on the way back to the reservation.

Again in 1983, the Indians were caught selling fish to McCarthy Bodin. This time the charges were put against James McCarthy for 6500 pounds of walleyes. This arrest was not made by any Minnesota State Wardens. It was made by the Fish and Wildlife Service. The fish were sold over a two-year period of 1981 and 1982.

In regards to the fish (mainly walleye pike) in the Red Lakes, I was constantly being complained to by the Indians on one hand and the hook and line fishermen on the other hand.

Each group had their own theory as to who was taking and entitled to take the walleyes from Red Lake.

The Indians feel that as their reservation encompasses four-fifths of the water, they are entitled to the bulk of the harvest. However, the biologists say the harvest should be based on the reproduction six years prior to the taking.

The hook and line fishermen and the resorters complain that they can only take six walleyes per day and at no time can they possess more than six walleyes.

The Indian fishermen are told they can take fish with their nets and sell to Redby Fisheries on the average year one million pounds of walleyes. They fill this quota in four to six weeks. However, they keep on fishing, some of them the year round and they sell the fish to the whites. The whites complained to me about this.

McCarthy also bought illegal fish from Canada.

I have friends in Minneapolis and St. Paul that told me they had bought sacks of walleye fillets from Indians in the beer joints. I have told them that was an illegal act and they should report it to the authorities. Their response was, "If I didn't buy them, someone else would."

It's like which came first—the chicken or the egg?

Chapter 40/ RED LAKE INDIAN FISHERIES

This is about the way it was in the sixties and early seventies at Red Lake.

There are two Red Lakes, upper and lower, and these are huge bodies of water with a total of 288,800 acres of water. Upper Red Lake has 107,800 acres of water and Lower Red Lake has 181,000 acres of water.

All of Lower Red Lake and over half of Upper Red Lake are within the boundaries of the Red Lake Indian Reservation. The Red Lake Indian Reservation is a closed reservation, almost a nation unto itself. Only registered personnel are allowed to fish, hunt, or trap on the Red Lakes within the reservation.

There are a number of small lakes south of Lower Red Lake that outsiders can fish in, providing they purchase a license from the Indian Council and have registered personnel for guides. Their fees fluctuate and are in excess of the fishing permit.

The Red Lake Reservation have their own lakes for their own people and they have their own police force, game wardens, courts, judges, etc.

However, when an outside violator is found within the Red Lake boundaries, they are usually put in the jail at the town of Red Lake. At the convenience of the tribe, they are transferred to the Federal Court at Duluth for a hearing.

A lot of the game and fish laws are compatible with the Minnesota Game and Fish Laws. I have had occasion to be called to the police station at Red Lake to take outsiders that were caught within the boundaries in violation of a game or fish law that was compatible with a Minnesota State Game or Fish Law. They have me charge them with the violation and process them through the Justice of the Peace Court. Most of them were no problem, however, there are a few instances where our courts of justice screwed up. (I will relate some of these instances in the following stories.)

The Indian people are allowed by their laws and the Minnesota laws to take certain kinds of game fish and sell them on the open market. However, their own laws as to the manner of taking and the quantity govern them.

This is where the outsider and the Indian bump heads, and I, as a conservation officer, find both parties in severe violation of the fish laws especially from the Red Lakes. Greed and money is the name of the game.

The Red Lake fishermen have a quota on the number of pounds of walleye pike, northern pike, and whitefish they can take with nets for commercial purposes out of Lower Red Lake and their part of Upper Red Lake. I have been told some experts from the University of Minnesota determine the poundage that can be taken on each given year governed by spawning conditions five or six years prior to the year of taking.

The average poundage was about a million pounds of walleye pike, three hundred thousand pounds of northern pike, and three hundred thousand pounds of whitefish with no limit on rough fish. <u>All</u> the fish are to be sold through the Redby Fisheries located at Redby, Minnesota, on the south side of Lower Red Lake. Indian personnel fillet the fish out for the buyers. Booth Fisheries, out of Chicago, seemed to be the biggest buyer. The Redby Fisheries have a large ice-making machine to pack the fish in for transporting. The Indian fishermen will usually fill the quota in a month or less.

The Indians are allowed to continue to fish for their own consumption, but some continue to fish all year and sell their fish illegally. Some outsiders will go on to the reservation and purchase walleye pike from individual Indian fisherman. Some of the Indian fishermen will fillet out a couple of hundred walleyes, pack twenty-five walleye fish fillets into a plastic bread bag and haul them to Grand Rapids, Duluth, or the Twin Cities, and peddle them in saloons and beer joints. When the Indian fishermen sell their fish this way, they realize more money per pound and they get to keep all the money providing they don't get caught.

When the Indian fishermen sell their fish in the proper and legal way, they are given about 75% of the cash value of the fish when they turn their catch over to the Redby Fisheries.

To explain it a little more clearly, we will assume the average value of walleyes delivered to Redby Fisheries by the Indian reservation is one dollar a pound. The fisherman gets seventy-five cents a pound guaranteed on delivery. The market may vary from ninety cents to a dollar and a quarter a pound by the time Redby Fisheries sell the fish to Booth Fisheries or whoever is the high bidder. That difference, that is accumulated, goes into the Indian Council. At the end of the season, that money is divided equally among every legal registered Indian on the Red Lake Indian Reservation. That way every Indian, whether he fishes or not, gets to share in the reservation resources.

Also, by the same token, those fish being sold by the Indian fishermen to people on or off the reservation are in a way stealing from the council and the non-fishermen Indians.

Chapter 41/ INDIAN UPRISING

This incident occurred in the fall of the early seventies. It occurred in the district of my neighbor, Leo Manthei, the warden from Blackduck. I did not make out arrest reports or confiscation reports so I do not have dates to refer to.

One day in October sometime in the afternoon, Terry Clairmont of Kelliher, Minnesota, who was a part time deputy sheriff, had picked up several inebriated members of the Red Lake Indian Reservation. He had them locked up in the cell at the Municipal Building in Kelliher pending a hearing by Justice of the Peace Clara Quale of Kelliher.

Terry called me and asked if I would use the state patrol car to haul him and any of the members of the Red Lake band if the justice of the peace found them guilty of whatever charge he had on them to the county jail in Bemidji, forty-five miles south of Kelliher. He, more or less, wanted me on a stand-by basis depending on the judge's sentence.

Around 4:00 p.m., Terry Clairmont called and said he would like to have me leave Waskish as soon as possible. The judge had the first person into court at the time. The penalty was a $100.00 fine or thirty days in the county jail. The man elected to sit it out. Terry said, "I think all four of them will probably end up doing the time." Actually, the Indians didn't mind going to jail. They would get three good meals a day, get themselves cleaned up, and have clean bedding and clothes every day. Usually they were better off than on the reservation. Also, after thirty days, they would be pretty well dried out.

Eventually the judge finished with the men, made out

commitment papers, and gave them to Terry. We loaded the men into the back seat. It was a bit crowded and we headed down Highway 72. We were a few miles past Blackduck when I received a call from Leo Manthei at Blackduck. I answered. He wanted to know where I was. I told him about six miles south of Blackduck headed for the county jail in Bemidji. I also told him I was accompanied by Deputy Terry Clairmont and four 10-15's (prisoners).

He claimed he had an emergency call of deer shooting up south of Saum and he was wondering if I couldn't come immediately to help him. I told him I was obligated to finish this assignment. Terry and I would come back later and give him an assist. I don't think he was too pleased with this arrangement.

At any rate, we hurried on into Bemidji and unloaded our cargo, turned the commitment papers over to the deputy on the desk, and hurried back to the patrol car. I called Leo on the car-to-car channel and he didn't answer. So I called the dispatcher at Thief River Falls to see if he could contact Leo. The dispatcher was glad to hear from me. Leo had called in a few minutes earlier and said he had an Indian uprising on his hands and he needed help now! I told him we would be there within a half hour. Then I asked the dispatcher of Leo's location in case conditions changed before we got there.

We could hear the dispatcher question Leo but we couldn't hear Leo's response. The dispatcher came back to us and said, "Warden Manthei has taken refuge on the first farm on the east side of the road just north of the Joe Jerome Road."

We knew where he was, so we concentrated on getting there. When we came on to County Road 23 leading to Saum, we expected or suspected to see several Indian cars and all kinds of activity. Instead there was no one in sight. So we drove up to the farm and found Leo sitting in his patrol car with one other man. It was starting to get pretty dark.

Leo got out of his patrol car and walked over to me. I also

was out of our car. Leo told me he caught one Indian and had him in his car.

The complaint came from this farmhouse. There was shooting in back of this place and a little south. When Leo arrived at the farm, the farmer told him to go south about an eighth of a mile. There was a little old logging road that was parallel to his south line. He was sure the shooting was from a high power rifle. No one lived back there.

So Leo went down to that little old trail, turned east, and met this old red Buick coming out. It was getting dusky out so every one had their lights on. This car came to a stop and Leo drove up to it. But instead of letting Leo check it out, they started backing up with Leo driving forward with his bumper up against this red Buick. Then Leo started pushing the car and somehow it stalled or hit something. The car was full of Indians and they started coming at Leo. Leo captured one, got him in the car, and backed out of there and drove over to this farm. He was sure the car was still back in there somewhere.

Meanwhile, Terry Clairmont, who by the way is one-half Chippewa, went over and talked to the Indian in the car.

I told Leo that Terry and I would drive back in there and see if we could find the car and the Indians. By now it was pitch dark.

Terry and I got in the patrol car and we started down this little trail. About a half a mile back in there, we came across this red Buick on the south side of the trail pulled back into the bush. There was an inch or two of snow on the ground in the woods. We could see from the tracks in the snow behind the Buick that there were about half-a-dozen people, some clumps of deer hair and spots of blood in the snow. We could see that the tracks led off to the south and they were dragging that deer. It would be safe to say they had shot that deer east of there, probably dressed it out, and loaded it into the trunk of the car. When they started to go back to the reservation, they met Leo coming in on the logging trail.

Terry had started to tell me of his conversation with the Indian in Leo's patrol car when we came across the Buick. Now after checking the area in back of the car, he wanted to finish his narrations. He said he was a young fellow, probably a juvenile. He, along with three other male and two female residents of the Red Lake reservation, went for a ride. They had one rifle in the car and they drove around parts of the reservation looking for deer with no luck. The owner of the car then drove off the reservation. Several of them were opposed to shooting any deer off the reservation where it was illegal. However, there were some, especially the driver, who were more or less thrill seekers. They ended up back on this trail where no one lived. They spotted a little deer grazing, and the driver of the car took the rifle and dropped that deer about a hundred feet from their car.

They thought they were far enough away that no one heard the shot. So they were in no big rush to dress out the deer and load it in the trunk. Then they started back to the reservation when they met this car. The trail was so small that there wasn't room enough to turn around. So they just put the car in reverse and started backing up. The car that was approaching turned on a red flashing light and started pushing them backwards until they were pushed off the trail and got stuck. All the young people got scared, jumped out of their car, but this one young man ran to Leo's car. He jumped into the passenger's seat and told Leo he wanted no part of what his friends were doing. He was even sure two or three more would have come with him except Leo started backing down the trail to the county road, and then into the farmer's yard. He told Leo that the young man who owned the car thought his car would be seized because he had the deer in the trunk.

With all this information, I called Leo on the radio and said, "I will leave Terry in my car with the radio along side the red Buick in case these young people circle around and get back to their car." I told Leo, "The trail is quite plain and I will see if

I can find these young people." I didn't figure they would go too far dragging that deer. It was dark now so I took my five-cell flashlight and started following the trail. I went about two hundred yards through the woods then I came out on an open area. The sun had obviously melted the snow and there the trail disappeared. I hunted everywhere on that frozen ground and could not see where they had gone. They must have carried the deer because there were no deer hairs from dragging. About two hundred yards south of me, there were some farm buildings.

The bachelor farmer that lived there was friendly with some members of the Red Lake band. Occasionally when we drove down County Road 34, we would see cars full of Indians in his yard.

Trying to figure out where they had gone, I backtracked. Finally I was back to our car. I told Terry, "I lost the trail and I was thinking they had time to get over to that farmer's house on County Road 34." I suggested the same thing to Leo on the radio. I told Terry, "I hate to leave that car but we have to find that deer or we have no violation." I was afraid they might come back if we left. Terry who was an auto mechanic said not to worry. He had removed the distributor cap. They could never start the car without that.

Terry and I drove over to the farmyard on County Road 34. The farmer was sitting in his kitchen reading when we drove into the yard. We got his attention and he came to the door. We asked him if he had three young men and two young women stop in the last hour. He claimed he had no visitors all day.

Leo said, "That's enough, we will knock it off until tomorrow morning."

The following morning with the aid of Bum, my dog, we followed the trail of the deer. It turned out that where I came out into the opening, they had gone east about two hundred yards carrying the deer between the four of them. Then they apparently carried the deer back into the woods and abandoned it. That's where Bum led us. There were no people. Leo cut about four feet off a small tree that had a fair sized limb near the bottom. He cut that off at an angle and hooked it through the deer's lower jaw, and we dragged it back to our patrol cars.

Bill's springer spaniel, Bum

Now we had the evidence and the car, but not the violators. When we came out on County Road 23 and turned south, as we passed the Joe Jerome Road, we saw our young violators walking back toward the reservation. We drove down and picked them up. They were cold, hungry, and tired. There was no resistance left in them.

I took them down to Bemidji and reported to the county attorney. The young people got hold of the public defender, Fritz Weddell, and they were out of the courthouse before we were. Fritz Weddell used to be the municipal judge at Bemidji and he was good. I kind of chastised him for getting those Indians released as they would get back to the reservation and we would never get them into court. His response was, "That's your job now."

Chapter 42/ RON STRAND

This episode started in October of 1972. I was stationed at Waskish, Minnesota. My supervisor had sent a trainee up for me to work with. On this day I had elected to take this new man up on Pine Island to see what we could stumble into.

Ray Himes from Ray, Minnesota had been doing a lot of coyote trapping in this area between Little Fork and Waskish. Unfortunately he would often catch a fisher in his traps. These animals were protected and their pelts weren't worth much. Game wardens were given authority to give the trapper a pelting fee for skinning the animal out, stretching, and drying the pelt when a trapper would catch a fisher. Then he was to bring the pelt back to the warden that made out the original seizure tag and confiscation papers. The pelt then would be turned over to the regional supervisor who would in turn haul it to the St. Paul office.

At various times during the year, the state would notify fur buyers of a fur sale. Each buyer would inspect each fur and put in a bid on it. The highest bidder would get the pelt. Whatever the buyer paid for the pelt, a check was made out to the trapper for one half the selling price. This would usually, then, amount to between five and ten dollars.

The fishers were starting to make a strong comeback in Minnesota. The trappers and Department of Natural Resources personnel were recommending the animal be taken off the protected list.

Also about this time, one local trapper took a fisher pelt up into Ontario and attempted to sell it to a Canadian fur buyer. Canada is extremely alert to the fur trade. They have really severe laws and regulations that their trappers and fur buyers must follow and it wasn't long before this trapper was hopelessly entangled in the Ontario web.

The Ontario warden called me at my office and left a message with my wife to call him back at the earliest possible moment. When I got home on that particular day, I returned the call. The Ontario warden told me whom they had and what he was trying to do. I told my Canadian counterpart that fishers were protected in Minnesota and that this individual had caught fishers before and he knew exactly what he had to do with them. Also, the Canadian warden said the price of fishers was going up quite rapidly and that we should be alert to future illegal activity.

I asked if there was any possibility of the pelt being returned to Minnesota in which case I would write a complaint against this individual for the State of Minnesota. His response was, "Sorry, mate, that pelt is now the property of the Queen."

Ray Himes seemed to pick up one or two fisher every time he came across Pine Island to clerk his coyote sets. For a while, Ray would skin out the fisher, stretch and dry them. He sometimes waited three or four months for the checks. Then when he saw how small the checks were, he started just dropping off the whole carcass and I had to skin them out. One day he came with four. I was explaining all of this gobble de gook to my trainee. I don't know if it was sinking in or if he even knew what a fisher was.

About this time, we came to Christiansen's Corner, and we met a pickup with a grubby older man and a young woman. I stopped the vehicle, and then I noticed it had an Ontario license plate on it. Looking in the back of the truck, I noticed that there was a pile of traps and a small buck deer head.

I asked the fellow for some identification and he produced an Ontario driver's license. His name was Ronald Strand of Rainy River, Ontario. I then said, "What the hell are you doing back in this country?" He told me he was born and raised in Big Falls and the woman was his daughter. He had moved to Canada and had become a citizen of Ontario. His daughter was married to a fellow in Big Falls and she was a Minnesota resident.

His story was that he was teaching his daughter how to trap coyotes. I then asked him if he had a nonresident small game license and he admitted he didn't know he had to have one. Then I said, "How about that deer head in the back of your pickup?" He said he shot it that previous Saturday over in Ontario and he was using the meat on the neck for coyote bait.

I knew in my own mind he was over here trapping fishers. He could sell them in Ontario because he was a licensed Ontario trapper with a specific district over there to trap in. I remembered what the Canadian warden's statement was about fisher prices going up rapidly.

I asked Strand how many coyote sets he had between Big Falls and where we were. He then said his daughter might have made a half a dozen sets. Then I asked, "Can your daughter set those traps?"

He assured me she could. He went on to say she had been trapping all of her life. Then I pulled a double spring trap out of the back of the pickup and gave it to her. I told her to demonstrate her ability to set traps. In thirty seconds, she was in trouble and obviously knew nothing about setting a trap.

Also, I advised Strand that I could and was seriously thinking of charging him with transporting a big game animal or parts there of in closed season. This would be a gross misdemeanor. I would seize his truck and the penalty could be up to one thousand dollars and/or a year in jail.

At that, I told him I knew exactly what he was up to but I couldn't prove it. However, I could charge him with helping another person to take wild animals without first obtaining a nonresident small game license.

I got him in the car and showed him in the Minnesota game and fish law book how many ways I could charge him. Then I asked him how he got along with the Canadian game warden at Rainy River. He claimed they were on good terms. I asked for the name of the Ontario warden at Rainy River and he gave it to me. I picked up my radio mike and called the Thief River Falls dispatcher. Asked him to call the Ontario game warden at Rainy River and ask him what kind of person Ronald Strand was.

I had my trainee counting the traps that I intended to seize. I made out the summons for a nonresident helping a person to trap without first obtaining a nonresident small game license. I also made out a seizure slip for fifty-four number fourteen double-spring traps.

About this time, the dispatcher called me and said he got hold of the game warden at Rainy River. When he asked him what kind of person Ronald Strand was he said to put it in his words, "He is a bandit," and he went on with a few more explanatory words that I need not mention here.

I booked him and brought him to the Justice of the Peace Court at Northome before Justice Elhard. He pled guilty and was fined fifty dollars and five dollars cost. I told Strand to take his daughter back to Big Falls and stay out of Pine Island until I had time to find his sets. Better yet, I suggested he go back to Ontario, his new chosen home.

Ten years went by, and I reluctantly retired from the Minnesota DNR as a conservation officer. It was due to the fact that I had developed arrhythmia, a problem with my heart. I was very much aware that I could not give the state a full day's work for a day's pay. So in January 1981, my wife and I went to the St. Paul office and announced my retirement. Fred Hammer, the chief, couldn't believe it. He suggested that I had enough sick leave so I could sit it out for a year.

I let him know I had gone to Fargo twice for shock treatments. They held up for about a month. But as soon as I would get really active, the old heart would revert back to erratic pumping. So for the good of everyone all around, I told him I was retiring. I think my wife was pleased. She worried so much about me. In the spring of 1982 my son, a state patrol officer, from International Falls called up. He asked if I would like to take a few days and go to an outback lake in Canada for a free fishing trip. I told him that was the best offer I had that day. Then I asked him what the circumstances were.

Then he was, in his spare time, flying for Bohman Airways. Fred had a commercial license and he was a knowledgeable bush pilot. He told me some Canadian individual was building a fishing camp on Pekagoning Lake. The lodge building was a rough structure at best and it was still being worked on by a couple of jack-knife carpenters. There was no road into this lake other than logging trails. Most of the rough-sawn lumber, gas refrigerators, and bunk beds had been brought in on the winter logging trails.

Fred said the owner of this property had turned the lodging scheduling over to Bohman Airways. The average package was three days and two nights for $295.00. There were two fourteen foot Alumacraft boats and two 9.8 Evinrude motors. The fee included flying in and out, the use of the building, gas stove, gas refrigerator, boat, motor, gasoline, and minnows.

Now here is where I would come in. Fred would need help to rassle a fifty-five gallon drum of gas out of the Beaver onto the dock at Pekagoning and build a stand for it. Then he would like to have me fish the lake and learn where the best fishing would be for their guests. The first guests were due in about a week.

Fred told me to bring my sleeping bag, clothes, food and fishing gear for at least a four-day stay. I was to be at Bohman Airways the following day by 8:00 a.m. At this time, Patricia and I were living in Baudette so I would have to leave home no later than 6:30 a.m. With a lot of enthusiasm on my part, I started to gather up what I would need. I think Patricia was glad to see me go. She fried up a whole chicken and packed up a whole mess of grub.

Callies' Baudette home

The following morning, I took off for Bohman Airways. I loaded all my gear in the Beaver, and Fred and I took off for Pekagoning. It was about a forty-minute flight. We set down and taxied up to the dock. The dock consisted of two twelve-inch spruce logs lashed together that set on questionable posts.

Somehow or another, we got that barrel of gas onto the dock and rolled into shore without falling in. Then Fred took me up to this lodge building. Frankly, I have seen better barns. He introduced me to the two carpenters. They looked like a couple of cutthroats. However, I figured I could manage. The lake looked good and I was anxious to get my gear up to the building, get the stand built for the gas tank, and go fishing.

Fred went down to the plane and he was out of there. He had promised he would come back in three or four days to pick me up.

I told these two workmen I had brought some rolls if they had some coffee for a snack. I also had a whole, good chicken all cooked up that I would share with them at noon. That seemed to go over big with them. So we sat down to a cup of coffee and some rolls. These men got to talking about the problems they had building this lodge, hauling the materials in on a winter road across lakes and beaver dams. Then they got to telling about shooting moose and deer and doing some trapping on the side. They used gill nets under the ice for fish. It was soon obvious to me that they thought game and fish laws were for other people. I didn't dare tell them I was a retired game warden. They really laid it on me about their hunting, trapping, and fishing. I tried to remember some of their exploits with the idea of advising Roy Brown, the supervisor for the Ministry of Natural Resources in Fort Francis. These two men would do anything to turn a dollar and they went all out to tell me about it.

Eventually, we drank the coffee and ate the rolls. I asked them if they had a hammer, a saw, a square and a few nails to build the gas barrel stand. I also asked if it would it be okay if I used some of the scraps of lumber lying around outside. These two men were real cooperative; they fixed me up with everything I needed.

So I went down by the lakeshore. I started in measuring, cutting and nailing and finally created a stand that would support a fifty-five gallon drum full of gasoline and the spigot would be high enough off the ground to put an outboard motor gas can underneath for refilling. I wrestled the drum of gas up on the stand and was in the process of cleaning up the scraps and returning the tools to the carpenters. It was just past noon and I suggested to the men maybe we should warm the chicken up and that they should call me when they were ready to eat.

I went back down to the lakeshore when I heard a motor. I thought it might be a boat, and then out of the sky came a little J3 on floats. It set down out on the open water and taxied into the dock. A small bearded man with fairly long hair crawled out on to the dock. I notice there were about six 1" x 6" x 8' pine boards lashed to the top of each float. The two carpenters came down to the dock and inquired if this pilot had remembered to bring some tobacco and a can of coffee. The pilot reached into the back seat and pulled out a small packsack and announced, "I've got your whole order right here in my pack sack."

Then one of the carpenters asked me if it was all right to share my chicken with Ron. I told him, "We will just quarter the chicken." The carpenters said they would make some fresh coffee. The spuds are almost done and the chicken would soon be warmed up. The three men went up to the lodge.

I started to get a boat and motor ready so I could go fishing after lunch. The man that flew in looked a little familiar but I couldn't remember if I had ever met him before. He did seem to look at me kind of hard.

About ten minutes went by when one of the carpenters hollered to come and get it. I had washed up down at the lake so I went up to the lodge and sat down at a homemade picnic table. Everyone was rather quiet. There was no one bragging about their hunting escapades. Everyone was busy gnawing the meat off the chicken bones. Finally, all the grub was eaten up and these three men were lighting up cigarettes or pipes. There were some queries of Ronnie, the pilot, as to what was going on in the big city of Fort Francis.

Then it hit me, could he be the Ronald Strand I had run into on Pine Island? I started to feel a little uneasy. One of the carpenters went outside to drain his bladder so after a couple of minutes I moseyed out. I found the carpenter and I came right out and asked, "Is that pilot Ronald Strand from Rainy River?"

His response was loud and clear, "Yes and you're a G__ D__ game warden."

I told him that is true, I was a Minnesota Game Warden but now I have been retired since 1981. I said I had a minor altercation with Strand about nine years ago. I could see things were starting to get ugly but all I could do was try to weather it out for the next two or three days. So I loaded my fishing gear in the boat with the hopes I could catch a few walleyes or lake trout for dinner that evening. Hopefully things would cool off some.

I got out on the lake and started trolling when I heard an airplane motor. Then over the trees came the Beaver that Fred flew me up in. It was Dave, the aviation mechanic from Bohman Airways. I jumped up in the boat and started waving my arms. I was frantic. I must have looked like a windmill. At any rate, Dave sensed I wanted to talk to him now so he set the Beaver down. I ran my boat over to him and told him what a mess I was in. He told me that Bohman had some guests in another lake about twenty miles away. He was bringing supplies in to them. He said, "I will unload this stuff and come back and pick you up."

I went right into shore and got my gear down to the dock. When Dave came back I threw it into the plane and I was thankful to get out.

Chapter 43/ NEW SYSTEM FOR LICENSING DEER HUNTERS

The following incident occurred during the deer season in the early seventies. The game managers had set up a new system for licensing deer hunters. As a deer hunter, you selected three concurrent days during a nine-day period in November as the days you could legally hunt.

I don't remember the date but it was a Friday. I had spent most of that day checking deer hunters and was especially watchful that they were hunting on the days they had chosen to be marked on their licenses.

After sundown I went home and had dinner with my wife at Waskish, Minnesota. After dinner I thought I ought to go out for a while to watch for illegal night hunters. My wife packed me a lunch and a thermos of coffee and I started out south of Waskish on Highway 72.

About two miles south of town, I saw, with the aid of my headlights, a small doe grazing on the east side shoulder. I figured I had bait but not a real good place to pull off the road to hide my car. I finally settled on an approach to a ditch grade that led to the Lausnick boys' home. I would be about three quarters of a mile straight south of that little deer. There were no obstructions between the deer and me. Occasionally, when a car came from the north, I could see the shadowy form of the deer with the aid of my binoculars.

When cars came from the south, I would come out of my hiding place in the ditch and, with the aid of my glasses, I would see the brake lights of the car come on when the car got near where the deer was. Most people just like to look at a deer. Others approach cautiously for fear the deer will jump out in front of their car. The car and the deer could sustain serious damage. I would guess I saw a half a dozen cars slow up as they passed the deer. No one came to a full stop. This occurred over a period of about two hours.

At around 9:30 p.m., a pickup coming from the south passed me so I rose up to watch what would happen when they saw the deer. When the pickup got close to where the deer was, the brake lights came on. After about a minute they went off and I assumed they had driven past the deer. Then the brake lights came on again and stayed on for at least thirty seconds. Then, I heard two shots. They did not sound like a big high-powered rifle.

I immediately ran for my car, drove out onto the blacktop without lights. The pickup was still sitting there with the brake lights on. There were no other cars around. I could see the roadway real well without lights. I was driving about forty miles per hour.

Then the brake lights went off and I had the feeling the pickup was moving off at a slow pace. I caught up to it within a half a mile of where the deer had been. I pulled along side of the pickup turned on my headlights and red flashing light and started to crowd the pickup onto the shoulder. They finally came to a stop and I bailed out of my patrol car and ran to the driver's side of the pickup. I pulled open the driver's door and announced "State Game Warden" as I was reaching across the driver to the man in the middle. He had a holstered semi-automatic pistol strapped to the front of his body.

There were three men in the vehicle. I pulled the handgun out of the holster very carefully and quickly because I could see the hammer was cocked. I quickly lowered the hammer down and ordered the men out of the car and up in front of the headlights. Then, I saw an uncased high-powered rifle lying on the floor. I pulled that out and opened the action and found it to be loaded in both barrel and magazine. I shut off their motor and took the keys. The man in the middle, whose gun I had pulled out, pretended to be asleep. The other two men got out of the truck.

Now, the driver of the truck started to get a little belligerent about being stopped and ordered around and of course denied shooting any deer or even seeing a deer.

They all had Minnesota resident deer licenses and they all submitted them to me. I checked their hunting dates and their licenses expired as of sundown on that day.

I told the driver, "Turn your pickup around and drive back to the place where someone in the car shot at that little deer."

He was getting kind of smart now, and he asked "What deer?" Then he said, "You have no right to detain me. I wonder whether or not you're even a Minnesota Game Warden?"

I showed him my shoulder patch and badge. I told him, "Just sit in your pickup and hold your tongue while I look for that deer."

About that time Kelly Petrowske came by headed for Kelliher. He stopped and asked, "What's going on?"

I told him, "These three men shot at a little doe with a nine millimeter Smith and Wesson hand gun."

I had checked the hand gun, and the clip was short of three

shells and there was one shell in the chamber. So assuming these men started out with a full clip, there were two shells missing.

I spent about a half an hour looking for the deer and the two empty shells and could find neither.

I told these young men that I figured they were just stupid opportunists. I told them they were guilty of a gross misdemeanor and the fine could be up to a $1,000 and/or a year in jail and they would lose their pickup. However, if they would go before the local justice of the peace, I would reduce the complaint to "Attempting to take deer in closed hours" and the fine would probably be $300 and court costs, each, which would come to $915.

I made out the summons for the men and told them to appear before the justice of the peace the next morning in Kelliher at 9:00 a.m.

I then released the men on their own recognizance. They were Minnesota residents. I had their Minnesota deer licenses, one rifle and one handgun. At sometime later, I returned to my home and went to bed.

The next morning Kelly Petrowske awakened me. He was headed south on Highway 72 and he was curious about the evening before. He spied a little dead deer on the west side of the road just a few feet back in the bush. He assumed it could have been the deer I was looking for the night before so he offered to lead me to it. I pulled on some clothes and followed Kelly down there. When we got there some other deer hunter had seen the deer and was just starting to dress it out. I told him it was a deer that had been killed illegally the night before. He swore up and down he had just shot it, which was true. He had a 20-gauge single barrel shotgun with slugs and you could see a big hole in the neck right behind the head. I took hold of the deer and it was obvious the deer had been dead for many hours—rigor mortis had set in.

I told the fellow I was taking the deer until after court and if he wanted it, he could have it. I did tell him I would be concerned about the meat lying all night like that with the entrails in it. So we removed the entrails. There was a bit of an odor in the body cavity. I told this young fellow where I lived and what time court was. Providing these three men plead guilty at 9:00 a.m. that morning, I would come back to my residence and he could tag and take that deer.

I then went home with the deer on the trunk. I went in the house, cleaned up, had breakfast, and left for the Justice of the Peace Court in Kelliher at about 8:30 a.m. I arrived in Kelliher, located the three night hunters and took them over to the justice of peace's house. Mrs. Quale asked me what I had and I told her these three young fellows shot a little doe about a mile and a half south of Waskish on Highway 72.

I gave her the court's copies of the summons and she made out her forms, had me read her copies and then had me swear that this was a true and accurate account of the activity that occurred the night before.

I told her who the driver was, so she read his complaint first. When she asked for his plea, he pled not guilty. Then he made a remark about this was a phony court at her kitchen table and the whole deal was a set-up and a rip off.

I asked him, "Is that what you really think after Mrs. Quale showed you her qualifications?"

So I said, "You don't want to be heard by this justice of the peace?"

He just responded that he didn't think this was a real court or that Mrs. Quale was a real justice of the peace.

So again I asked this man, "You don't want to be heard by her?"

He responded, "No way."

So I told him, "Give me the keys to your pickup."

He asked, "Why?"

I told him, "I am going to charge you men with just what you did, 'Take one deer with the aid of your headlights'. Your truck is involved and I'm taking the three of you to Bemidji to County Court. You will be tried in a municipal court."

He gave me the keys to his truck. Then he asked, "When will I get it back?"

I told him, "If the judge finds you not guilty, the truck will be turned back to you. Otherwise, it will be held as evidence if you are bound over to District Court." I also told him, "I have the deer you shot. I put it in the trunk of my state patrol car." I showed the men the deer. He claimed I went out and shot this deer to have more evidence to hang them.

So I told him, "The young man that stopped the night before to ask what was going on, found it early this morning on his way to work."

Also, "This young man will so testify if it goes to District Court."

The men took a few things out of the pickup and I locked it

up. I told them I would store it in the fish hatchery garage until after court.

I loaded them up in the state car and hauled them down to Bemidji and booked them into the county jail. They were quite upset about this so I told them, "The Municipal Court will not be open until 9:00 a.m. Monday. I will be back then with the county attorney Monday morning. If you want to hire an attorney, the deputy sheriffs will assist you."

Also, I told the deputy, "I am charging them with a gross misdemeanor." This was Saturday so these three men would be guests of the county unless they wanted to put up bail.

I went back down to Bemidji early Monday. I went up to the county attorney's office and told the whole story to the county attorney. He allowed I had as good a spot-lighting case as one could get.

The county attorney and I went over to the courthouse. The county attorney had to get the case on file. In the meantime, I ran into Leo Manthei, the warden from Blackduck. Leo wanted to know why I was down there. I told him I had three men for spotlighting from last Friday night. I told him the whole story including their response to the Justice of the Peace Court. Leo admitted I had a good case. Then he asked where the three men were and I told him in the county jail. They would be brought over by a deputy whenever the county attorney set up the trial time with the clerk of court.

I can't remember where I went, it may have been the rest room or maybe I ran into someone and got into a conversation with someone. I may have been gone for about a half hour. At any rate, I walked into the courtroom and the three violators were sitting in the courtroom and a deputy sheriff was with them.

The deputy told me when he brought them over, Leo came in and talked to them for about ten minutes, then left. I sat down by the deputy and we got in a little conversation.

Then Leo came in and told me, "I've got the whole case

settled."

I asked, "What do you mean?"

Then he told me, "I talked to these men and let them know that you have an excellent shining case and that for sure they will lose the pickup and the handgun and they are each liable for a fine of up to a $1000 and/or a year in jail. I also told them they should hire an attorney."

Then he told them they should have pled guilty to the justice of the peace, and the most she could fine them was $300 and costs, and they would lose the deer and the handgun.

I guess Leo got them pretty shook up because they asked Leo if they could go back to Kelliher and enter a plea with the justice of the peace. He told them they had gone too far, but if he had their assurance they would plead to the original charge, "Take or attempt to take one deer in closed hours", which would be a misdemeanor, the most they could be fined was $300 and/or ninety days in jail. They would also lose the gun they shot with. He would go find the county attorney and convince him that I really didn't want to go through with the gross misdemeanor trial because they drag out for two or three months sometimes.

They told Leo to go talk to the county attorney and they would plead the lesser charge.

So Leo approached me proud as punch. He had plea-bargained the whole thing. The county attorney and the county judge went along with the whole thing.

In a way I was glad it was settled, but I sure came down on Leo for intervening. I know Leo never liked it when I would come in with a gross misdemeanor charge.

Chapter 44/ MEMORIAL DAY, 1971

Another Memorial Day long weekend was upon us at Waskish, Minnesota, on Upper Red Lake. There were people everywhere out on the lake in their boats fishing for walleyes. All the cabins and resorts were filled. There were tents, motor homes, and trailer homes. People were fishing from shore on both sides of the Tamarac River—it was bedlam.

On these long weekends, the sheriff would send up his deputies, Howie Schultz and Ron Solberg, and this year a new deputy who was stationed at Kelliher. There was also usually a narcotics enforcer. These men usually headquartered at the warden station. There were accommodations for six men in one cabin and two men in the other cabin. There would usually be three wardens sent there to assist in keeping things under control. The usual wardens were Supervisors Les Borning, Don Fearn and Ted Znajda. There was also me, the warden stationed at Waskish, and the two forest rangers, Roger Anderson and Hugo Kornell. We had our hands full from Friday evening to Monday afternoon.

We were caught up with auto accidents, taking too many fish, fighting, stealing, drinking and drunkenness. In fact, this year we started to become aware of lots of young people becoming inebriated. Several of them were getting sick. I'm now talking about boys and girls as young as thirteen and fourteen. It was an epidemic. There were a few resorts in the area that had liquor, and they were checked and warned by sheriffs about underage people acquiring alcoholic beverages.

Finally, around Saturday evening, we realized there was a lot of traffic on a little dirt trail that went east of Waskish for about two miles to a dead end. There were the remains of old log buildings of the early settlers that came into that country back around 1900. We drove back on this trail and we found several campfires, a lot of small tents and a mass of young people and several cars. In the middle of all this was a large four-wheel u-haul trailer. There were three or four young men in their twenties more or less overseeing the contents of this trailer.

Several of us law enforcement people inspected the contents and found it full of beer, wine, and whiskey. There were teenagers around these campfires drinking every kind of alcoholic beverage. We started gathering these people up and seized the trailer with all the alcoholic beverages. I believe the deputies charged the men with furnishing alcoholic beverages to underage people. The new deputy sheriff offered to haul all the booze to his home for safe keeping until it could all be hauled to Bemidji headquarters.

There were so many young people drinking or drunk that the deputies didn't know how they were going to handle this situation. There were enough people to fill every jail in Beltrami County four times over.

Then the process started of writing up the names, addresses, gender, birth dates, age, etc. It soon became evident that the bulk of these young people came from either Thief River Falls, which is a hundred and twenty five miles west, or from Bemidji which is sixty miles south. The trailer came from a rental unit in Thief River Falls.

Because this was primarily a problem for the county sheriffs, I was more or less a standby doing the bidding of the deputy sheriffs. I was not privy to their decisions.

Eventually, I was told that we just can't swamp the courts with this mass of people. It was decided that the wardens were on the same frequency as the Thief River dispatcher. We were to give the dispatcher the names and telephone numbers of all the young people that came from over west. He was to call the parents of the children and give them the option of either come right now and pick up your children or they would be booked in

Bemidji the following Tuesday and charged, and the parents would have to be there for juvenile court.

The deputy sheriffs called their office in Bemidji and had their dispatcher do the same thing in and around Bemidji—come now, pick up your boy or girl and that will be the end of their problem. If you don't, they will be booked the following Tuesday and then the parent will be required to attend juvenile court.

Of the two options, it was obvious the smart thing would be to head for Waskish to pick up their offspring right now.

The parents came and the sheriffs that thought that treatment up should be commended for the way they handled an awkward situation. If nothing else came of it, at least the parents were being made aware of what their children were up to. I would imagine a lot of youngsters were grounded for a long time with a loss of privileges.

Eventually, one of the deputies told me on the quiet that when they went up to Kelliher to pick up the seized alcoholic beverages they found this new deputy had disposed of it already. It seems he thought it was up to him to dispose of it. He admitted he and his family consumed some and the rest he gave away.

I think that was just before I received a letter from Sheriff Tom Tolman who was in Washington DC attending an FBI school. He wanted my opinion of the new deputy.

Chapter 45/ *GET US OUT OF HERE*

It was about 5:30 p.m. on December 12, 1971. I was at my home in Waskish, Minnesota. My wife was in the process of making our evening meal. The telephone rang. My wife just said, "Now what?" We both knew I probably was being called out for something. Usually I was called because a car had killed a deer or moose. I answered the phone. It was a police sergeant at the Red Lake Indian Police Station.

He said, "We have three white men here in jail and we would like to get rid of them."

I asked the sergeant, "What did they do?"

He said, "Two of my policemen caught them fishing for rainbow trout through the ice on Kinney Lake and they had not acquired an Indian permit, nor had they hired an Indian guide."

I told the Sergeant, "That is not a violation against the fishing laws of the State of Minnesota. However, the season is closed in the State of Minnesota for the taking or possession of rainbow trout."

Then I asked, "Is your season for taking rainbow trout on Kinney Lake on the reservation closed also?"

He came back with, "It's closed to all white men and I would like to have you come down here and get them out of here now. I don't have any money to feed them."

So I told him, "OK, I'll leave here now, but it will take me at least an hour." It is close to fifty miles from Waskish to the town of Red Lake.

So my wife put our meal on hold. I put on my heavy coat and went out to a cold car and headed south on Highway 72 through Kelliher and Shooks then west on Highway 1 through Redby to the police station at Red Lake.

When I walked into the station, there were two big Indian policemen talking to an Indian woman. The sergeant came out of his office and gave me a run down on these three fishermen. The police saw them fishing on the ice of Kinney Lake around noon that day. They found their vehicle. I believe it was a 4-wheel drive jeep enclosed sort of like a station wagon. One of the policemen walked out to check the three men and found them to be on the uncooperative side. So he gathered up their fish and gear and marched them back up to the vehicles. When the owner of the jeep produced the keys, the policemen seized the guns and put them in the trunk of their squad car. The three men were put in the back seat of the squad car. Then one of the policemen drove their jeep and they all went back to Red Lake and the men were charged and locked up.

All the while the sergeant was relating this to me, the two big policemen were questioning the Indian woman. The only problem was she would not answer them. She would not talk. About this time, the sergeant, who was obviously agitated, excused himself and told me, "I'll be back with you in a few minutes."

He went over to this Indian woman and flung her through the front door, went outside grabbed her by the arm, and disappeared into the dark behind the police station. We were all inside with the windows and doors shut but we could hear about five or six heavy thuds.

A minute later, the sergeant came back into the police station pushing this woman ahead of him. You could see some swelling starting to show on her head, but now she could talk in English and Chippewa.

The sergeant showed me the fish and winter fishing sticks then he pointed the way back to the jail cells. I walked back in there. There was one small light bulb out in the walkway and there was little or no heat. I had their names so I called out, "Moberg, Detschman."

There were two Detschman (brothers). They responded, "Over here."

I told them where I was from and who I was and that I might be able to get them out of here. They just begged, "Get us out of here. We'll do anything you say but just get us out of here. We'll be dead by morning if you don't." They thought they could hear someone talking about doing away with them and dividing up their guns and the jeep. I told them normally they would be transported to Duluth and tried in a federal court the following day. However, if the federal courts were tied up, they might have to sit in jail in Duluth for a few days waiting for a trial date opening.

Then I told them, "It's against the law to take rainbow trout in any Minnesota lake or stream at this time. The season is closed. The sergeant might turn you men over to me and I will run you through the Justice of the Peace Court in Kelliher. The charge will be taking rainbow trout in closed season and you will be expected to plead guilty. I have the trout for evidence. The judge will give you a fine or days in jail or both. Are you agreeable to this?"

"Yes! Yes! Just get us out of here."

I told them, "The sergeant would want me to make out the summons and have you sign them before you will be turned over to me."

The response was, "We'll sign anything. Just get us out of here!"

I told these three fellows I would go back and see if the sergeant will approve of it. Then one of the fellows said, "How about the car and guns?"

I told him, "Let's just get you out of here for now and don't make any smart cracks if you want us to all get out of here."

I went back to the sergeant and told him, "They will do almost anything to get out of here."

I then said, "How about the car and guns?"

The sergeant said, "We will hold them here until they plead guilty and pay their fine."

So we brought them out into the office, made out the summons and the seizure slip for the fish and fishing equipment. Everything was signed up and we all thanked the sergeant and we went out to my patrol car and drove east on Highway 1. When we went through the eastern entrance of the reservation, all three of them whooped it up.

I took them to Kelliher and to the justice of the peace. I explained the whole agreement to Justice of the Peace Quale. She said the fine would be $30.00 and $5.00 cost. These boys didn't have it. They suggested I take them to Bemidji and their wives would give me the money and I could bring it back to the judge.

I told them I had a better idea. I told them, "Call your wives and tell them to come to Kelliher to pay the judge then they can take you home." With that, I went home to Waskish and another screwed up meal.

The next morning, I got a call from the fellow that owned the jeep. He wanted to get his car back. He said the fine had been paid to the Justice of the Peace Clara Quale. I told him I would meet him in Kelliher at the judge's house.

We met, went to the reservation, told the police they had posted bail and the justice of the peace had the money. The car and firearms were released and everyone went to their homes. Later on that day, some attorney called the justice of the peace and was told Judge Marcus Reed of the Municipal Court in Bemidji had approved a change of venue. The attorney said a letter would follow to confirm this latest action on Moberg and the two Detschman. Justice of the Peace Quale was to send the money to the Municipal Court in Bemidji along with the summons and seizure slips.

I found out later that one of the violator's wives was a secretary in the county attorney's office.

The clerk of court of the Municipal Court in Bemidji told me that the men appeared before Marcus Reed on the 21st day of December and pled guilty.

I have my suspicions, but I believe they may have been fined $35.00 each but in the end, the fine was suspended. There was too much maneuvering and vague responses to my questions.

I did go back and tell the Red Lake sergeant my suspicions. He felt that was par for the course. He assured me in the future that route would not be taken and it never was. I did remain friends with the sergeant.

Chapter 46/ *ALMOST GOT BY WITH IT*

I was at Baudette working with Harland Pickett on October 24, 1971. We finished up whatever we were involved in and I headed home to my wife at Waskish, Minnesota at about 8:30 p.m.

I arrived at my residence at 9:15 p.m. and when I pulled into the yard, I noticed a light on in the big cabin. The yard light was on, and there was a car parked near the cabin. This is state property. We pay rent to the state for the house. Although it is my duty to maintain all the buildings and grounds, any state employee can stay at the cabin if he is working around there. Occasionally, various law enforcement personnel will take a holiday and come up to Waskish to go fishing or hunting. However, they usually advise my supervisor or me and get permission. When they are there, if I can use their assistance, I don't hesitate to call on them.

Waskish outbuildings

I went into the house and asked my wife, "Who's up in the big cabin?"

Patricia told me, "It's Lloyd Hoffman, the area supervisor from Sauk Centre, and a couple of friends. They came up here to net white fish but they didn't bring a boat and I didn't see any nets. You figure it out."

Then she told me, "I heard a shot that sounded like it came from across the river and south. I went down and talked to Lloyd about it but he told me they didn't know the country, so it would be best they not get involved."

I asked her, "When did you hear the shot?"

She said, "It was after dark, around 6:30 p.m. Also, someone reported hitting a deer north of Waskish about seven miles on the west side of the road. That occurred shortly after these men arrived. I asked Lloyd to go look for it and pick it up. Lloyd wasn't sure where that would be, so, I rode along with him but we did not find the deer."

I went up to the cabin to see what was going on. To the best of my knowledge I don't remember seeing any netting gear and I had no intention of loaning my nets to anyone. I asked Lloyd, "Did you guys hear the shot?"

They all said, "Yes, we heard the shot." They pointed to an area southeast and across the river.

I got in my car and drove through the Sunset Resort down to a resort, which was at the end of the road. I couldn't find anything in the dark and as I remember, the people that owned that resort were from Kansas City, Kansas, and they had closed up for the season.

The next morning I went down in that area across the river and started walking around. Around noon, I came across a deer gut pile. The bow deer season had been closed in this area. There were some areas south and west of the Indian reservation that were open to bow hunting and that is at least seventy miles away. So, naturally, I put two and two together, and it was obvious that someone had killed a deer illegally. The firearm season was closed, so the shot my wife and Lloyd heard probably was the one that killed that deer. Even during the firearm season, it would be an illegal act to shoot a deer after sundown.

I came back to Sunset Resort that was being operated by Chuck Beck. He was kind of an opportunist. He had gone down to Minneapolis and rented a room from Mrs. Frank Persons. I had known Frank for many years when I was in the floor covering trade. At one time, we had worked together at Pliam Linoleum, and later on when I became shop foreman at St. Paul Linoleum, I hired Frank Persons. Frank Persons and his wife used to come up to Waskish and visit with Rudy Beck, Chuck's brother.

Frank Persons developed cancer and passed away. That's when Chuck Beck moved in on Frank's wife. Some how or other, he talked her into selling her house. He married her and talked her into buying the Sunset Resort in Waskish that was up for sale. They purchased the business from the Davidsons, when Harry Davidson wanted to get shut of the resort business.

This resort is on Minnesota state land and what they bought and owned were the buildings and the business. They paid for an annual lease to the property. Actually the state was considering terminating the lease, but the Beck's hung tough because a liquor license went with the business.

I started walking around the rental cabins at the Sunset Resort, looking in garbage cans and any place I might find something. At the first cabin south of the main lodge, I came across a scrap of new carpet about ten inches by twenty inches. It was typical of the small scraps we would throw in our vehicles on completion of a floor-covering job. I knew that Frank had been instrumental in teaching a lot of his offspring, nephews, and sons-in-law the floor covering trade. This piece of carpet had a big splotch of blood on it and some deer hair.

I went into the lodge and found Chuck Beck just being served a big breakfast of eggs, sausage, toast, and coffee by

Mary. I asked the Becks, "Who is staying in that cabin?"

They said, "We didn't get their names. They just stayed two or three nights. They paid cash so we never entered them in our logbook. Why are you so interested in who they are anyway?"

So I kind of took the bull by the horns and told them, "I know they killed a deer just south of your resort last night, and I want them and the deer."

Then Beck said, "They had deer bow licenses and I thought they had gotten a deer."

I countered with, "This area is not open to taking deer with a bow and arrow and the gut pile is just south of your resort."

Then Beck said, "Well, we don't know who they are and they are gone."

I came back with, "I know they are floor layers and it is against the law for you to put up lodgers and not record their names, addresses, make of car, and car license. I will give you ten minutes to come up with these people or I'm going to get your lease terminated and you will be kicked out of this property."

Chuck Beck said, "You can't do that!"

I just said, "Try me."

That was too much for Mary. After all it was her money that was in this venture. After they gave me their names, I told her, "Call these men."

Both Mary and Chuck talked on the phone and when they hung up Chuck Beck told me, "They killed a deer with a bow over south of the Indian reservation on the west side of Highway 89. They brought the deer back, guts and all, and dressed it out where you found the gut pile."

I then told Chuck Beck, "To transfer the deer back to their residence, it had to be checked by the closest game warden in the county it was taken in to be sure it had been killed with an arrow."

Chuck Beck said, "We didn't know that."

I assured him, "All bow and arrow hunters are aware of

that."

With that I told Mary, "Get this person back on the phone. I want to talk to him."

So she called him back. He was Paul Furth of New Ulm, some relative of theirs.

I got on the phone and asked him, "Is it a buck or a doe?"

He said, "A small doe."

I then asked, "Where is the deer now?"

He said, "It's in the locker plant in New Ulm."

I then asked him, "Why didn't you bring the deer to my office for checking to see if it had been killed with an arrow?"

He claimed, "I didn't think there was a warden in Waskish. So I took the deer to Dave Mick at New Ulm and Dave signed me off before I took the deer to the locker plant."

I asked, "What is your partner's name?"

He said, "Stephen Stotka of Mankato."

I said, "Thank you", and hung up.

Then I told Mary and Chuck, "Paul Furth had taken the deer to Dave Mick, the warden at New Ulm and Dave signed his license and the deer is at the locker plant being processed."

Both of the Becks seemed relieved and even jovial.

I went right to my office and looked up Dave Mick's telephone number. He was a relatively new man. I had never met him.

I called and got Dave on the phone. I told him, "I'm Bill Callies the warden stationed at Waskish. I talked to a Paul Furth of New Ulm and he told me you had checked out a small doe taken with a bow and arrow and signed him off."

He said, "That is correct."

Then I told him, "You didn't check that deer because it was shot in the head or neck with one shot at night by a high power rifle."

To that Dave said, "I live in an apartment house and I was involved in something else and I was sure the guy was honest."

I let him know, "The deer is in the locker plant and you

should go there immediately and seize the carcass. Be sure to have the head. Call me back as soon as you have done this. Also check around the rib area and see if there was evidence of an arrow cut."

About a half hour later Dave called me back and said, "I have the deer but the head is missing. The man at the locker plant said that is the way Paul Furth brought it in."

I told Dave, "You better sharpen up or go find some other job. Be sure to hang onto that deer."

Then I called Paul Furth and told him, "I am reasonably sure you are lying to me and I am going to charge you and your partner with 'Taking a deer illegally and in a zone closed to the taking of deer' unless you and your partner come up to Waskish and take me to the site where you killed the deer."

He said, "I will be glad to do that but my partner and I have to work. However, we will be up there on October 30."

As I remember that was on a weekend. I told him, "Get up here as early in the day as possible so we will have good light."

These two men showed up at my office around noon. Paul said, "I wish I would have known that you were that handy to Sunset Resort. I could have had this cleaned up a week ago."

I had alerted Leo Manthei, the warden at Blackduck, to be at my office that morning to accompany us on this investigation.

I would guess these men had been well-schooled by Chuck Beck because they started to tell me we would have to go to Shooks on Highway 72 then turn west on Highway 1 through the Red Lake Indian Reservation on the west side back on a trail a couple of hundred yards to get to where they killed that deer.

Paul Furth was in the front seat with me and Stephen Stotka was in the back seat with Leo. After we had passed through the reservation on Highway 89, I started driving slowly and I told Paul, "Let me know where to stop."

He thought a couple of places were the trail he was looking for. It started to rain a little and then all of a sudden he hollered,

"That's the place, back up." I backed up. It was an approach to an old logging road.

The four of us got out. Leo asked, "Did you drag or carry the deer?"

I then told Leo, "They didn't gut the animal out until they got back to Waskish so they must have dragged it." We all walked down this trail for almost a quarter-of-a-mile.

Finally, Leo turned to this fellow and said, "How long are you going to keep this up? No deer has been dragged out here."

These two fellows finally said, "I guess you got us." I almost had to give them an "A for effort".

So when we got back to the car, I wrote them up and charged them with a misdemeanor, "Take one deer in a closed area".

We all went back to Kelliher where I looked up Justice of the Peace Clara Quale. She fined each of them $75 and $5 costs or ninety days in jail.

On the way back to Waskish to get their car I told these two men, "If you had been stopped anywhere on your way home you could have been charged with 'Transporting an illegally taken deer', which would be a gross misdemeanor. The fine would have been somewhere between $100 and $1,000 and/or up to a year in jail and you would have lost your vehicle."

Chapter 47/ BELTRAMI ISLAND FOREST

It was the third or fourth day of rifle deer season in northern Minnesota. I was stationed and lived at Waskish in an old log house that belonged to the State of Minnesota. There was a circular driveway around this house. The house also served as my office. This incident occurred in the early 1970's.

I had left home early that morning to get out and patrol around my district to look for any illegal activity and check hunting licenses. My wife was at home to answer the telephone and respond to any questions from deer hunters that elected to stop at our residence.

Sometime around noon, I came back to our home to grab a bite to eat and check on any problems my wife may have solved. She was my number one unpaid assistant. She knew more about what was involved with my job as a game warden than anyone else in the area. When I came through the door, I could tell she was obviously upset and frustrated. She told me, "Don't you dare leave this house until you see what some idiots are doing down in St. Paul!" She was mad!

When I said, "What is the matter?"

She told me, "Just sit still and listen to the AM radio." Then she reached over and turned up the volume. The radio was set at 830 AM—WCCO in Minneapolis.

I told her, "Give me some idea."

She said, "They are about to repeat the message. It comes on every half hour."

It was the news period and it started out, "This is the Department of Natural Resources of the State of Minnesota. We have been advised by our representative in the Beltrami Island Forest area that we have too many deer in this area and not enough deer hunters. If we get a severe winter, there is not enough food to sustain this deer herd and we will lose these deer through starvation. We need more hunters to harvest this big surplus of deer."

I couldn't believe my ears and I said as much to my wife. She told me, "You haven't seen the rest of the problem." Again, she wanted me to witness for myself.

She started to get a little lunch together for me when I noticed a car that drove into the yard and stopped near the front door where my office was in the enclosed front porch. These men bounced out of their vehicle with a lot of enthusiasm and headed for the office door. At least it looked like there was no problem because they were all so happy. When I answered the door they asked, "Are you the game warden in the Beltrami Island Forest?"

Patricia at the Waskish Warden's Residence

I told them, "I never heard of the Beltrami Island Forest, however, this is the north part of Beltrami County and there are woods and forest all around." Then I asked, "What can I do for you?"

With a big smile on the spokesman's lips he asked, "Where do you want these deer killed?" I happened to look toward my wife and she had a bright little smile on her face.

I turned back to these men and I told them, "As long as you abide by the law, you can hunt almost anywhere around here that you want to because it is almost all state land. However, even the locals are having poor success. There were a lot of hunters up here over the first weekend and very few of them got their deer."

These guys didn't believe me. I think they thought I was saving some secret place for my friends. The way they acted, it would seem that we had herds of deer in some corral or tied up and I just wouldn't tell them where.

I told these men, "Stand by and I will find out if the district forester might know where the Beltrami Island Forest is."

So, I called Roger Anderson. He laughed when I told him the problem. He said, "We have had hunters in here all morning asking that same question." He did not know where the Beltrami Island State Forest was. In the meantime, a couple more cars pulled into the driveway. Some of these hunters let me know they had driven all the way up from southern Minnesota and the Twin Cities.

I told these hunters, "I'll call my supervisor in Bemidji and maybe he can tell us where all these deer are."

I got Supervisor Tarte on the phone and told him about my problem. He said, "Willie, are you having problems up there too?" He went on to say the hunters were in the Beltrami County Courthouse, the sheriff's office, the city police, and out at the Regional Department of Natural Resources Office, and no one knows where the Beltrami Island Forest is. However, he had a call in to the St. Paul office and WCCO. Both places said they would get back to him and he would put it out on the air.

We finally got the word. It was the game manager at Norris Camp that had called St. Paul with all this good information. That surprised me because I had checked some hunters on the Lost River Trail that said they had been hunting over the first weekend near Faunce, which is under Norris Camp, and they had told me there were no deer there and very little sign.

At any rate, now we knew where to send these hunters. We very carefully told them to go out onto Highway 72, turn right, and go 40 miles north to Baudette, then go west on Highway Number 11 to Roosevelt, then turn south on the gravel road about 20 miles to Norris Camp. I assured them there were signs pointing to Norris Camp. "When you get there, look up Herman

Anderson. He is the head man and he will tell you where those deer are that he wants killed."

I never heard what happened up there, but it had to be worse than what we were experiencing. I'll bet Herman will never call the St. Paul office and make a statement like that again.

Chapter 48/ FOUR LOCAL SPORTS

I believe it was on a Friday night or I guess I should say Saturday morning. Anyway, it was October 27, 1973.

I had myself set up on old Highway 72, about four miles out of Kelliher. It was a quiet night. Most of the time I was sitting on the hood of my state car. I had my little portable radio and I would alternate listening to WBBM out of Chicago, or KOA out of Denver—talk shows. My car was back in the brush, but I was situated so I could see down a long straight stretch to the northwest. No one lived along this stretch of road. McCarthy lived up on the northwest end about six miles away. There were a half dozen farms between me and Kelliher.

I had been sitting out there since about 7 p.m. No one had come by. I could hear cars going north on the new Highway 72. I don't remember the exact time. I had eaten my lunch around midnight and it was some time after that. I heard one shot off to the north. It sounded like a high-powered rifle. I couldn't even guess how far away it was, because, to my knowledge, no one had driven up the old Highway 72 that I was on. I assumed it may have been one of the cars I heard driving north on the new Highway 72.

I knew a place back near the new Highway 72 that I could pull off out of sight and observe anyone coming back towards Kelliher on either the new or old Highway 72. I drove back to this new location to sit and watch. Also, I called on the radio to see if Leo Manthei, the warden from Blackduck, was around. He didn't answer but Lonnie Schiefert from Northome responded. I told him I may have some activity, gave him my location, and asked him how close to Kelliher he was if I needed assistance. He said he was east of Kelliher, near Mizpah, and wanted to know if he should head over my way.

I told him to stay where he was, but I would appreciate it if he would stand by.

About an hour went by and an older model four door car came from the north with four occupants in it. I called Lonnie to advise him I was going to follow this car into Kelliher with my lights off to see what would develop. This car turned east one block short of the main street. It went one block east, then turned south one block, then turned east on the main street, crossed the railroad tracks about a hundred yards more, and turned into a house. I could see quite a little movement towards a garage to the west of the house. I called Lonnie on the radio and told him I was going to pull into this garage and confront these people to see what was going on.

There was an old style garage door hung by rollers on a track so you could slide the door to the west. It was apparently hooked, as it would not slide open, so I just took a good hold of the door and pulled it towards me. It opened just enough so I could squeeze in. The four people were inside. They had turned on the single light bulb that hung from the rafters.

There was a stack of lumber in the middle of the garage floor. Along side of the stack of lumber was a nice eight-point buck. There was a lot of scrambling of bodies so I hollered. "Hold it. Don't move, Game Warden!"

Two members of the group tried to hide on the west side of the pile of lumber. One of the individuals was to my left in the corner, and one person was near the small door on the east side of the garage. Everyone just seemed to freeze. I recognized all of them—local young men.

About this time, Lonnie burst through the small door on the

east side of the garage. As I recall, he hollered, "Game Warden, freeze." Then he saw me and the deer lying on the floor.

I turned to the young man in the corner to talk to him. His name was Stephen Mohs, the son of a dairy farmer that lived north of the busy corner. His mouth was open and appeared to be talking, but no sound was coming out. I thought he was on drugs and I asked him if he was. He still could not utter a sound. Lonnie and I started to get around to the job of writing them up. I took the oldest person, Dennis Poxleitner, out to my patrol car. It was his or his folks' car that had been used. I had examined the car and found deer hair and fresh blood in it.

I told Dennis I could charge all four of them for transporting an illegal big game animal and all of them would be subject to a fine up to a $1,000.00 and/or up to a year in jail. I also told him he would lose the car. Dennis begged me to just charge him for this mess. It was his idea and he talked Mohs and the two boys into going along.

I told Dennis, "I am going to charge all four of you, however, you could pay their fines if you felt responsible and wanted to."

I went on and said, "I have never had any problems with any of you before and if you will give me assurance that you won't try this dumb stunt again ever, I will reduce the charge to 'Taking one deer in closed season'. That is a misdemeanor." I would have him up before the local justice of the peace. The maximum fine she could hand out was $300.00 and/or ninety days in jail. I told him if all four of you go into her court and act like gentlemen she may not give you any jail time but I was reasonably sure they should have $300.00 each on them.

I did tell him if I ever caught any of them again pulling a stunt like this I would seize everything involved. They could count on it.

Next, I took Stephen Mohs in the car to write him up. He now was able to communicate. I asked him what was the matter with him that he couldn't talk. He just said, "You just scared the shit out of me."

I told him what I had told Poxleitner. Then I said, "I had you in firearm safety class about ten years ago when you were in the sixth grade. I told you then what could happen if you pulled a stunt like this. Now, you will know from personal experience. You best have $300.00 on you when you go before Justice of the Peace Clara Quale."

Next, I took the third young man in the patrol car to write him up. At that time, I found he was a juvenile, but in a matter of days he would be classified as an adult. So I booked him into juvenile court before Marcus Reed in Bemidji, Minnesota.

Apparently, the judge thought he was close enough to eighteen, because he was fined $150.00.

The fourth lad was sixteen, so I sent him to Marcus Reed's juvenile court. Of course, we never know what the courts decide to do with the juveniles.

We sent the four of them on their way. I believe Lonnie had dressed the deer out. I sure thanked Lonnie for being out working and available.

It was just possible if Lonnie hadn't burst in like he did, one or two of them might have taken off on foot. At any rate, we both thought we had accomplished something that night.

Chapter 49/ GIVE THEM 'A' FOR EFFORT

It was a nice pleasant day on October 5, 1974, when I drove over to the boathouse located next to the Minnesota State Fish Hatchery in Waskish, Minnesota.

I noticed a man and two women comfortably set out in folding chairs in the fish hatchery yard and each holding fishing poles with their lines extending out into the mouth of the Tamarac River.

They looked to be people in their late 20's or early 30's. I asked them, "Have you had any luck?"

They acknowledged with, "Yes, we have a few on the stringer."

I then asked, "Can I see your angling licenses?"

The man pulled out his billfold. He searched and searched through the papers in his billfold and finally concluded. "They're all in a pocket in my life jacket at home."

The state issues the wardens a book of "Acknowledgement of no license". There is an original and a copy for each person that is written up. There are many questions to be answered as to when and where the license was purchased, a description of the individual, a place for the person to sign, the warden's signature, and an address to mail the license and acknowledgement to within five days or a warrant will be put out for the arrest of the person.

This was a man and his wife from Nisswa and a lady from Brainerd.

About five or six days later, I received a combination-angling license for Mr. and Mrs. Leo Rice and an individual angling license for Margaret Zander. The issuing date on both licenses was for a few days prior to when I contacted them. They were all issued at the same establishment.

I had been suspicious of them when I made out the acknowledgement but now I felt certain they were cheats.

Minnesota Game Warden Art Gensmer was the closest warden to the establishment that issued these licenses so I packaged all of this and mailed it to Warden Gensmer in Pine River, Minnesota. I explained my suspicions in a letter that I included with Rice's and Zander's fishing license and the originals of the "Acknowledgement of no license".

He advised me by mail that he checked the copies of the angling licenses in the books at the establishment where they were issued. He found in the books several licenses had been issued on October 5 and October 6 in both the combination and individual license book. Then the licenses issued to Rice and

Zander were issued on October 3.

Warden Gensmer questioned the purveyor of the licenses, "Was there a request to back date the licenses or did you do this on your own?"

The man that issued the license said, "I was alone in the shop that day and it was quite busy. When the man started to fill out the licenses, Mr. Rice offered his services. He told me to go wait on the other customers then when they got the licenses filled out, I could come back and sign them and take the money."

Also Warden Gensmer said, "I chastised the purveyor of the licenses and threatened to remove the right to sell Minnesota game and fish licenses. However, that decision would have to be made by my regional supervisor."

When I received all of this information back from Warden Gensmer, I made out the summons for each of the individuals along with a letter explaining what the purveyor of the license told Warden Gensmer as to the date they were actually there to purchase the license.

I scheduled them into the Justice of the Peace Clara Quale at Kelliher, Minnesota on October 30, 1974. All three of them posted bail in the amount of $29.00, $25.00 for the fine and $4.00 for cost.

Chapter 50/ WILD DOGS

People that live on the south shore of Upper Red Lake and along the eastern boundary of the Red Lake Indian Reservation refer to them as "Indian Dogs". I'm sure some of these dogs come from abandoned dogs on the reservation, but also a lot of these animals come from tourists passing through the area and just dumping off unwanted pets.

I have had many opportunities to see some of these animals

and they range from terriers up to German Shepherds. They run in packs of up to fifteen or twenty animals. They are muscular and powerful animals and don't have the fear of man that timber wolves and coyotes have.

Only the most powerful of these animals survive in the bush. The weaker animals are killed and eaten.

The farmers, loggers, and settlers have a lot of respect for these animals and some of them have lost livestock to them as well as to the timber wolves.

I will relate two of many incidents that I personally had experience with.

There was an elderly couple that lived on about ten acres on the south shore of Upper Red Lake. They called me one evening and said a pack of wild dogs came through their yard. Two of the dogs went into their barn where they used to keep a horse and a few pigs. The man ran out and closed the barn door capturing the two animals. He requested that I come down to his place and go in the barn and kill these two animals.

I left my home immediately and started for his place. It is about twenty miles, so I assume it took me about twenty minutes to get there. The old resident came out of the house when he saw my headlights coming into his yard. He then informed me there was only one dog left in the barn. After he talked to me on the phone, he and his wife heard their pet cat that obviously was in the barn let out horrible screams. The wife panicked and urged her husband to go and save the cat. He ran out to the barn. The cat quit screaming and when he opened the door one of the dogs burst out past him so he quickly slammed the door shut again.

Now, I only had one dog to deal with. I got out my double barrel twelve-gauge shotgun. I then took two twelve-gauge shells out of a box loaded with double ought buck shot. I put the shells in the gun, took my five-cell flashlight, and cautiously opened the door and stepped inside. I saw a movement through a crack in two boards of the stanchion. He came around the corner toward me about fifteen feet from me when I fired the first barrel at his head. The shot knocked him backward and down on the barn floor. In a flash, he was back on his feet, so, I gave him the second barrel. He went down again, but, then I could see there was still some life in him and I was out of shells.

I got out of that door fast and slammed it shut. I went over to the car and got my rifle, loaded it up, and came back to the barn door. I opened the door just a crack and shone my light in. I couldn't believe it. He was on his feet. His head looked like a mass of pulp. I took quick aim at the center of the head and fired again. The dog stayed down for keeps then. We found bits and pieces of the cat. The dogs had eaten most of it.

To say the least, I was amazed at how much punishment that animal took before he died.

The second incident occurred one morning about 8 a.m. I had just gotten home from having been out all night looking for deer shiners. My wife was up and started to get breakfast for me. I was pooped out. I just wanted to get a bite to eat and go to bed.

Then the phone rang. It was Mrs. Wistrum. They have a small farm on the south shore of Upper Red Lake, right next to the Red Lake Indian Reservation. They lived in a house on the north side of the county road. Their private drive is about an eighth of a mile from the house to the county road. She had three school age children and the school bus was due in about a half an hour. Mrs. Wistrum had looked out the window and saw a pack of wild Indian dogs jumping around in a weedy, abandoned pasture on the south side of the county road. She wanted me to come down immediately and chase the dogs out of there because she was afraid to let her children walk down to the school bus on the county road. Also, she was afraid to go down near the dogs. I told her I had just gotten home from working all night and I was beat. I finally said, "All right, I'll come."

My wife asked me what the problem was. She wanted to know if I was going. I told her "Not until I get something to eat. It is twenty-five miles down there. I have to gas up the patrol car and it would be a half hour before I got there. By that time, I think those dogs will be long gone."

About fifteen minutes after I received the call from Mrs. Wistrum and while I was eating my breakfast, another call came. It was Mrs. Wistrum. When I answered the phone, she just screamed, "Haven't you left yet?"

I asked, "Are the dogs still there?"

"Yes!" she screamed.

"I'm on my way," I said. "Are the dogs still there?"

Another screaming, "Yes!"

It took me roughly a half hour to get there. I looked out on the field and there the dogs were jumping around in the high weeds about a hundred yards south of the county road.

I took my Remington 700 rifle in the caliber 25-06. It would hold one cartridge in the chamber and three in the magazine.

I started to think that the dogs must have killed a deer or a moose out there to stay that long in one place. I leaned the rifle over the top of the squad car. I could just barely make out the tops of the larger dogs that were standing. However, the smaller dogs showed up when they were jumping around. I got a good shot at the first dog standing. Then it was just a blur of dogs and shooting, as those dogs took off to the east into the thick bush.

As I started to reload, I heard Mrs. Wistrum hollering behind me, "How many did you get?"

I answered, "I'm not sure if I hit any of them. The weeds are so high I couldn't see any of them go down. I can go check to see if I hit any of them as soon as I finish reloading." There could be a cripple out there. Also, I wanted to know why they stayed in one area so long.

I hunted around in the weeds and found three dead dogs. The first one I shot standing was a big female, mongrel dog.

You could see she was a muscular animal. She weighed about 80 pounds. It is my belief that she was in heat, because, as I remember, she seemed to be the center of all the dog activity.

At least Mrs. Wistrum was somewhat appeased. So, chalk one up for public relations northern Minnesota style.

Chapter 51/ BELTRAMI COUNTY DEPUTY SHERIFFS

I was awakened by the telephone this night. It was pitch dark inside and outside of the log house that was our residence and office at Waskish, Minnesota. I had hoped to get to the phone before it woke up Patricia, my wife.

I found I was talking to the dispatcher at Thief River Falls. I asked him, "What time is it?"

He responded with, "It's twelve forty-five on the sixteenth day of October."

"I've got a Beltrami Deputy Sheriff relaying some traffic through his dispatcher office in Bemidji to the effect he was chasing an Indian car that had shined and shot on a field north and west of Saum on the dead-end road that goes into the Mohstad farm."

He, Dave Bergstrom, and his partner Deputy Sheriff Ronnie Solberg witnessed the shining and shooting and attempted to stop the station wagon with three occupants believed to be Native Americans from the Red Lake Indian Reservation. The chase had been going south on County Road 23. They finally managed to get the vehicle stopped near the County Aid Road 104, south of Saum.

Two of the Indians bolted from the station wagon, one carrying a rifle and the other carrying a spotlight. They ran into the woods on the west side of the road and disappeared. The driver of the station wagon saw an opportunity to drive off to the south on County Road 23. The deputies saw a dead deer in the back of the station wagon.

The deputies abandoned any idea of taking after the two men in the woods and instead were in pursuit of the station wagon south on County Road 23. They wanted me to come out and assist them.

I told the state dispatcher they were at least thirty miles from me and heading toward Bemidji. It would take me five minutes to get dressed and start out. Also the violations occurred and were occurring in Warden Manthei's district—call him out of Blackduck. I will be in my patrol car within five minutes to assist.

Eventually, I was in my state vehicle heading south on State Highway 72, then on to County Road 23 down past Saum into the area of the first stop made by the deputy sheriffs. I continued on south as fast as my vehicle would go for about eight or ten miles. I came across a small doe lying in the roadway. It looked to be a car kill. I stopped, picked it up, and threw it into the trunk of the car and reported my find to the state dispatcher at Thief River Falls. He relayed the information to the sheriff's dispatcher at Bemidji.

About five minutes later, through three relays, I was told the station wagon they were chasing had several deer run across in front of it and had hit one of them.

At the same time, I was advised they were coming into Turtle River and not driving too fast. However, every time the sheriff's car attempted to come along side the fleeing vehicle, that driver would swing from one side of the road to the other.

I realized I was getting close to them when the state dispatcher told me the station wagon turned north on Highway 71.

Within a couple of minutes, I came up and passed the sheriff's car and attempted to pass and force the fleeing car to a stop. The station wagon was all over the road. I was within a hundred feet of the sheriff's car but could not communicate because we each had our exclusive channels—frustrating. Then the state dispatcher called me and said, "Don't force that car into the ditch. There is a small two or three-year-old child in the station wagon."

We were coming up a little grade into the town of Tenstrike. I saw my chance and shot my car on to the left side of the fleeing vehicle. Looked to my right and the station wagon had disappeared. He had made a right hand turn on the first street we came to in this little town of Tenstrike.

I came on around the block and saw the taillights heading east. The driver of the station wagon didn't know it, but he was heading east on this small dirt road that had a dead end about three miles east of Tenstrike.

I sent this information to my dispatcher, "We've got him now." The road was through small rolling wooded hills. In a few minutes, I found the station wagon. The driver apparently lost control and went off the trail downhill and was wedged between two large popple trees. The driver could only get out by climbing over the dead deer carcass through the rear gate.

The man was reluctant to attempt to get out of the vehicle when he saw the two deputy sheriffs come walking down behind me. He was under the impression Deputy Solberg would beat him with his nightstick. I assured him that no way was that going to happen.

Solberg did alert me this Native American was inclined to kick people and he advised me to be extremely careful if and when he comes out of the station wagon.

I then got into a long conversation with the Indian. His name was Howard Hart and he lived on the Red Lake Reservation. I let him know he would be charged with spotlighting deer and shooting at them. Also he would be charged with transporting an illegally taken deer and a third charge of attempting to escape—three separate gross misdemeanor charges.

I finally talked him into coming out of the car. He seemed

to fear Deputy Solberg, but I finally assured him no harm would come to him or his son as long as he behaved himself and did what he was told.

I then asked the deputies to transport Mr. Hart to the county jail and contact social services to take care of the boy. Also not to do anything to antagonize Mr. Hart.

I then took the deer out of the station wagon, locked it up until I could get a tow truck out there some time in the future to tow it out. Also, I took a few minutes to dress out the two deer and load them on my patrol car.

I got the exact location from the deputies where the two partners of Howard Hart ran into the woods and returned to that location. It was here I met Warden Manthei. He suggested he could imitate the sound of a couple of hounds. We started to talk real loud about releasing some trailing dogs that we had in the car. Leo seemed to think the two escapees were close enough to hear us. Then he went into his dog yelping act but nothing developed.

Then Leo stepped on something in the grass a few feet in from the graveled road. It was a beat up 94 Winchester 30/30 rifle with cartridges in the chamber and magazine.

I then told Leo I wanted to check the area where the sheriffs had witnessed the shooting. The two of us went to this area and out on to the fields. There was a snow fence set up on this field in anticipation of the coming winter.

With the aid of our flashlights, we found a dead deer on the backside of the snow fence. Obviously, when the Indians shot the deer it either jumped over the snow fence or ran around the end of it before its life ran out.

Leaving a dead animal is typical of illegal night hunters if they can't see the quarry dead or disabled from where they fired the shot. They are inclined to assume they missed or only crippled the animal and they make a hasty departure.

There was some body heat in the carcass so we dressed it out and piled it on to the two deer I already had on my car.

I suggested to Leo that he take over the case because it all ran out in his district. He wanted no part of it, claiming I had been the first one called out and was more aware of the circumstances.

That meant I would be able to go home, get about three hours of sleep before I would have to be up and about and on my way to Bemidji to report to the county attorney.

Nine o'clock in the morning found me sitting in the county attorney's office spelling out the circumstances earlier on that day. Because Mr. Hart claimed to be indigent, the public defender was brought in to defend him.

The public defender and the county attorney got into a private conversation that finally took the two of them to go see Judge Phillip Nelson, who would be hearing the case.

Actually, no one wanted anything to do with this problem. I had the feeling they would like me to drop the complaints and everyone could just go home.

Finally, Mr. Hart was arraigned in court. He was to be charged only with spotlighting and transporting a big game animal. The escape charge was dropped.

I believe it was Deputy Sheriff Dave Bergstrom that did most of the testifying. Mr. Hart pleaded guilty to both charges. He was told he could post a $250.00 bail bond and be released on his own recognizance. He was unable to post bail so he was put back in jail.

Eventually, Mr. Hart was brought up before a district judge and was found guilty. He was fined the minimum penalty on a gross misdemeanor charge of a $300.00 fine or ninety days in jail. Also, I was to return his vehicle to him.

Mr. Hart was placed in the county jail in Bemidji. Then a couple of weeks later he was transported to the jail at the Red Lake Indian Reservation.

I went to see him there to see if he would give me the names of his confederates. He would not. I told him to be sure to hang onto that receipt for his station wagon that I had given him out in those woods east of Tenstrike.

Then he asked, "Can I have my gun back?" Obviously, his two partners saw Leo find the gun and turn it over to me.

I asked Mr. Hart, "Do you have the receipt from me that I took a gun from you?"

He answered, "No."

I then said, "We found a 30/30 Winchester laying in the grass near where your two partners took into the bush. I will make a deal with you. I don't know who that gun belongs to that Leo stepped on and turned over to me. However, I will give it to you if you will give me the names of the two other men that were with you and testify in court after I have them picked up and charged."

He refused to do that.

At the end of his ninety-day jail time, he came to Waskish where I was holding his car. He returned his receipt and we dug his car out of the snow that had accumulated on and around it. We got the motor started and Mr. Hart left.

The state also got stuck with a $180.00 bill for towing the station wagon from its wedged spot to Waskish.

This whole incident was typical—no one is really a winner.

Chapter 52/ O'BRIEN LAKE

It was on July 29, 1975 when I received a call from Mr. Balmer on O'Brien Lake. I had been at my new station less than a week. Mr. Balmer was upset about some beaver on the lake. He said he had called Walt Heineman in previous years but Walt never did anything to relieve the problem.

He said he had called Walt the previous day and he was told he had retired and that he should call his replacement, meaning me.

So I asked, "Just what is the problem?"

He told me, "Many years ago the home owners and summer cabin owners had, in conjunction with the state, built a concrete dam at the outlet of the lake in order to maintain a stable water level. Some beaver had moved in and built a dam on top of the concrete dam, which in turn raised the water so high it was over our boat docks."

Callies' home in Ironton, MN. Bill's office was in the basement.

In years past when Walt failed to show up, the building owners would go down and try to remove the dam by hand. It was an ongoing problem. I asked Mr. Balmer, "Just where do you live on O'Brien Lake?"

He described it and then added, "You can't miss it, and my name is on the mailbox."

I located his home. Mr. Balmer got in the car with me and instructed me to drive down a small trail on the west side of the lake. Finally, he told me to stop at what appeared to be a turn around. We got out of the car and walked down through the brush. He stopped where the brush was getting real thick and pointed in an easterly direction and said, "The dam is right down there about a couple of hundred yards. We always come down here by boat. Maybe you should come down that way too."

I agreed with him. I told him, "I have to go home to get some explosives and my hooks if I have to take it apart by hand. Where is the public access to the lake?"

His response was, "We don't have one and we don't want one." He said, "You can go to Corky Hewitt's Resort on the southeast side of the lake. They have a little launching place." I took Balmer home and thanked him.

I told him, "With any luck, I should have the lake down at least a foot by sundown."

I went back to Ironton, picked up the state boat, motor, trailer, explosives, moss hook, toolbox, cushion and life jacket. I returned to O'Brien Lake and located Hewitt's Resort. It wasn't much of a resort. They had a few fourteen-foot boats to rent and a make shift access to the lake.

Corky wasn't home, but Mrs. Hewitt said she thought it would be OK to use the ramp and she would not charge me if I would get that beaver dam out of there and lower the lake water so they could use their docks.

On the way to the dam, I passed a small boat with a fisherman in it. I was sure the license was expired on the boat.

At the dam site, I could see the beaver dam was on top of the concrete dam. I decided two sticks of explosives should loosen the beaver's portion of the dam. I was remembering the time Lonnie Schiefert, at Northome, had a similar situation at Island Lake. He did not know there was a concrete dam under the beaver dam and he put a really heavy charge in the dam. It took out the beaver dam and the concrete dam and practically drained Island Lake. He was in a hell of a spot for a long time until the state replaced the concrete dam.

At any rate, I got my charge down in the dam with the fuse

sticking above the water. I started my outboard motor and left it in neutral, went back, lit the fuse, jumped in the boat, and got out of there. After the explosive blew, I eased down near the dam and could see I had punched a good hole and there was a tremendous flow of water.

Beaver dam exploding

With the job done, I came back and checked the fishing and boat license of the party I had passed. He had an angling license but he said, "Almost everyone on O'Brien has quit renewing their watercraft license."

So I wrote him up for no watercraft license and told him, "Take the boat back home and pull it out of the water until you get a new license."

Then I started checking boats and fishermen. I had about six tickets in my summons book and I soon ran out of summons. I went back to my patrol car and got a new book of twenty-five summonses and almost filled that up. I wrote up a county attorney, a policeman from Breezy Point, an Internal Revenue Service officer, a college professor from Iowa, and a few other porky people that were going to have my job.

However, I did lower the lake and the residents were thankful for that. So I loaded up my boat, thanked Mrs. Hewitt and went home. I had spent the whole day on O'Brien Lake.

Four days later, I thought I best go back to O'Brien Lake to see if the beaver had rebuilt their dam. I had the boat on behind the car and explosives in the trunk. I returned to Hewitt's Resort and parked my car and boat over near the ramp. I got out of the car to go over to the house to again ask permission.

About half way to the house, the back screen door just exploded open and out came a big man with shaggy hair and an even shaggier beard. He opened his mouth with a roar that I couldn't understand and he had a big meat cleaver in his right hand. He was running at me and I knew that was no place for me. I turned and ran for my car, opened the car door, and grabbed a club that I had made from a broken hickory oar.

I whirled about with my club. The man was about twenty-feet away. He stopped, buried that meat cleaver into a log and started to laugh.

I wasn't sure how to take him. Then he came forward with his right hand out-stretched and announcing, "I'm Corky Hewitt." I shook hands with him after I transferred my club to my left hand.

Then he said, "You sure shook the hell out of a lot of important people on this lake." Then he went on to say, "They came down on me because my wife had let you put the state boat in the lake. I keep my boats licensed but I know that it is a popular concept to not renew boat licenses on O'Brien Lake. Walt Heineman, the former warden, never came around."

I then asked Corky Hewitt, "Can I use your ramp again to go down and check to see if the beaver have rebuilt the dam?"

He let me know I was welcome to anything he had within

reason and I need not ask. Then he insisted I come in the house while he put the coffee pot on and we could sit and talk. That is our status as of this day.

Chapter 53/ COLLEGE BREAK

It was a beautiful morning in spring. The sun was coming up, warm and bright. The ice was out of the small lakes formed by the removal of the iron ore in the region. This was the Cuyuna Iron Ore Range, northeast of Brainerd. The miners are gone and so is the high-grade ore. All that remains of the mining are the pits and the small ridges formed by piling up the over-burden in quest of the ore. Some of the pits are over 500 feet deep and are now filled with water.

There are small trails winding all through this area. I was on patrol alone through this area checking for any violations of the Department of Natural Resources.

On the trail I was on, I was heading toward the Mississippi River, which was about two miles ahead. It was here I started meeting pickup trucks with young people riding in the cab and a lot more riding in the back. I could see what looked like tents, sleeping bags, and coolers. Some of the people had pop or beer cans in their hands.

I decided to stop one of these rigs to find out what was going on. They were for the most part an exuberant crowd, although, some of them looked pretty sick and some were ugly.

It seemed that most of the vehicles and passengers were from the Mankato State University and some were students from St. Cloud State University. Some of the young people said things had gotten out of hand and they were on their way home.

I continued on down this trail meeting more vehicles. Some of the occupants were jovial. Some of them called me the "Fish Cop" and some called me the "Game and Fish Pig".

Eventually, I came to an open area about 200 yards from the Mississippi River. There were cars and pickups all through the woods. There were young people everywhere and they looked filthy. Most of the young men had a three or four day growth of beard and the bulk of them were bare chested. There were beer and pop cans all over the area on the ground. There were a number of small Norway trees chopped down. This was a forestry plantation area. These people had all kinds of battery-operated radios, some of which had speakers hanging in the trees. When they saw me, they turned up the volume until the sound was deafening.

These young men started to surround my patrol car. They climbed up on the hood and some stood on the rear bumper and started to bounce my patrol car. When I tried to talk to them, all I got was, "You got a problem, man? You come down here to harass us, man?"

I told them, "You can't leave a mess like this and this area is a state plantation. It is against the law to chop down these trees."

The situation got worse by the minute, and for the first time since I went to work for the state, I was pretty sure they were going to work me over.

I don't know where they came from but four young women showed up and started to bawl these men out. I'm sure the men were either drunk or on dope. They didn't even act like human beings; however, when these women started to call these men by their names and commanded them to back off and give me room, they moved away.

These ladies said, "We agreed to come on this bash providing the group do whatever they are told to do." They were in charge of this mob of men and women.

I told these women, "The entire area would have to be policed." I started to write down license numbers of the vehicles.

These young ladies assured me, "Everything will be

cleaned up and left the way we found it." They claimed the tree chopping had been done by some unwanted people that moved in on them the day before, and that to the best of their knowledge, those people had left the night before. They advised me, "We have to be back in school tomorrow and we will get everyone cleaning up the area as soon as you pull out."

I told them, "I'll be back tomorrow and if this isn't cleaned up, I will put charges against the owners of the vehicles."

With that, I got back in the patrol car, turned around and found about twenty young men blocking the road. I drove real slowly up to them. Little by little, they opened up enough for me to drive through. Some of them made remarks to me. As I passed, I heard one of the women chastise these men.

I was sure thankful to get out of that mess and I went straight home and told my wife what I had run into. I also put down eight hours on my daily report. I know I didn't physically do the eight hours but mentally I felt like I had put in twelve hours.

The next day at sunrise, I went back there. The cans and garbage were all gone. However, when I walked back into the woods, 55 feet from the clearing, there were piles and piles of human body waste.

I went to the Forestry Department and reported the damage to their plantation. They were amazed that I went down there. It seems that was a yearly event. I was new to the district, having moved into Ironton the summer before.

I then went to the sheriff of Crow Wing County and reported the problem. He just shrugged his shoulders and said, "Those young people have to go some place to let off steam and that's as good a place as any."

I just wished someone had advised me.

Chapter 54/ A BURRO IN DEERWOOD

On the 6th day of April in 1976, I was patrolling around my district when I crossed a small creek that drained out of Serpent Lake. From the car I could see a lot of the high weeds trampled down. I got out of the car to check this situation. Then I could see the creek went under the country gravel road through a three-foot culvert. The downstream end of the culvert was about ten inches above the creek level at the outgoing end. Also, I got a glimpse of several small northern in the pool on the downstream end of the culvert. It was obvious these small northern were trapped attempting to go upstream to spawn.

I was aware that some of the locals like to catch these small northern and pickle them. The season for taking northern pike was closed. I figured I best spend some time around this creek to see if someone was actually taking these fish or just stopping by to look at them.

There was no place close I could hide my car and still observe this site for violators. I did notice a small stand of sweet corn stalks within seventy-five yards of the road and culvert that I could hide in and have good observation of the site.

I then checked around this area for a place to hide my car so no one would stumble on to it. I finally located a good place to hide the patrol car but I would have to walk about a quarter-of-a-mile to the stand of old corn stalks.

Eventually I went home to dinner. I told my wife what I had come across and where I planned to work.

About 8:00 p.m. I took leave of my wife and home and drove to the gravel road that led to the creek. There were no cars around when I turned out my lights and drove the one-and-a-half miles to the place I would leave my car.

Then with my five-cell flashlight in hand in the off

position, a summons book, seizure tags, and a heavy jacket with a sandwich in the pocket, I took off to the old standing corn site to see if someone would pay me a visit.

I slipped into one end of the standing corn and went down on my knees to rest and get my breath. There was no moon that night and everything was really black and extremely quiet. I then decided if I moved to the other end of this corn patch I could observe the creek even better. About half way through this corn patch something let go with a loud roaring "BRACHCH". I swear I jumped five feet straight up. Then I could hear the animal making the noise on the other side of the barn wire fence. It was a western burro. I believe he was as shook up as I was. After about ten minutes, my heart got back to normal and I continued on to my observation location.

As I remember I sat there for close on to two hours when I saw my first car come down on the country road. It stopped just short of the culvert and three people came out of the car. Two of the people each took a dip net out of the trunk and with the aid of their flashlights waded out into the water thirty or forty feet down stream from the culvert.

Fish thrown up on shore

Immediately there was excited talking and they were throwing objects from the dip nets into the weedy areas on either side of the stream. The third person was busy throwing the objects further back from the stream.

I finally guessed they had at least thirty of these objects up in the weeds so I got up and without the use of my flashlight I walked almost up to the one person that was on shore before she realized I was there. Then I turned on my flashlight and announced, "Game Warden! Come out of the water and give me those dip nets." They all complied so I asked for identification from the two men and one woman. They all submitted their drivers' licenses.

We all went over to their car where I could make out the summons using the hood of their car for a desk. When I submitted the summons for their signatures, one of the party was missing. It was the woman. She was busy throwing the fish back in the stream. She had thrown all the fish back on one side of the stream. I just thanked her and told her I had planned to put all of them back except three or four. I told her I had kept count every time the men in the water threw a fish in the grass.

Two of the party appeared in court that following Friday, pled guilty and paid a fine of $25 each—the third had skipped town. I picked him up on a warrant that summer when he came home to visit and then he too made his donation to the county court.

Chapter 55/ NO PLACE FOR AMATEURS

It was April 17, 1976 that in response to a request from Brad Burgraff, the warden at Garrison, Minnesota; I went to assist him in searching for gill nets in Mille Lac Lake. Brad had the northwest portion of the big lake along with at least thirty smaller lakes in his district. He also requested the assistance of Don Slinger, the warden stationed at Pierz, Minnesota.

Brad had about a twenty-foot inboard, outboard boat to work the Mille Lac.

The first night we patrolled the lake from about 9:00 p.m. on Saturday until 2:00 a.m. on Sunday. We operated with me sitting up on the bow holding a heavy line attached to a hook affair made out of iron rods welded together forming four 8 to 10 inch hooks which, when dragged through the water down near the bottom, would snag any gill net we came across.

Brad operated his boat from inside the cabin. He ran as slow as the motor would go. He had his running lights shut off. He paralleled the shorelines by about one hundred yards.

When, and if, I hooked a net, I had him stop the boat or even back up a bit. Then I would work the net back to Don Slinger and we would pull the net into the boat and release any live fish.

This first night, we only hooked one net believed to belong to an Indian who would disclaim any ownership.

On Monday, April 19, I again accompanied Burgraff and Slinger looking for gill nets on Mille Lac Lake from 9:30 a.m. to 3:30 p.m. and then again from 6:00 p.m. to 8:00 p.m. We worked the west shore of the big lake. Then we started to move up into the northwest part of the lake. We were operating with no running lights and the slowest speed the boat would operate at.

As we came into an area just out from the Myr Mar Lodge Resort, we saw some one-gallon plastic white bottles.

Our suspicions were that someone was jug fishing or these were the locating markers for gill nets. There were three or four jugs. We backed out of there real carefully to make plans to catch these people in the act of clerking their nets.

There were a couple of lights on in the lodge and a huge yard light in the front of the lodge. We backed out of there and moved in to shore and then up through the woods to get where we could place the lodge building under surveillance with the aid of our binoculars. We watched for any movement through the windows of the lighted rooms. We believed we had three young men moving around inside of the Myr Mar Lodge.

Burgraff contacted Jim Bryant from Isle to come up by boat and assist us. Jim was stationed at Isle on the southeast part of Mille Lac Lake. Jim had an eighteen-foot Alumacraft Queen Marie. He came up to the marina located about halfway between Garrison and the Myr Mar Lodge. He had another law enforcement man with him.

I can't remember for sure, but we also had a young ex-marine, 21 or 22 years old, that was some relation to either Burgraff or Slinger who was real anxious to tag along. I normally don't like strangers along when you are taking on a bunch of two bit punks like we had under surveillance. As I remember, we had between us, two portable radios.

The plan was for Jim Bryant to move up in his boat with his partner to within about a quarter-of-a-mile of the plastic bottle floats and sit there until he was told by Burgraff to move in. Burgraff and Bryant had the portables.

Burgraff, Slinger, the ex-marine and myself were to station ourselves in the woods surrounding the resort. We had also noted a sixteen-foot boat with oars in it pulled up on the beach about a hundred yards northeast of the lodge. There we were all to sit and wait until the men went down to their boat, picked up all their nets and fish, and rowed back to the beach. Then we all would move into the fishermen. We knew we could expect some kind of a Donny Brook from this trio.

Sometime around midnight I could see some activity inside the lodge. The people inside appeared to be putting on additional clothing—sweaters, jackets, or rain gear. Eventually, they came out the front door into the well-lit front yard and headed to the east in the direction of the boat on the beach.

From where I was, I could just barely see the men pass down into the ravine and out of the yard light. Then I heard one of the three men say, "Wait, I forgot my six pack of beer." He turned and came back into the yard light and at that same time that ex-marine was right out in the yard light. He was going to follow the three men and of course there was no way to stop what happened—both men met right there in the front yard under the bright yard light.

One yelp from the man going back to get his six pack and the whole thing was blown. The other two men came up from the beach and all three of them went back into the lodge.

At one time, I could see two of them lift the cover of a deep freeze that was in front of a window that was so dirty you could hardly see through it. I could not make out what was being removed from the deep freeze. If I could have seen fish, we would have at least a weak excuse to break in. We did not even think of getting a search warrant and I doubt if any judge would issue us one anyhow. Also, we didn't know but what the owners of Myr Mar Lodge were in on the netting scheme.

It turned out Brad knew of someone that might know who the owners of the lodge were so we could contact them.

Jim Bryant was notified by the portable radio about what had happened so he was told to move in and pick up the gill nets if that was what he would find under the plastic jugs. We suggested he should release all the live fish but keep a count as to specie and quantity.

Eventually, somewhere around 2:00 a.m. on April 20, 1976, we got the names of the owners, their addresses and telephone numbers. I called the party and told them exactly what happened. Of course, they denied any knowledge of what the men in the lodge were doing. They were in the lodge legally we were told. Also at my request, the owner verbally gave us authorization to go in and search for fish. Actually, we were on pretty shaky ground. We searched everywhere but could find nothing illegal so all we could do was apologize and back off.

We were involved in cleaning up this goofed-up mess until 6:00 a.m. I took some pictures of the mess of nets and fish in the boat and then finally of several tubs full of walleyes and northern. There were some huge walleyes full of eggs because those females were in there to spawn.

At a later date, I was shown an article in a local paper about a local bait dealer. He and his wife were giving a Ford car to the fisherman that brought in the largest walleye on the opening day of the walleye season on May 14th. One of the men we believed was involved in this incident claimed he caught the 11-pound / 12-ounce walleye and was given the car.

The fish was a big female full of eggs with the marks on its body and head from a gill net.

Chapter 56/ MC CLINTOCK—BLACK LAKE

It was June 20, 1976. I was out doing my normal patrol—basically checking lakes in my district for unlicensed watercraft and fishermen using illegal methods to catch fish. My normal approach was to look the lake over with my spotting scope or binoculars. I towed the state 14-foot boat and motor behind my patrol car on a trailer in the event I witnessed a violation out on the water.

I had visited a half dozen lakes east of Crosby, Minnesota in Crow Wing County without observing any violations.

I was near Black Lake, a lake I had never seen anyone fishing on. There was an access on the lake—just dirt, rock and sand. It was a very poor access if it was raining.

I drove into the access, and off to my right, I saw a pontoon boat tied up to the end of a dock. That was always there. To my knowledge there were no cabins on this lake.

Only this time, there was a fisherman sitting out on the pontoon. I thought I could see fish poles but because of the brush and leaves, I was not sure. The road from the access turns to my left or north. It parallels the lakeshore about 100 feet from the lake.

I followed up this road about a half mile to where I found a good place to turn my car and trailer around. I came back toward this fisherman looking for an opening from which I could observe the fisherman with my spotting scope. The scope would be clamped to the car window while I could sit comfortably behind the wheel observing this fisherman.

I got myself set up with the spotting scope and started my observation. I could see there were several poles so I moved the magnification from 15 power to 30 power. Now I was able to even see the lines. He had two casting outfits with lines running out east into deeper waters and one casting outfit with line going straight down to a small bobber on the north side of the pontoon. I was not sure if there were hooks on all the lines and I was curious about what he was using for bait.

He apparently got a bite on the pole by the pontoon because he lifted it up and he had a small sunfish on the hook. He then reeled in one of the lines to the east. It had a lively small sunfish hooked through the back with about a No. 6 hook. He cast that back out to the east and reeled in the other line. That also had a sunfish for bait but it appeared dead so he removed it and hooked on that small sunfish he had just caught and cast that line out to the east. Then he baited that hook on the pole next to the pontoon with a worm and lowered it into the water.

That was enough for me so I started my motor, drove back to the access, and turned west as though leaving the area. About two hundred yards down the road I locked up the car, took a summons books, a synopsis, and a ballpoint pen and took into the woods south. I wanted to approach this fisherman from the south, where he probably would not be watching for anyone. Most times these guys like to try to get the extra lines out, and in some cases they cut the lines or throw the whole fishing outfit in the lake.

I approached the dock from the southwest and walked out to within ten feet of the fisherman before he was aware I was there. I told him who I was and asked for his fishing license. He produced that which was OK. Then I told him he was in violation of angling with more than one line and using a protected fish for bait. I reeled in all his lines and made out a summons for angling with more than one line and then for using a protected fish for bait.

About that time he said, "You're no game warden or even a law enforcement man." So I showed him my badge, my patch on my shoulder, and my ID card with my picture on it.

"But you don't have a gun on you", he said.

I told him, "I don't need a gun for a simple arrest like this."

Then he came on strong and said, "I went through the Los Angeles Police Academy, left them, and now I'm a deputy sheriff just south of St. Paul. No law enforcement man in the United States can write a summons or make an arrest unless he has a full uniform on and that includes a side arm."

So I told him, "I never wear my side arm except when I work nights on spotlighting. I'm not a very good shot with a handgun so I have an old 92 Winchester 25/20 converted to a 38 special. I'm a much better shot with a rifle if I need a firearm and I always have that in the patrol car along with the state side arm."

I booked this Harlan McClintock into county court in Crosby before Judge Longfellow the following Friday.

The following Monday, I checked with the clerk of court and found everyone pled guilty except this McClintock. He had pled not guilty and wanted a twelve-person jury. I couldn't believe this guy was stupid enough to say he was not guilty and ask for a jury trial. The clerk of court advised me, "I'll let you know when the trial will be."

I said, "Thank you," and left.

About two weeks later, the chief of police in Crosby asked me if I knew the county attorney had received a letter from McClintock and was considering dropping the complaint. I asked the chief on what grounds he was going to. Then the chief showed me a photo static copy of the letter with a pencil mark around the chapter regarding a 38 special rifle.

I contacted my supervisor in Brainerd. The county attorney had told him what he planned to do. Supervisor Jovonovich was well aware of my struggle in my district especially with black people up around Adney Lake and Goggleye Lake. He found I had always been careful to have a good case before I started charging anyone. So he started in digging up the facts and background of this McClintock dude.

The trial was held on July 30, 1976. Forty days after I pinched this guy. He was found guilty on both counts and fined.

The county attorney ended up with egg on his face.

Chapter 57/ INDIANA FISHERMEN

One summer day, in 1976, while I was stationed at the Crosby/Ironton station in Crow Wing County, I got a telephone call from a man who wanted to meet me regarding some information he thought I would like. He didn't want me to come to his home so he told me when and where to meet him.

I made the contact. He told me, "I've tried to tell your predecessor, Walt Heineman, on several occasions but he didn't seem to be interested in the information."

I asked him, "What have you got?"

He then said, "There are four men from Indiana that are staying at the resort on the southwest side of Lower Mission Lake. They are out fishing every day. This is their third day and I have no idea when they will be leaving. They have a fourteen-foot boat with a small motor. Two men will go out on the lake fishing while the other two men stay at the cabin and clean fish. When these men fill up their limit (30 sunfish, 15 crappies, 6 bass, and 3 northern), they will come back to the cabin and then the other two will take the boat and go out and do the same thing. If you ever check them on the lake, they will never have over the limit in the boat."

I asked him, "Do you have any idea where they might be storing the fish?"

He said, "I have no idea. There are several places that would freeze and store the fish."

I thanked him for the good information and said that I would let him know how I made out if he would tell me how I could contact him. This was on a Wednesday.

I checked around the lake where I could set up to use my spotting scope. I wanted a place with cover and where no one would see me and become suspicious of my activity and possibly alert these Indiana fishermen. I finally found a place I could drive to without arousing suspicion. I had a 15' X 60' Bausch and Lomb telescope with a window mount. I could sit in the patrol car and observe most of the lake. I finally located a boat with an IN prefix on the numbers on the license of their boat. Like the man said, there were two men and I kept track of the number and species of fish. Then, like he said, they went to their cabin. So now I knew where they were staying. About fifteen minutes later, two different men came out and went fishing.

At sunrise, on Thursday, I was back again and spent the day with them. They kept every fish they caught regardless of size. However, when they were on the lake, they never had over their limit of any species. So went Thursday.

On Friday, the same thing happened.

One day, I actually witnessed two of the men come out and fill up their limit three times. I was afraid to check their cabin because I was sure they wouldn't be dumb enough to have too many fish in the cabin.

Friday evening was different. After taking the fish up to the cabin one of the men came down to the boat, took it over to the boat access where a station wagon with a boat trailer was backed down into the water. They loaded up the boat and drove up to their cabin. I was concerned they might be planning to pull out that evening. I drove my patrol car to within a couple hundred yards of their cabin. It was pitch dark by now. They loaded some of their gear into the boat and then covered the boat with a canvas cover. The cabin was well-lit, and occasionally I could see one of them pass one of the windows.

Around 7:30 p.m. all the lights were out. Their station wagon with the boat and trailer behind it were parked along side of the cabin. I was exhausted, hungry, and I felt cruddy. I hoped they were in bed for the night so I could go home and clean up, get some food inside me, and catch a few hours of sleep.

I went to my home in Ironton. My wife got after me for not calling in some help. However, she knew how bullheaded I could be, so she gave up, and fixed me a meal while I took a bath. Then, I hit the bed and set the alarm clock for 4:00 a.m. I asked my wife to be sure I got up when the alarm went off.

Bill and Pat in California on vacation from their DNR duties

However, I woke up before the alarm went off. I was sweating, I thought I had slept through the alarm and that my wife had let me sleep because she was concerned for my health. I got up, looked at the clock and I realized I had misread it in the dark. It was around 3:30 a.m., and my wife got up also. She had put up a couple of sandwiches and made a thermos of coffee before she came to bed. I never could have done my job without her help.

I hurried back to the resort. All the way I was thinking they might have gotten up around midnight and took off. I pulled into the area I had left the evening before. The cabin was black. My Indiana fishermen were still there. I remember I had a hard time staying awake. I think I was more exhausted than I liked to admit.

Around 5:30 a.m. it was getting quite light out. Then, I could see activity in the cabin. About this time my informant came up to my patrol car. He lived near there and he had seen me pull into the area the evening before. He asked, "Do they have the fish loaded yet?"

I told him, "I don't think so. They have put some gear in the trailer but no coolers are in evidence anywhere yet."

Then he said, "I'll get out of your way. Good luck."

About 7:00 a.m. some grips were brought out and loaded into the boat. Then, the men put the canvas boat cover on the boat and tied everything down good. Two of the men walked over to the resort office. I assumed to pay their bill. I was concerned as to where the fish were. The other two men drove the station wagon over to the resort office.

Then it happened. The two men that went to the office earlier came out with a huge white foam cooler. It appeared quite heavy. Then the other two men went into the resort office. Eventually they came out with seven coolers and were in the process of packing them in the station wagon. It was then that I heard Dave Mick, the warden from Brainerd, check in with the dispatcher. I called him and asked, "Where are you?"

He said, "I'm on the east side of Brainerd."

I told him, "Drop everything and immediately go north on County Road 3 to just past the Y, south of Edward Lake, and find a place to pull off."

I told him, "I have four men in a station wagon pulling a boat trailer with an Indiana license. They are just getting ready to pull out from a resort and I think they have too many fish. I'll follow them until we get away from the resort and then when they come to the stop sign at the Y, I will pull them over. However, if they spot me behind them and try to make a run for it, I will alert you and you can try to block them."

Dave Mick understood what he was to do. He managed to come north on County Road 3 passed the Y and had his patrol car parked off the road facing north with a good view of the road.

About this time, the Indiana vehicle pulled out onto County Road 3 and headed south. I pulled out and stayed about a quarter-of-a-mile behind them. As we got closer to the Y, I closed the distance to about a hundred yards.

Dave Mick called on the radio and said, "I see the outfit coming and now I see you right behind them."

I told Dave, "Pull in behind me, and when they pull up at the stop sign, at the Y, I will pull along side of them and motion to them to pull into the parking area across the street. We will see how they behave."

The Indiana vehicle came to a stop at the sign. I pulled along side and motioned to the driver where to go. The driver nodded compliance. Dave was up tight behind their trailer.

We followed the rig into the parking area and we all came to a stop. Everyone got out of their vehicles. The driver of the station wagon asked, "Is there something wrong?"

I told him, "We are game wardens and we want to check your angling licenses and count your fish." The men almost acted as though someone had knocked the wind out of them. Three of the men had non-resident angling license. The fourth man who was the driver and owner of the vehicle and the boat trailer had failed to acquire an angling license. I told him, "We have had all of you men under observation for three days, and you were fishing at various times on each of the three days, so you will get a summons for no angling license."

Then, I told them, "You can legally have 120 sunfish, 60 crappies, 24 black bass, and 12 northern." We took one of the containers out and opened it up. All of the fish on top were filleted out and frozen solid. I told the men, "We will all go over to the fisheries building and thaw out the fish so they can be counted. Some of the fillets are no bigger than the face of a watch."

One man spoke up and said, "We've got about a total of all our possession limit in one box."

I told them, "I am aware of that because while watching you, I noticed you keep every fish regardless of size."

Another man said, "We probably have seven times more fish in those coolers than we are allowed to have, maybe more."

So I told them, "I will charge each man with three times their possession limit and we will hold the coolers in a refrigerator area until court Monday morning in case the judge demands a count. The maximum penalty you can be charged is $300 each, plus, $50 for the one man with no license. You can plan on a total of $1,250."

I told them, "We will lock you men up until Monday so you don't leave the country."

One of the men said, "Can't we post bail and be on our way?"

I told him, "Yes, we will have to allow you that courtesy, but it has to be cash." They didn't have over $200 between the four of them. So, I said, "We will put you in jail until court, Monday. The judge will give you your options."

Then one man said, "Could we go to the Western Union and send a message to our wives to gather up the money and have it sent back via Western Union?"

I allowed them, "That can be done."

We held the men for about four hours. Then the Western Union said they had the $1,250 so we turned the men loose.

Chapter 58/ PRESEASON BASS FISHING

It was on May 4, 1977 in Crow Wing County that I received a call from the highway patrol dispatcher at Brainerd to contact my wife as quickly as possible regarding an ongoing violation. It was obvious to me that the information was hot and imperative or she would have given it to the dispatcher to relay to me. I had been made cognizant that many people had monitors tuned to the state police frequency and Patricia was aware that the people involved could have a radio monitor.

Patricia

I was not too far from Ironton so I went directly home. It turned out some individual had called in and reported that a man was fishing and catching largemouth black bass on Hamlet Lake. This individual also reported that this man had been doing this for years but Walt Heineman could never catch him.

The black bass season was closed and these fish are very vulnerable at this time of the year. The males are on around the clock guard of the nest that the female has laid her eggs in. The male will slam into anything with his head to drive away any kind of an intruder. The male also slams into any plug a fisherman puts near the nest, and then usually gets snagged on one of the many treble hooks on the plug. The male will stay at his post until the young hatch out. The season usually opens around Memorial Day.

This party would not leave his name but he did say that, at the time he was calling, the fisherman was out on Hamlet Lake in a small white rowboat and he was casting with false bait and catching black bass. This caller also said this party lived in the west bay of Hamlet Lake. Then he hung up.

I had never heard of Hamlet Lake so I dug out my inventory of Minnesota lakes book. The identification number was 18-70. It was about ten miles southeast of Ironton—a 313-acre lake.

I took off immediately and located the lake but when I arrived there was no boat out on the water. I was concerned that I might alert the fisherman or one of his friends and blow the case. With the aid of my binoculars, I did locate a small white boat that was partly pulled up on the shore on the south side of the west bay. I watched this lake for about an hour. No one went out fishing. I concluded that he must have caught all the fish he wanted for that day.

That evening, I called my neighbor, Brad Burgraff, and told him what had transpired that day. I told him, "Meet me. I will leave my vehicle and ride with you to Hamlet Lake. We will go close enough to the house where the boat is. If the boat is not pulled up on shore, I will jump out of my car near the house in question." Brad was to go to an area about a quarter-of-a-mile north of where I was and we could use our portable radios for contact.

The following day we met as planned. I directed Brad to Hamlet Lake. I had Brad slow down when we got near the house where the supposed bass fisherman lived. I was able to look through the brush to where the white boat had been beached the previous day.

The boat was gone so possibly our bass fisherman was out on the lake fishing. I told Brad to slow down almost to a stop about two hundred yards short of the house. I would slip through the brush and get as close to the house as possible without anyone seeing me.

Brad was to follow the road around the curve and to the north for about a quarter of a mile where he could find a place to pull off the road.

I got up close enough to the house so that I could see the walkway from the house to the beach from where I was. I could not see more than half of the lake. I could see Brad up north of me come out in the open between two cabins.

I could see him signaling me with his arms and holding up his portable. I hadn't turned on my radio yet. I knew where the on-off switch was and when I turned it on I got a real loud squawk, so I quickly turned it off. I reached for my glasses, as I have trouble reading up close. I didn't know which channel I had the set on. Again, I looked at Brad and the way his arms were swinging I thought he was doing the St. Vitus dance.

I crawled out to a big birch tree in the yard of the house to better see out on to the lake. Then I looked down and to the right and here was the white rowboat about seventy yards from me.

The man was really rowing the boat hard and he was coming into the beach right below me. I just dropped as flat to old mother earth as I could. That man beached the boat, baled out of it, and headed for the house on a dead run. He passed within twenty feet of me and he did not see me.

I didn't know if he had any bass in the boat and I didn't want to let him know I was there if he didn't have any fish. When I heard the door slam, I made a fast run for the boat and there was the evidence—seven largemouth black bass.

We had him. I turned to look for Brad and I could see him. I motioned for him to come to where I was. I sat down on the bow of the boat to wait for my fisherman. In about ten minutes, he came out, took two long steps before he realized I was there. Then he stopped and stared at me for a good minute and told me to get off his property.

I told him whom I represented and that he was under arrest for having black bass in possession in closed season. About that time, Brad showed up so we wrote him up and scheduled him into county court the next day. This fellow didn't feel he had done anything wrong so when I made out the seizure slip on the fish, I also made out one for his spinning rod. He got quite upset about that. He said he had just bought that outfit for his wife and it really belonged to her.

He wanted the rod and reel back. I told him that after a conviction in court the next day, it would be confiscated and he could go down to St. Paul the next time they had an auction. If he bid high enough, he could get his equipment back. He still thought he was being abused.

I then told him if he ever pulled this stunt again and I caught him I would also seize his boat. That seemed to get his attention.

He elected to post bail in the amount of $85 to us. I delivered it to the clerk of court the next day.

Oh, by the way, the reason the man was in such a hurry to get to his house was that he was having a nature call.

Chapter 59/ THE BANKS

It was around four p.m. on the twentieth day of November in the northeast part of Crow Wing County. The deer season was open. Those were the days when the game managers of the Conservation Department set the seasons and what could be taken. It was a complicated mess for law enforcement in that each hunter could select his three days to hunt within a ten-day period. Also, in this district, does were protected. It was bucks only.

I was just on a general patrol to check licenses, firearms, deer tags, and a dozen other requirements of anyone hunting deer. My area supervisor, Fred Hammer, chose this day to deadhead along with me to give me assistance if it was needed.

We drove north on County Road 106 to a dirt trail or township road that went east between sections five and eight in Ross Lake Township.

About two-tenths of a mile in on this trail, we came upon two hunters. The man on the south side of the road I recognized as Charlie Banks. Charlie and his wife lived over on Island Lake in Ross Lake Township. According to rumor, Charlie lived pretty much off the land. However, as of this date, I had no reason to believe he was a game and fish poacher. I checked his license, firearm, clothing, and there was nothing amiss.

I then turned to the young man sitting on the ground on the north side of the road. He, too, was dressed in red. Behind him laid a gun case. I opened the case and found a 94 Winchester 30-30 rifle, a popular rifle in Minnesota for hunting deer. I asked to see his deer hunting license and he produced a Minnesota small game license. I then had him empty out his pockets and he had eight 30-30 rifle shells in one of his pockets.

His license had been one where the license dealer used the buyer's driver's license to fill in the information for filling out the license.

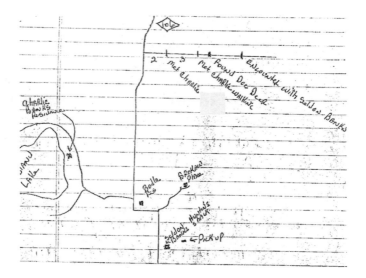

The birth date on the license led me to believe that he was 18½ years old. He was in deer hunting territory with a rifle and shells capable of killing a deer. I charged him with hunting deer without first procuring a deer hunting license.

After I had checked Charlie out, he told the lad he was going to start walking east on the trail. It took me about five minutes to do the paper work on the lad. About three-tenths of a mile further on, we caught up with Charlie. I stopped and asked him if he wanted a ride. He declined our offer.

About four-tenths of a mile further on, we saw a vehicle about a half a mile away coming toward us. It was across a ravine and was moving very slowly. As the trail is only wide enough for one vehicle, I knew of a pull-off just behind us. I quickly put the patrol car in reverse and hid the car in the pull-off spot.

We got out of the car and hid in the brush along the south side of the road. Looking through the brush, we could see the vehicle still coming at a very slow pace. There were two men in the pickup that we assumed were looking for a deer. There was a possibility that they would have a loaded, uncased gun in the pickup, so we stayed in the brush, listening and waiting, until the vehicle was about thirty or forty feet from us. It was coming up the hill on this side of the ravine. Then we stepped out. Fred was in the north rut and I was in the south rut. We held up our hands to command a halt. Both of us were in uniform with our badges shining.

Then something totally unexpected happened—the truck raced straight at us! The rear wheels were spinning and throwing up a cloud of dust higher than the truck. The back end of the truck started to whip one way then the other. It seemed I was right between the headlights when I made a mighty lunge into the brush on my right. I took a fast look to my left and it looked like the side of the truck box hit Fred. He was half hanging in the side of the truck box. I didn't know if he tried to get in the truck or if he was hit as the truck was whipping back and forth in their attempt to escape.

In a fraction of a second, the truck and Fred disappeared into a rolling cloud of dust and were gone. I ran to the patrol car and came out onto the trail. The dust was so thick that I couldn't see to drive. At that same instant, Fred came out of that huge cloud of dust. He was badly humped over and absolutely covered with dust. He told me his shoulder or collarbone was broken. He told me he almost ended up on the truck box and there was a deer there.

We started in pursuit but the dust was so thick I had to wait about three or four seconds before I could see to drive. I asked Fred if he could stand the pain from his broken bones while we continued the pursuit. He just said, "Go get those bastards."

About three-tenths of a mile back west, we came across a dressed out doe deer with an orange nylon rope for pulling around it's neck. I stopped and threw the deer in the trunk. This was about where Charlie should have been. A little further on we found that the lad was gone also. The dust tracks on the blacktop turned south but they soon disappeared so I headed for Charlie Banks' house. The truck was not there. I ran up to the door and a young lad answered my knock. I asked him if anyone in his or her party had a green pickup. The lad said, "Seldon does." Mrs. Banks came to the door and said no one in his or her party had a green pickup.

While in the vicinity of Charlie's house, I put in a call for assistance from any law enforcement. I wanted to get someone to take Fred Hammer to the hospital.

I then drove to the Bodle residence, Charlie's in-laws. Mr. Bodle said that Seldon Banks had a hunting shack on the east side of 106, south of the Bodle residence. He also verified that Seldon had a green pickup. I drove south into the old Brokaw place that now belonged to Seldon. No one was there.

We came out of there, went further south, and turned into a camp on the east side of the road. We drove past an old barn that had been converted into a hunting shack onto an old logging road. It was getting pretty dark by this time. I followed along on this trail until the ground seemed pretty soft. I could see in my car headlights a Minnesota license reflective license plate. I stopped the patrol car and walked up to the pickup. It obviously got stuck and was abandoned. It was too dark to try to track these men.

About this time, I saw the lights of a car pulling into the shack in back of me so I walked out to that car. The driver was Chester Banks, another brother. I told Chester what had happened and I wanted Seldon Banks and his partner in the encounter. I told him I would take my patrol car out to the county road if he would call them out.

About a half hour later, two sheriff cars came with Sergeant Dick Ross and Deputy Skip Rundquist. Also to the aid was the Emily police, Al Jensen, and a Breezy Point policeman, Al Orr.

About this time Chester came out with Seldon Banks. Seldon was put in Rundquist's car and his rights were read to him. At first, he claimed he was alone but finally admitted his brother, Coy Banks, was with him. Eventually, he admitted to transporting a doe deer and attempting to escape.

In the meantime, Al Orr transported Fred Hammer to the hospital. He was to undergo surgery the following Monday morning.

Pickup with dead deer

I went home and got my wife to help me get Seldon Banks' pickup truck to my residence where I also had the deer. I went back the next morning to measure out the distance for the county attorney's information in the event they pled not guilty.

The lad now claims to be a juvenile stating the date on his small game license was wrong. He also claims that he was born in Crosby. I checked court records and found he was a juvenile. Obviously, he had changed some numbers on his driver's license.

Eventually the following spring, trial was held in District

Court in Brainerd before Judge Spellacy. The Bank's attorney arranged to have separate trials and Seldon was to go first. He entered a plea of not guilty and had a twelve-person jury trial.

After Fred, the two deputy sheriffs and I testified. Seldon Banks' attorney offered to enter a guilty plea providing they could retire to the judge's chambers to do some plea-bargaining.

I never heard what happened to Coy Banks. I was told later by someone that was privy to the plea bargain that Seldon said when the two wardens stepped out into the road Coy hollered, "Step on it."

After the trial was over, the state set up the proceedings to transfer the title on the truck from Seldon Banks to the State of Minnesota. About a month later, I auctioned off the truck in front of the courthouse in Brainerd. It seems to me the highest bidder was around twelve hundred dollars.

Guilty Plea Cuts Short Criminal Trial

Seldon Banks, a 38-year-old man from Savage accused of trying to run down a game warden with a pickup truck last November, pleaded guilty in District Court yesterday to illegally transporting a doe and obstructing a peace officer by force or violence.

Banks' guilty plea cut short a jury trial scheduled in the case before Judge John Spellacy, Grand Rapids.

A third charge against Banks, of aggravated assault, was dismissed. The county attorney's office said that testimony from the four prosecution witnesses called in the case indicated that Banks had not actually intended to run over the game wardens involved.

Spellacy sentenced Banks to one year in jail on each count. Nine months of each count was suspended, and Banks was ordered to serve three months in the county jail on each count, for a total of six months.

He was also fined $500 on each count, for a total of $1,000. He was placed on probation for two years on condition that he do no hunting whatsoever.

Stephen Rathke, county attorney, had called four witnesses and had rested his case by 3 p.m. yesterday before Banks entered his guilty plea. Attorney Harold Fritz of Nisswa represented Banks.

Witnesses included the two game wardens involved, Fred Hammer and William Callies, and two sheriff's deputies, Dick Ross and Earl Rudquist.

The jury was excused about 5:30 p.m. yesterday.

Chapter 60/ TRAPPING SEASON

It was the first day of the mink and muskrat season. The trappers could start setting their traps at noon. It was just a few minutes after sunup when I was launching the state fourteen-foot boat at the access at Riverton to go into Little Rabbit Lake. The sun was coming up and it promised to be a really nice day. It was my intent to go through the outlet from Little Rabbit Lake into the Mississippi River to check duck hunters, fishermen, and possibly, some early trappers.

While still in Little Rabbit Lake, I came across three black people in a boat fishing—an older man, a young man, and a young lady. They had just started fishing, so they didn't have any fish at this time. I pulled along side their boat and asked to see their angling license. The young man produced a resident individual angling license. The older man produced a combination husband and wife resident angling license. The license showed their age as well into their sixties. I then asked the young lady for her license and the old fellow said, "You already saw it. She is my wife."

I told the old fellow, "Give the license back to me so I can recheck the age on the license." It showed the wife to be in her sixties. I then asked the young woman, "What's your name?" The old fellow responded with the name. I told him to keep quiet and then I asked her, "What's your address?" She didn't say anything and again the old fellow blurted out the address. That was enough, so I finally got the correct information from her and it did not match the combination license. I wrote her a summons, to wit, "Did angle for fish without first obtaining an angling license".

The old fellow was quite put out. He said, "My wife wasn't fishing today so in her absence this young lady was just taking her place."

I told him, "Explain that to the judge." I then moved through to the outlet onto the river. Directly ahead of me on the west bank I saw some buildings and a number of beehives.

When I was a kid down in Iowa we had bees. The most we had were eleven swarms. Mostly we got the honey for our own consumption, but we did sell the surplus of maybe a hundred pounds, more or less.

This party had a boat dock straight ahead that had room to tie another boat or two. So I tied up the boat and went up to talk to these people. I met the man out in a small shed and introduced myself as the new warden in the area. I then got into the art of beekeeping. This man was more knowledgeable on the subject than I. We got into a real compatible conversation.

I also noticed a lot of animal traps and stretch boards in the little shed.

This man allowed that this was about the time of the morning he would go into the house and have a cup of coffee and a homemade roll. He only had to ask once if I would join him. This man introduced me to his wife and we all sat down to hot coffee and fresh, hot, cinnamon rolls. The conversation was about beekeeping. Then, I finally got around to trapping. It finally came out that this man was very upset about early trappers. He told me there were three men from the Merrifield area that made it an annual thing to get into that area of the river and skim the cream of the mink and muskrats.

I asked him, "Have you ever reported this to anyone from the Department of Natural Resources."

He said, "I told Walt Heineman and Walt always told me he had other complaints but he would try to get down there and clean up the problem. To the best of my knowledge, I don't think Walt got down in this area."

I then asked, "Would you divulge the name of these early trappers?"

He said, "You bet I will." His wife tried to downplay this

information. I think she was afraid of some reprisal. I assured her there was no way these men, if I was fortunate enough to catch them, would ever be told by me that they, the beekeepers, ever gave me any information.

The man was in the process of writing their names down. He had to use the telephone directory to get the addresses.

I thanked them for the coffee break, got in my boat and started to move down stream about a half mile. Some distance ahead of me, I saw two people in a boat, close into shore. The person in the front seat raised a firearm to his shoulder. Then he took the gun down and they motored ahead and picked something up out of the water. I shut off my outboard motor, picked up my binoculars, and watched them as they started to move on. I could see their boat seemed to slow down and then stop. Again, the person in the front seat lifted a gun to his shoulder. I didn't hear a shot but again the gun was lowered and the boat moved up and away, and the person in front using a dip net scooped something out of the water. I took after this boat in earnest.

It was a father and son. The son was the gunner. They had several muskrats in the boat, all of them shot and they had a loaded uncased twenty-two rifle in the boat. Muskrats can only be taken by trapping, so I charged the men for taking the rats illegally—taking them in closed season (it was around 10:30 a.m.) and transporting a loaded, uncased firearm in a motorboat. I made out seizure slips for the gun and rats and told them that I could also seize the boat and motor. If I ever caught them doing this again, I would. I also made out the summons for them to appear in court and released them when they signed all the papers.

I then continued onto a small island. I pulled the boat up and tied it to a small tree. I picked up my binoculars and sat down on an old log. I sat there for about a half an hour when I saw a canoe on the west side of the river with two men in it. They were paddling upstream when they pulled into shore.

Using my binoculars, I saw the front man get out of the canoe. He had hip boots on and walked to a place ahead of the canoe. He had a small stick or club in his hand that he struck at something next to the shore. Then he lifted up a single spring trap with a muskrat in it. He took the rat out of the trap, stuck it into his hunting coat, and appeared to set the trap. He went back to the canoe and the two men started upstream again about a hundred yards where they pulled the canoe up out of the water.

Then the man pulled the rat out of his coat and started skinning it out. All of this was being done before they were legally allowed to even set their traps. These two had obviously set their traps at least the day before the season.

When the man finished skinning the rat, he tossed the carcass in the river and put the pelt in the back of his hunting coat. Then the two men started walking in a westerly direction along what looked like a small creek until they were out of sight.

I got into my boat and went across the river to the place where the trap was, snapped it off, and pulled the stake. Then I moved the state boat to the canoe. I located the rat carcass, pulled it out of the river, and put it in the state boat with the trap.

I sat down by their canoe and waited. About a half-hour later, I saw one of them coming toward me. He saw me about the same time. Just that quick, he disappeared. Within a minute, he came boldly walking down the trail toward me. I asked him, "Where is your partner?"

He said, "I have no partner."

Then I told him, "Give me the muskrat pelt."

He said, "I don't have any muskrat pelt."

Then I told him I had both of them under surveillance for a half hour. I had the rat carcass and the trap in my boat. Then I said, "I will give you five minutes to go back and get that muskrat skin and call out your partner or I will seize your canoe for the state." I also told him, "I will charge you and your partner with trapping and taking a muskrat in closed season and I can find and identify your partner if I have to. Now, either call your partner out and go back and get that rat skin or kiss your canoe goodbye."

It was beginning to look like too great a loss, so he went back and picked up the rat skin and hollered for his partner. I wrote up a summons on both of them, plus seizure tags for the trap and rat hide, and released them.

Later on I checked out some duck hunters. Then I started to think about the list the beekeeper had given me. It turned out that I had written up all three of the men that were on his list— the boat operator, on the first incident, and the two men with the canoe.

On my way back to my patrol car, I stopped in at the beekeepers place. After a few pleasantries, I showed him my summons book. He was elated. He told me, "Anytime you are near my home and you want something to eat, our kitchen is open to you anytime of the day or night."

Chapter 61/ *STURGEON AT CLEMENSON*

One summer day I was in my patrol car. I was just coming into Clemenson on Highway #11. Clemenson is a town of about ten people.

There is a gas station that also carries some groceries with a pool table in the back room. The owner also has a half-a-dozen small cabins across the highway that he rents out to tourists.

There were several people ahead of me selecting pop, candy, etc. I had a light tan jacket over my warden shirt and although the owner knew who I was, I don't believe any of the customers realized I was a game warden.

The entrance door opened behind me and a small man in his fifties interrupted the owner and said, "Quick put this in your deep freeze." He had a long piece of butcher wrapping paper in his two hands partially covering a fair-sized fish.

I moved in, pulled up one corner of the paper and noted it was a sturgeon with the head and entrails missing. I made the statement, "The fish is short on one end."

This man assured me, "The fish was legal when the head was on."

I asked, "Where is the head?"

He said, "It's over in the fish cleaning shack."

So, I told him, "We will just take this fish over to the cleaning shack, hold the head on one end and measure it."

We found the head, and with the fisherman holding the head loosely against the carcass it measured 39 inches. I told the man, "The minimum length on a sturgeon to be legal is 45 inches."

Then this man asked me, "What's this going to cost me?"

I told him, "The bail schedule on an undersize sturgeon is $100.00."

Then this man said, "I caught the fish on the Canadian side of the river and they only have to be 36 inches over there."

I then asked him, "Do you have a Canadian angling license?" I was really surprised when he came up with one. This man was from Iowa and he had both a Minnesota and a Canadian license.

I then told him, "Sturgeons have to be 45 inches in Canada also."

He told me, "You're wrong, the Canadians use the metric system but I can't remember the figures but it amounts to 36 inches."

I asked him, "Do you have a Canadian synopsis?"

He said, "I do, but, I don't know where it is."

I looked in my patrol car and I didn't have one either. However, I told him, "As long as you said it was caught on the Ontario side of the river, I will have to turn you over to the Ontario wardens and when we go through customs we can check on the synopsis at their office."

When we got to the customs office, we went inside and I got ahold of an Ontario fishing synopsis. I showed him where it showed 45 inches.

Then I thought I would have a little fun with him so that he would realize in the future that the laws included him.

I asked him, "Do you have $200.00 on you?"

He asked, "Why?"

So, I told him, "The fine or bail is $200.00 over in Ontario and I am going to turn you and the fish over to Roy Brown who is the warden supervisor at Fort Francis and he will set up a court date. If you don't have enough money to post bail, Roy won't fool around with you. You will go to jail and it could be a week or ten days before your trial comes up." He just begged me to run him through the Minnesota court.

Chapter 62/ SOUTHERN MINNESOTA FARMERS

One winter day, I was on my snow sled checking fishermen up north of Longpoint on Lake of the Woods. I pulled up by one man and he produced an angling license and he didn't have any fish.

I decided to sit on the sled, kind of close to him, while I started to look over other fishermen with the aid of my binoculars. The man seemed a bit nervous with me staying so close to him, but he tolerated me. There were two men and a boy fishing that caught my eye. They were quite active pulling out fish. The fish appeared small so I assumed they were saugers and they could legally have forty-two.

Bill owned this snow sled even before snowmobiles were issued to wardens. He used it on the lakes to check ice fishermen.

One of the men filleted fish in between pulling them out. He put the entrails, heads, backbones, and skins back down a hole. Also, I noted the sack holding the fillets was pretty good size. They kept the sack underneath a sled that was towed by their snowmobile.

Then the operator of the snowmobile started off with his snowmobile towing the sled and leaving the sack of fish exposed. I figured I had better go with my snowsled and check out that sack. This fisherman went about a quarter-of-a-mile west and was meeting another fisherman. I had about the same distance to get to the sack. This man spied me and he came back just a flying. He beat me to the sack and ended up with his sled between me and the sack of fish. I walked around and looked in the sack and I could see he had way too many fish. Also, I told him when the fish are filleted out we had to count them as walleyes and they could only have eighteen. But, I said, "I'll count them."

I laid out a large plastic bag. Two fillets made one fish. They had 168 fillets, which would be eighty-four fish. I said I would give them a break and count them as saugers. So they had forty-two saugers over their legal limit.

The other partner came over and asked what the problem was and I told him. "You guys have too many fish."

He just said, "What's that going to cost us?"

I told him, "You can mail in the bail and forfeit."

Then he said, "What does bail come to?"

I said, "I'll make it $400 and I'm seizing the fish and you guys are done fishing today."

He said, "That sounds reasonable, will you take a check?"

I said, "Yes."

They were residents of Minnesota so he borrowed a pen from me, got down on one knee and he muttered as he was making out the check, "I'll just go home and sell another cow."

GRANDPA'S OLD SHOTGUN AND DAD

It was the second Saturday in December of 1929. Just a month or so after the big stock market collapsed. Our family was extremely fortunate in that my dad was a Train Dispatcher for the M & St. L Railroad. The dispatcher's office for the central division was located in Fort Dodge, Iowa. It was absolutely compulsory that a train dispatcher be on duty twenty-four hours a day, seven days a week, or the trains would not move.

My dad had the four to midnight shift which he enjoyed. It gave him the better part of daylight hours to hunt, fish, trap, and gather berries, nuts and firewood.

On this particular day, I was allowed to accompany Dad to check his trap line up at the ore beds on the Des Moines River about eight miles north of Fort Dodge. We left home about 6:00 a.m. in Dad's Model 'A' Ford sedan. The day was overcast, cold, with little or no wind. There was frost everywhere on the ground.

When we arrived at a place that was as close as a car could be driven, we got out and pulled out our gun cases. Dad removed his old double-barrel twelve-gauge shotgun from the case. The gun had been the property of my grandfather, at that time deceased. It was a trap grade, L. C. Smith made by Hunter Arms with two large exposed hammers that had to be cocked individually by hand. It was my dad's pride and joy.

I uncased my shotgun which was a double-barrel 410 gauge hammerless shotgun that fired the old 2½-inch shells. This gun had been given to me by my grandfather on my mother's side when I was eight years old. I am now twelve years old and at this day and age I had become quite adept at using this little gun. In fact, I made it a point when hunting with my dad to never touch off a trigger unless I was sure I would hit my target—be it a squirrel, cottontail rabbit, pheasant or a duck. Dad could not and would not tolerate a miss. Early on in my younger years he would grab a stick or a cornstalk and dust my britches if I missed what I was shooting at.

The air was sharp and cold as we made our way west to the river where my dad had a couple of dozen 1½ Victor traps set for mink and muskrats. Dad had told me when he was up at the river on the previous day, that the river was pretty well froze up except for a few spots that were shallow where the water flowed fast and the ice had not formed.

Also, he had told me he shot a pair of fat corn-fed mallards in an opening on the river about a quarter-of-a-mile ahead on the previous Thursday. Then he admonished me to walk quietly—don't step on and crack any sticks. Also, don't take a shot at a rabbit if one appeared until we had checked this open spot in the river for ducks.

We were finally within a hundred yards of the river. There were a few large trees and lot of high grass and weeds bordering the river. At this point, Dad stopped, got down on his knees and whispered to me that I should stay there while he crawled up to a big tree that he pointed out.

Off Dad went on his belly. When he arrived at the tree, I saw him very carefully peek around the tree, then his head came back. From past experiences, I knew there were ducks out there. However, I did as I was told. I laid back there waiting for a motion of my dad's hands as to what I was to do.

The next time I could see Dad, he was behind the tree near the ducks. He turned his face towards me and I could see he had two shells protruding from his mouth. His hand signal motioned me to move up and also be quiet. I knew there had to be a lot of ducks out there.

The normal routine under these circumstances was for Dad to take the pot shot on the water. He could kill a lot more with the 12 gauge than I could with the 410. Then he muttered to me,

"Get ready." With that, he touched off his first shot and as I was leaping to my feet, I heard his second shot and I could vaguely see another duck spin out. Then I got off my two shots picking two drake mallards. Dad had reloaded, cocked both hammers and two more ducks came down out of that mass of ducks. Seems to me we ended up with ten or eleven big fat corn-fed mallards.

Dad had hip boots on, so he waded out and picked up the ducks. Dad suggested I pack that bunch of ducks back to the car. Those birds weighed close to four pounds each so I had quite a load to carry back to the car.

I knew Dad would be working upstream checking his traps so on completion of my task, I started to follow the river upstream where eventually I came upon my dad. He was almost at the end of his trap line. He had picked up a couple of mink and a half dozen rats.

We skinned the rats out at the far end of his trapline so we wouldn't have so much to carry. He was so fussy about his mink that he would rather take them home to skin out and stretch.

While we were skinning the rats out, we heard a strange pierping sound which caused us to look in the direction of that sound. It was a small flock of geese—looked to be seven in all. These were the first geese I had ever seen. They were very rare in those days. I had seen pictures of them in sporting magazines. Dad said he had seen geese when he worked out in South Dakota as a train operator in his younger years, however, he never got close enough to one to shoot. Finally we got back to the car and returned to Fort Dodge and cleaned our pile of ducks.

While cleaning the ducks, and before Dad had to clean up to go to work, he said, "Tomorrow when we go to check the traps, should we go before church or after?" Church started at ten o'clock.

I answered, "Before!!"

So Sunday morning, we left home about 5:30. It was still

dark when we parked the car. We went through the same routine only it was harder to see as we headed for the river.

Again, we came to that place on the river where we shot all those ducks the day before. The same routine was carried out— Dad crawled down to the tree, took a peek, turned and looked at me then he took another peek. The next time I could see him he had two shells in his mouth. I couldn't believe those mallards would come back to that same open water. Dad looked back at me but he was real slow about motioning to move up.

Finally, he motioned me to move up to him but there was an unusual amount of motioning to be quiet. Then he pointed out to the river, which meant I was to take note of what was out there. I couldn't believe my eyes as I peered through the grass. There were seven long black and white necks. Dad told me later that my eyes almost popped out of my head. Then of all things, there was a big mink off to our left at the shoreline. I whispered to Dad, "Mink."

Dad just shook his head, "No." To me that mink looked like a ten dollar bill.

The mink knew we were there but also he was interested in those geese. The geese were all eyes on the mink which gave us quite an advantage. Finally Dad muttered, "Get ready." He fired one shot and I was bouncing to my feet when I saw a bird collapse to Dad's second shot.

I fired at the closest bird only to see both his feet fall down from its body. I hadn't led that bird enough, so I increased my lead by two feet and fired the second barrel. The bird came down. Out of the corner of my eye I could see the two shells from Dad's mouth spinning through the air and his right hand grabbing to catch them.

I was sure I was in for a licking for only getting one goose down with my two shots. Then to my surprise, the goose I shot at was still alive. Dad had three birds dead out on the water.

The goose I had crippled started honking and to our amazement the three birds that escaped started to swing back.

Dad said, "I believe that crippled bird could call those other birds back." Then he said, "Forget it. We have enough food now to take care of." With that, I picked up a stick and with a mighty swing dispatched the crippled goose.

Again, Dad said, "You carry both of our guns and the four geese back to the car. We have done enough killing." I would carry two geese and one gun a hundred yards or so then go back and get the other two and the gun. Eventually, I got everything up to the car and waited for Dad.

When he got back to the car, he even congratulated me for getting one goose especially as I only had number 7 1/2 shot in my shells where as Dad was using number 6 shot in his old L. C. Smith. Dad complained that he could only find one of the two shells that fell to the ground that he had in his mouth.

Bill and his Dad with geese

So, we got home. Mother came out with the old box camera and took all six pictures on the roll of film. Then Dad and I changed clothes and we were off to church.

Somehow or other, one of the pictures showed up with a story along side of our good fortune in the <u>Fort Dodge Messenger</u> and eventually in the state paper, <u>The Des Moines Register</u>.

All of a sudden, we were almost being treated like heroes. There was a sporting goods store in town known as "Kautzkys". They were a very prestigious family of gun-makers that had moved to the United States from Europe around 1900. They contacted my dad and invited him to join them at their trap-shooting club to take part in their annual turkey shoot before Christmas. The event was to take place on the Saturday before Christmas.

Dad got directions to get out to this gun club and Saturday morning found Dad, Mother, my sister and I driving out to this gun club. Dad uncased his old shotgun and deposited it in a gun rack along side about twenty other shotguns. As I remember, there were a few other double-barrel shotguns but none with exposed hammers. There were several slick looking slide-action shotguns and even some that were semi-automatic.

It was suggested Dad sign up to shoot. I believe the fee was a dollar. Sixty cents was for a box of twenty-five twelve-gauge target loads. The forty cents went toward the acquisition of the prize—one live turkey. I remember Dad kind of groaned because he thought he was invited for free. He did put up his dollar and his name was added to a sheet with four other shooters.

Finally, the five men were called up and they each selected their station on the sixteen-yard line. We had noticed the previous shooters always put their guns to their shoulders and pointed their guns out over the little building the clay target came out from. Then they would holler, "Pull." The clay target would then come out very fast in various directions.

When it was Dad's turn to shoot, he would insert a shell in the right barrel, cock the hammer on the right side, then without putting the gun to his shoulder, he hollered, "Let her go." Then he mounted the gun to his shoulder and smashed the target and so it went until every man had shot his twenty-five shells.

There was an occasional miss and the judge would call out, "Lost." If you broke the clay target he would call out, "Dead." Then he would make an entry onto the sheet.

It ended up that Dad and one other shooter broke every target so they had to have a shoot-off, which caused my dad to have to come up with another dollar for a box of shells

The two men started shooting from the seventeen-yard line where they each broke five targets then they moved to the eighteen-yard line. Finally on the nineteen-yard line the other fellow missed one and Dad broke his. Our family was elated.

Dad went back to claim his turkey at which time, Joe Kautzky suggested that Dad sign up for another round—Dad declined and told Joe Kautzky, "No thanks, one turkey is enough."

SHIELDS LAKE

This is a fishing story and it is actually what happened.

It was early summer in 1938. I was installing floor covering for anyone who would hire me. Most of my installations were in new construction mostly for Thomas Moulding out of Chicago or the C.O. Dunham Company out of Minneapolis. At this time, I worked a lot of time in Mankato, Albert Lea, and Faribault for Dunham. Some of the workmen on my last job were pretty enthused about sunfish in Shields Lake.

I was told that there was a boat livery on Shields Lake but if you wanted to get a boat on Sunday, you best get there early because that was the prime place to go after church by the local

German farmers.

I asked my number one girl friend if she would like to go fishing. She answered with an enthusiastic, "Yes!" However, I don't know if she knew what she was getting into. Anyway, on a Sunday after church, we went down to Faribault and made inquiries about how to find the boat livery on Shields Lake. I had two cane poles with fishing lines; bobbers, sinkers and a common single hook attached to each. The poles were about fourteen feet long.

At the boat livery, we found there were a couple of flat-bottomed twelve-foot boats to rent each with one pair of oars, an anchor, and about twenty feet of anchor rope. The rope went through a small pulley up on the bow of the boat. The person rowing the boat could release the anchor without leaving his seat in the middle of the boat. There was a bracket to attach the free end of the rope so that you could pull the anchor up to the front-end pulley and tie it off while moving.

The boat cost fifty cents for a half a day. I paid the operator.

Then I asked the boat owner if I could borrow a fork to dig in his cow manure pile for a mess of grub worms. That was approved and we dug up about forty worms for bait.

Patricia and I got in our little rented boat with our cane fishing poles, anchor, and a pair of oars for propulsion—no cushions or life jackets.

As I rowed out on the lake, I became aware of a huge cluster of boats off to our right. They were all using huge cane poles, maybe eighteen to twenty feet long. I kept my eye on them and I never saw one cane pole stand up indicating some one had a bite. Apparently where they were could have been a hot spot the weekend before.

At any rate, I baited the hooks on our two lines, set the bobbers so that our baited hooks would be about eight feet below the surface. There was a gentle wind blowing. All the time, I'm keeping my eye on that mass of fisherman to the west of us and not once did I see one of those cane poles come up.

We dropped our baited hooks in the water and started drifting about on the lake. Occasionally I would use the oars to change our movement. Then one of us got a bite—one beautiful sunfish that was almost a pound. We maneuvered close to the area and we each had a sunfish on our hooks.

I very quietly unhooked the anchor rope and let the anchor go to the bottom. We really had a rush of nice-sized sunfish. We had about fifteen on our stringer. You were allowed thirty sunfish for each licensed fisherman. I told my wife-to-be that we had enough. Then I looked to the west at that mass of boats each with two poles pointed skyward. They almost looked like masts on a sailboat. The boats were about half a mile away but heading towards us. There were oars flashing in the sunlight.

I told Patricia, "Don't take your fish off the hook. Instead put it back in the water and then pull the fish back out for the benefit of that mass of boats and fishermen coming towards us." I did the same thing with the last sunfish I caught. At the same time I took the anchor rope up and pulled the anchor up to just below the surface. The slight breeze took us away from that school of sunfish.

We kept up our ruse until the mass of boats was within about fifty yards of us. Then I eased the anchor back to the bottom. Then with one more display of pulling a sunfish out and putting it on our stringer. I pulled the anchor up to the pulley on the bow of the boat.

This mass of boats almost completely surrounded us. There were a lot of "oohs" and "ahhs" as I lifted our string of sunfish into the boat.

Then came the sounds of the water splashing as some of them plopped their anchors into the lake and the swoosh of air as those people swung their poles out to start fishing.

I had a difficult time to maneuver our boat through this mass of boats.

As I was rowing toward the boat livery, I kept an eye out

on that bunch of fisher people. Not once did I see a pole lift up pulling a fish out. Our ruse worked!!

The boat liveryman congratulated us on our nice catch. I told him that we had enough to clean and we were looking forward to some fabulous eating.

Pat and Bill in the '30s

MY WORST BOAT TRIP

The place was on Lake Kabetogama in northern Minnesota. I was nineteen-years-old. It was in the month of June 1937.

I had a job installing floor covering for the Thomas Moulding Floor Covering Company. The jobs were mainly in new schools, hospitals, and office buildings. Sometimes we worked for two or three months without a day off. Then there would be a two or three-week layoff. I had a 1936 Ford Coupe for transportation.

My folks had purchased about a twenty-five acre government lot from a commercial fisherman by the name of Ed Townes on the north side of Kabetogama, directly across from the Ash River Narrows. There was a one-room log cabin and an outside dubisary. My folks would allow me to stay at this place in between dry work spells. Occasionally, I picked up a day's work at the various resorts laying linoleum or tile. Sometimes Bill Palmer, from the Frontier Lodge, would have me go with some of his guests. Basically it was to see that his people would not get lost among the islands on Lake Kabetogama and Namakan Lake and to see that his boats were not abused on the rocks (they were all made of wood in those days). To catch fish was no problem. You could catch nice-sized walleyes anyplace. The limit was eight a day with twelve in possession. No one ever returned with less than their two day possession limit, which was usually caught in two or three hours.

A couple hundred yards west of the mouth of the Ash River Narrows on the south shore of Kabetogama was a family of commercial fisher people. John Slatinski was the name. My dad always referred to him as "Fisherman John".

Old John was a tall, rugged individual. He was rough and tough and he wouldn't back down from anyone or anything. John and Bill O'Conner, the game warden, were always at odds. John coughed a lot, some say he had TB, but that never slowed him down.

Off and on, when John knew I was at my folks' log shack, John would hire me as a helper to go along with him to lift his nets and gut and gill the walleyes caught in his nets. He had acquired a helper's license from the State of Minnesota. This license had no specific name on it, so whoever John could get to go along with him would be covered to legally assist a licensed commercial fisherman. To go with John to check his nets was a two-day affair. He had a large boat pointed at both ends similar to a lifeboat on big ships. It was powered by a four-cylinder marine engine with a drive shaft down through the keel. It had a rudder that was controlled by a small chain that was run through screw eyes just under the gunnel all the way around the boat. I would guess the boat was thirty-feet long and about seven-feet wide. It was well built—solid and heavy. The operator stood mid-ship with his hand on an iron lever to control the boat. When the lever was pushed forward, the boat would turn to starboard and back to port. Also, right along side the operator was a small cistern pump with a suction pipe down into the bilge. There was also a false deck to stand on.

There was no overhead or windshield—it was a bare bones work-boat. There was a small cabinet up in the bow and John told me he once came across a timber wolf swimming. He opened the door to the cabinet leaned over the gunnel, grabbed the wolf by the tail and the scruff of the neck, heaved the animal into the cabinet and slammed the door. That story sounded pretty weird but knowing John, I believe it could have happened.

John had arranged for me to be over at his dock about 6:00 a.m. one morning for a two-day fishing trip. It was against the law to net fish in Kabetogama. All the nets were in the border waters. John fished in Namakan Lake along with three other licensed commercial fisherman—Emil Torre, who concentrated on white fish, then there was Herbie Williams and "Prunes" who lived on Sheen Point.

We came to the first net in Junction Bay. We lifted the net, removed the walleyes, and put them in fish boxes half-filled with ice from John's icehouse. We rinsed the nets in a mild solution of lye water (the nets were made from linen). Then we would get out our cleaning boards, laying them across the gunnels, and start the cleaning process. The herring gulls were all around us gobbling the guts and gills as we pulled them out. It was a screaming process as the gulls fought to get the guts. Sometimes they lit on your head or shoulders and on the cleaning boards. Some of them gorged themselves so much they could hardly fly. When they got like that, some of them just jumped off the boat into the water.

Then we went from net to net and we finally ended up in Cameron Bay where John had an overnight shack. The next morning found us back out on the lake clerking the nets but heading for home. Quite often, John would pick up Prunes' and Williams' fish to be hauled down to the government dock at the west end of Kabetogama the following day. This area is known as Gappa's, a store and a small bar near the dock. We arrived at John's place, took the fish boxes into the ice house, and iced the fish down with fresh ice. John then asked if I was free to accompany him the next day to meet McCarthy's fish truck at the government dock. I agreed to go with him, but the next day I sure had some second thoughts.

This day I was up around 6:00 a.m., made myself a mess of pancakes, stuck a couple in my coat pocket, and went down to the dock where I had Dad's little flat-bottom boat tied up. There was a smart northwest wind blowing, creating some big roller waves. I had a pair of good six-foot oars for propulsion. I began to wonder if John would cancel the trip to Gappa's. I even was concerned about the quarter-mile of water I would have to travel to get over to John's. While sitting in my little boat at the bottom of the waves, the waves on either side of me were seven or eight-feet higher. I would roll up on one then slide down the other side. I can assure you I was busy with my oars.

I finally made it to John's dock and tied up. I found John carrying out the fish boxes with the fish and ice bulging out at the top. John growled at me for being late so I kept my mouth shut and started carrying fish boxes. I can assure you we had a load on that boat evenly distributed around on the false deck. John figured we had about a ton of fish and ice.

I was sincerely concerned and I let John know of my concern. We had about ten miles to go west, right into the wind. John just said, "The McCarthy fish truck will be at the government dock by noon and we have to get those fish down there." John had two old cork life jackets he picked up from World War I surplus. They were bulky to wear.

John cranked up that little four-cylinder marine engine and we were off. In no time that boat started to feel like a water-soaked log. There was a bilge pump hooked to the motor that shot a constant two-inch stream of water plus John was constantly pumping the little cistern pump.

It wasn't long when we realized the two pumps could not begin to remove the water that was coming into the boat from the spray and the boat got so heavy it would just plow into the middle of the next wave. The water was least a foot thick that just poured in over the bow.

I looked at John facing into the spray and water—his jaws were clenched. Finally, he could see it was a losing battle. John swung the boat side-ways to the waves and we would roll up one side and slide down into the trough on the other side. Then we could see there was water eight or ten inches deep on top of the false deck. I shifted some of the fish boxes so I could get a pail down in to help with the bailing. Between the bilge pump, the hand cistern pump, and my pail we got the water down below the false deck. John kept on for another twenty minutes then he announced we would pull into a bay on the south side where there was a blind pig (unlicensed bar). I don't know if it was Nebraska Bay or the Blind Ash Bay.

At any rate, we were out of those pounding, rolling waves. John told me to stay by the boat and keep pumping with the hand pump until no more water came out while he attended to some business in that shack on the hill.

I finally got the water out of the bilge and took off to the building I saw John go into. I found John standing up to a little bar with a glass of beer and a shot glass full to the brim. We used to call that combination "boiler makers".

After about a half hour, John and I walked down to the boat. The water was relatively quiet in the bay. John looked to the north, out on the big part of the lake, and announced it looked like the wind had gone down some and so had the waves.

I spoke up and told John, "The lake is as wild as when we left it."

John responded, "I have to get those fish down to the government dock. Anyway I've got my nerve up now." I'm sure I could have stayed there but I knew if I did, John would not pick me up on the way home nor would he ever hire me again. So I shut my mouth, untied the boat from the dock, and jumped on board.

When we hit the big water, it was just like when we left it. John stood there like a statute—face into the spray and wind. Both of us were soaked to the skin. When the boat started to lose its lift, John would put her sideways until we got most of the water out. Then he would put the bow heading west. To this day, I don't know how we made it but we did. McCarthy's truck was out on the government dock. We were an hour-and-a-half late but the driver said he knew John would make it through.

John instructed me to stay and help take the fish off the boat and load them on the truck. John, in turn, took off for Gappa's store and bar. At one time, we heard a big commotion coming from Gappa's. The trucker said, "I'll bet old John got in a fight at the bar."

I sat around the store drying myself off. John was taking on some more beer. He looked like his two front teeth were missing. Finally he said, "Young fellow, it's time to go home." He bought two picnics of beer (quart size). The wind had gone down to just a slight breeze and the sun was showing through the clouds.

We untied the boat, John crawled up on a small poop deck and instructed me to take us home. As I looked back, the sun was settling in the west and John was sucking on one of those big bottles.

John paid me $5.00 for three days.

The store on Broadway North in Minneapolis where Pat and Bill met

Double wedding ceremony of Bill, Patricia, Monica, and Jerome, 1941

Bill, Patricia, Monica, and Jerome, 50 years later

Dorothy (Doff) and Bill on their wedding day in 1998

William Henry Callies of Hibbing died at age 86 on September 21, 2003 at Leisure Hills Nursing home where he was a patient after having heart procedures done. He was born July 6, 1917 in Fort Dodge, Iowa to Ivanette and Edgar Callies.

Bill lived a most interesting, exciting life; a member of the Minnesota National Guard during the trucker's strike of 1934 in Minneapolis, a manager of F. W. Woolworth stores in Minneapolis, Rhinelander and Sioux Ste. Marie. As a manager in Minneapolis, he met his "Million Dollar Baby in a 5 and 10-cent Store", Patricia Sanders, and they were married in 1941. He was in the floor covering trade as a journeyman and joined the Navy in 1942. Bill served during World War II as a Gunner's Mate. Back in the Twin Cities after the war, he worked in the floor covering business again and was a foreman for Pliam Linoleum and St. Paul Linoleum. Eventually, he started his own business, Modern Floors in St. Louis Park.

In 1960, he became a Minnesota Conservation Officer and did that until his retirement from the state in 1981. He thought it was the best job in the world and won many awards, some for saving lives. While he was a warden, he was stationed at Waskish, Crosby-Ironton, Orr, and Baudette. After his retirement, he worked for the Lake of the Woods Sheriff's water patrol.

He and Patricia moved to International Falls where she died in July of 1993 after they had been married for 51 years. Bill then moved to Hibbing and in 1998, at age 80, he married a friend of Patricia's, Dorothy ("Doff") Osborne, who moved to Hibbing from England to marry him. Doff died in December of 2001.

Bill was always so proud of his family and he will be missed by his daughter and son-in-law, Ivanette (Ivy) and Herbert Hanson of Hibbing, his son and daughter-in-law, Frederic and Amber Callies of Carlton. He has seven grandchildren, Darrick Hanson, Two Harbors, Calisa Hanson, Mound, Darci (Charles) Graves, Texas, Robert (Jackie) Callies, Texas, Tricia (Steve) Yeathermon, Texas, Brenda Chute, Mankato, Paul (Erika) Chute, Alaska. Bill is also survived by one sister, Elizabeth (Bob Nunn) Olafson, Bloomington.

He has five great grandchildren.

There are two stepsons in England, David Osborne and Jonathan (Sandra) Osborne.

His brothers and sister-in-laws surviving him are Media Kozacz, Minneapolis, Monica (Jerome) Liemandt, Brainerd, Wayne Sanders, Minneapolis, Susan Celusnak, Minneapolis. There also are many nieces and nephews.

He was a member of Hibbing's American Legion, Hibbing Trap Club, Retired Conservation Officers' Association, NRA and Grace Lutheran Church.

Bill was the ideal son, husband, father, worker, and friend who could always be counted on to do the right and honest thing in any given situation. He will be missed but he was ready to go to his heavenly home.

Pall Bearers:

Robert Callies, grandson
Darrick Hanson, grandson
Bill Eicholz
Lloyd Steen
Howard Schultz
John Calgaro
Mike Jarvi

Honorary Pallbearers:
(Other grandchildren)

Calisa Hanson
Darci Graves
Tricia Yeathermon
Brenda Chute
Paul Chute